IMAGES
of America

TUMWATER

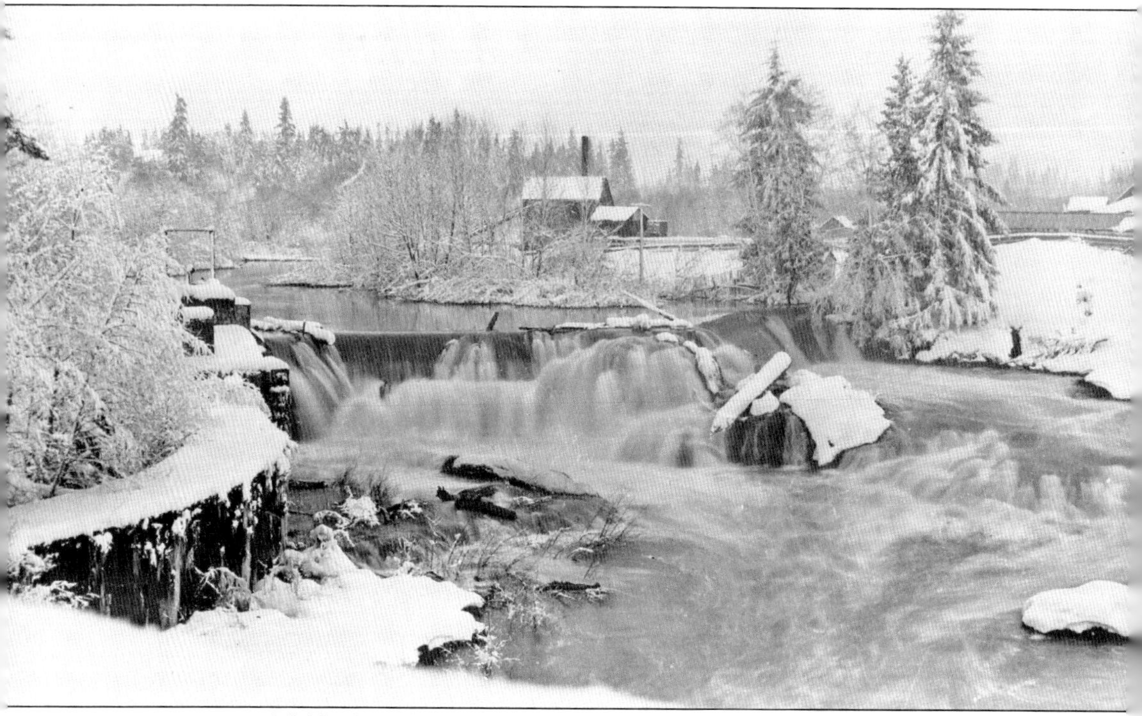

A winter snowfall blankets the banks of the Deschutes River in this view from the early 20th century. The buildings of the Lea Lumber and Shingle Mill stand in the background; the intake pipe of the Olympia Light and Power penstock is visible at the left. (Courtesy of Henderson House Museum, No. 621.)

On the Cover: The brick brewhouse of the Olympia Brewing Company towers above the train tracks and docks at the mouth of the river, as seen in this c. 1908 image. (Courtesy of Henderson House Museum, No. 150.)

IMAGES
of America

TUMWATER

Heather Lockman and Carla Wulfsberg
with the City of Tumwater's
Henderson House Museum

ARCADIA
PUBLISHING

ISBN 978-0-7385-8127-9

Published by Arcadia Publishing
Charleston, South Carolina

Printed in the United States of America

Library of Congress Control Number: 2010926134

For all general information contact Arcadia Publishing at:
Telephone 843-853-2070
Fax 843-853-0044
E-mail sales@arcadiapublishing.com
For customer service and orders:
Toll-Free 1-888-313-2665

Visit us on the Internet at www.arcadiapublishing.com

Contents

ACKNOWLEDGMENTS

The authors would like to thank Olympia Federal Savings and Loan, O Bee Credit Union, the Squaxin Island Tribe One Percent Commission, and the City of Tumwater for the financial assistance that made this project possible.

Historian Shanna Stevenson was unfailingly helpful in locating photographs and answering all of our questions. Retired brewmaster Paul Knight was equally patient in trying to explain to us the art of brewing great beer. We are also indebted to all those who shared family albums, clarified details, and read early drafts of our work, and to photograph assistant Katrina Repsch.

Our special thanks go to lifelong Tumwater resident Jim Brown, who saw the need for a local pictorial archive more than 30 years ago and gathered the first vital images for the photographic collection of the Henderson House Museum. Whenever we phoned with a question, he was at our doorstep in minutes, full of good Tumwater stories—some of which we'll never tell.

INTRODUCTION

Just before the Deschutes River reaches the south end of Puget Sound, it courses through a small canyon and down a series of three waterfalls—dropping more than 80 feet in barely a quarter mile. At least one traditional American Indian story has spoken of this stretch of the river as a haunted and mournful place. If you listen below the falls, it says, you'll hear the cries of an American Indian woman who drowned while gathering loon eggs at nearby Hewitt Lake and those of the husband who tried to save her. Both were mysteriously swept away through an underground passage, their bodies appearing later at the foot of Tumwater Falls.

When non–Native Americans looked at the cascading falls, they saw something else entirely: the waterpower they needed to turn industrial machinery. As early as 1829, the British Hudson's Bay Company made note of "the Puget Sound Falls" as a good location for a water-powered sawmill. At one point, the company considered moving its fur-trading post from Fort Nisqually, 10 miles up Puget Sound, to the falls of the Deschutes River. But some of the American Indian traders refused to travel so far south to bring their furs to the company, and the plan was soon abandoned. It was not until American settlers arrived in the 1840s that water-driven industries sprang up along the Deschutes River.

In October 1845, a party of 31 Americans, most of whom had journeyed together across the Oregon Trail, chose Tumwater Falls as the location for the first permanent U.S. settlement on Puget Sound. Within months, they built a gristmill alongside the Lower Falls. The next year, they added a sawmill. They christened their village "New Market" in the hopes that one day it would become an important industrial city. But the lofty name did not stick. By 1857, the town was calling itself Tumwater instead, from *tum-chuck*, a word meaning "noisy water" in the jargon used between settlers and American Indians.

For the next 40 years, the natural force of Tumwater Falls powered sawmills, flour mills, an ice-making plant, and even electric streetcars. When the age of waterpower was through, the falls remained an important part of the town's identity. An artist's sketch of the Lower Falls, incorporated into the logo of the Olympia Brewing Company, even appeared on the label of Tumwater's famous Olympia Beer.

Freeway construction brought big changes during the mid-1950s. The concrete ribbon of Interstate 5 sliced straight through the heart of Tumwater, essentially obliterating the historic center of town. And yet, in spite of everything, the falls themselves remain much the same as when early settlers first saw them. Thanks to two wonderful riverside parks (one owned by the City of Tumwater, the other by the nonprofit Olympia Tumwater Foundation), visitors now have access to the full run of waterfalls. Illustrated signs in both parks, along the banks of the canyon and down on the shoreline below the falls, help to tell the story of Tumwater's early years.

This book, too, is meant to help readers imagine how the city of Tumwater looked before the freeway came through. From Victorian homes near the waterfront to an elk farm at the Upper Falls, the pictures in these pages offer a glimpse of a civic past that is not always easy to see. Fortunately, more than 1,500 historic photographs—most of them gleaned from the attics and albums of local families—have been preserved and catalogued in the City of Tumwater's Henderson House Museum. The majority of the images in this volume are borrowed from the Henderson House collection. It's hard to think of a better way to make use of them than to publish them here, in context, for everyone to enjoy.

One

THE TOWN ALONG THE FALLS

In the spring of 1846, having survived their first winter, the earliest Tumwater settlers built a crude pioneer flour mill at the falls of the Deschutes River. "Benjamin Gordon and Mike Simmons started the first gristmill," Gordon's son Henry wrote later. "Indians told them that they knew where some fine rocks were that would make fine burrs. . . . They dug the rocks, loaded them on a raft, and took them to the lower falls at Tumwater & there started to make flour." The following year, Michael T. Simmons and other investors built a water-powered sawmill as well.

With its roaring falls, its thick stands of trees, and a tidal river basin that flowed into Puget Sound, Tumwater held plenty of promise. By the late 1870s, at least eight riverside factories clustered around the falls—not only lumber and flour mills, but a furniture factory, a tannery, and a wooden pipe factory, too.

While industries crowded the river's edge, a pioneer business district emerged on the west rim of the canyon. Hotels, saloons, boardinghouses, grocery stores, and a blacksmith's shop stood along muddy Reserve Street (now Deschutes Way). A promotional booklet published in 1890 touted the "seventeen residences and business buildings" erected the previous year and promised that Tumwater soon would "cast off the village swaddling clothes and rise to the dignity of a town."

But times were already changing. Steam engines and electricity began to replace old-fashioned waterpower, allowing sawmills and industry to move away from the river. Between 1891 and 1905, four riverside mills and factories—one of them already vacant—caught fire and burned to the ground. After 1895, only a single sawmill was doing business beside the falls.

Two new riverside industries kept Tumwater from disappearing. One was the Olympia Power and Light Company, which built its first powerhouse on the Deschutes River in 1890 and a second one 13 years later. The other was a small brewery that opened in 1896 and would, in less than a decade, become the largest employer in town.

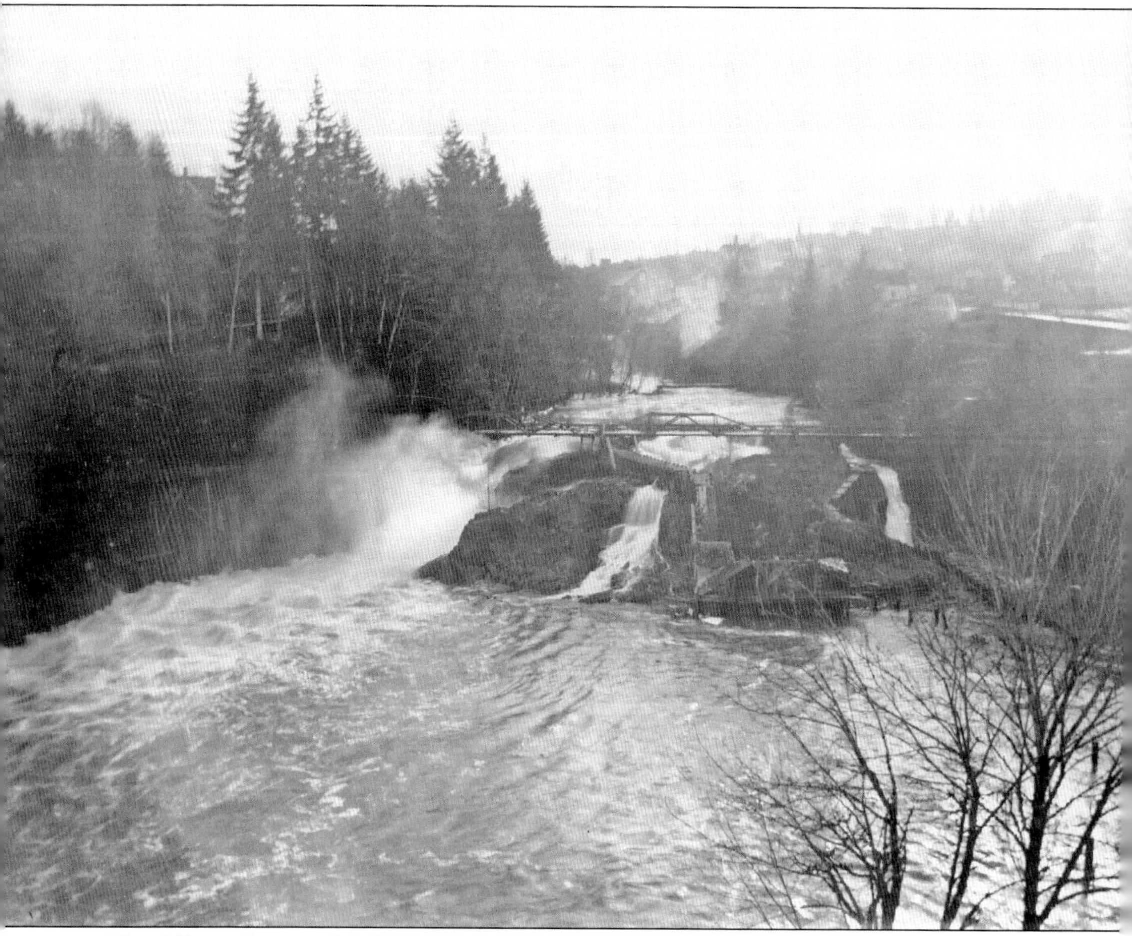

The falls at the mouth of the Deschutes River date from the end of the most recent Ice Age (about 12,000 years ago), when a massive layer of glacial ice covered present-day Tumwater. As temperatures warmed, the glaciers retreated, leaving behind the ice-carved bays and inlets of Puget Sound. The Deschutes River, which had flowed to the west while ice blocked its way, found a more direct route to saltwater by heading north to Puget Sound. The river cut through softer rock near the surface to a layer of ancient volcanic basalt, which wears away very slowly. This black basalt forms the framework for the three distinct cascades—Upper, Middle, and Lower—of Tumwater Falls. (Courtesy Henderson House Museum, No. 588.)

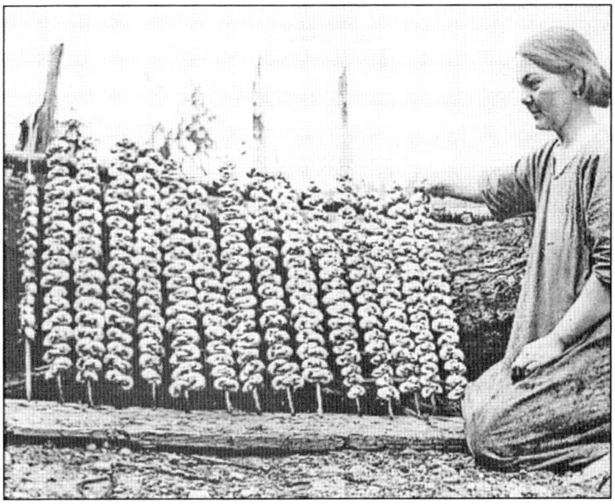

For centuries before outside settlers arrived, American Indians lived in a village on the west shore at the foot of the falls, where archeologists have uncovered heaps of shells dating back at least 2,000 years. The culture of the Coast Salish people revolved around harvesting food from both the land and the water. In this early-20th-century photograph, Squaxin Island tribal member Cecelia Bob dries clams in the traditional American Indian way. (Courtesy of Squaxin Island Tribe Museum, Library and Research Center.)

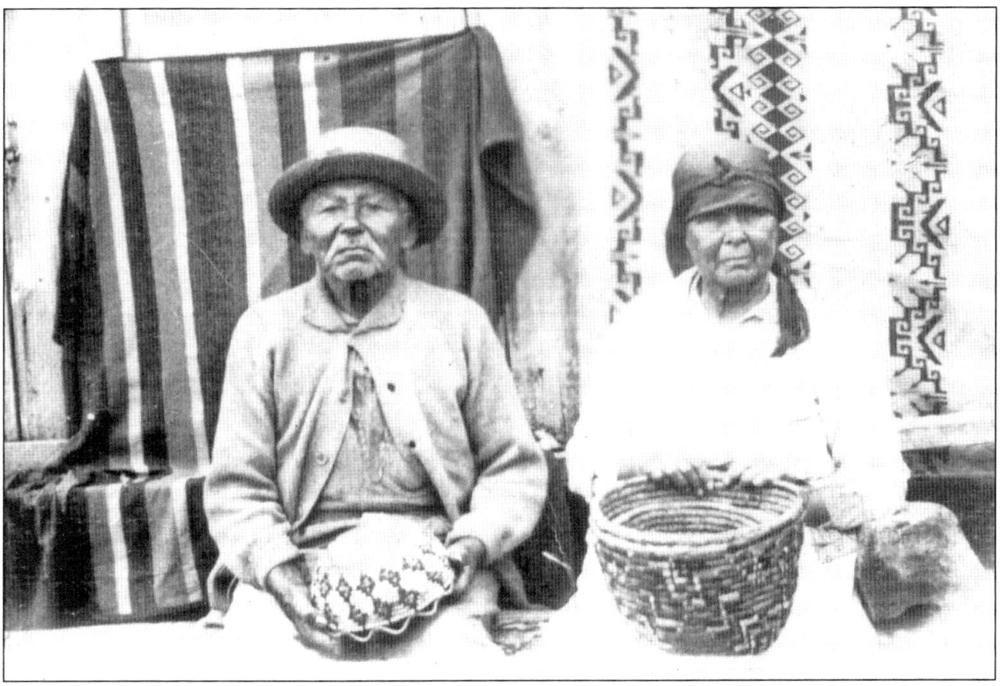

In 1854, the number of American Indians at Tumwater was counted at 20—about one-sixth of the town's total population. In the years that followed, most of the American Indians of Washington Territory were removed by the U.S. government to reservation lands. Native American people from the Tumwater area were relocated to the Squaxin Island and Nisqually tribal reservations, although some apparently continued to live in a camp on the east bank near the Lower Falls. Pictured here are John and Mary Skalapin, traditional medicine practitioners of the Squaxin Island people. Mary Skalapin was the grandmother of Cecila Bob, seen in the top image. (Courtesy of Squaxin Island Tribe Museum, Library and Research Center.)

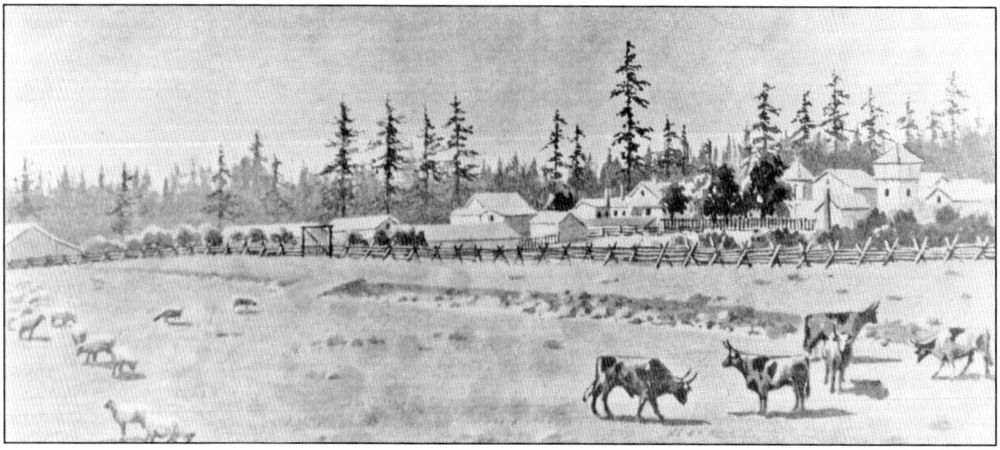

The presence of nearby Fort Nisqually, a British fur-tradition outpost built in 1832, was a huge advantage to the first Americans at Tumwater. When exhausted settlers arrived at the falls in October 1845, they bought wheat, potatoes, cattle, and peas on credit from Fort Nisqually. Short of cash, they agreed to work off their debt by splitting cedar shingles. (Coleman drawing courtesy of Fort Nisqually Living History Museum.)

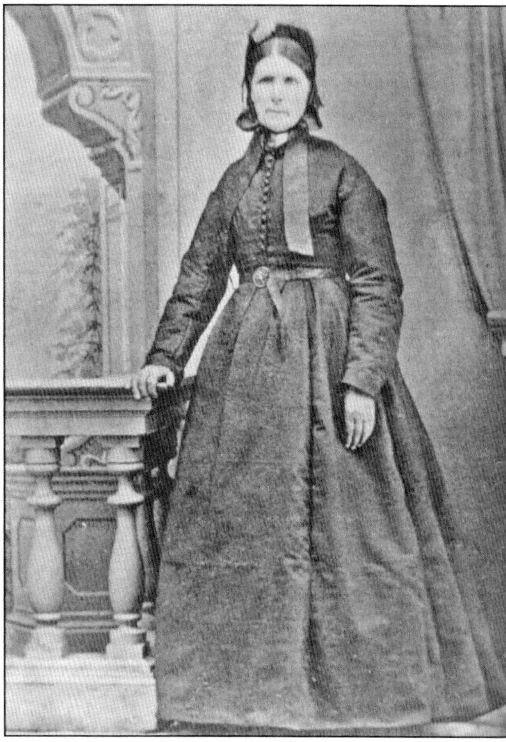

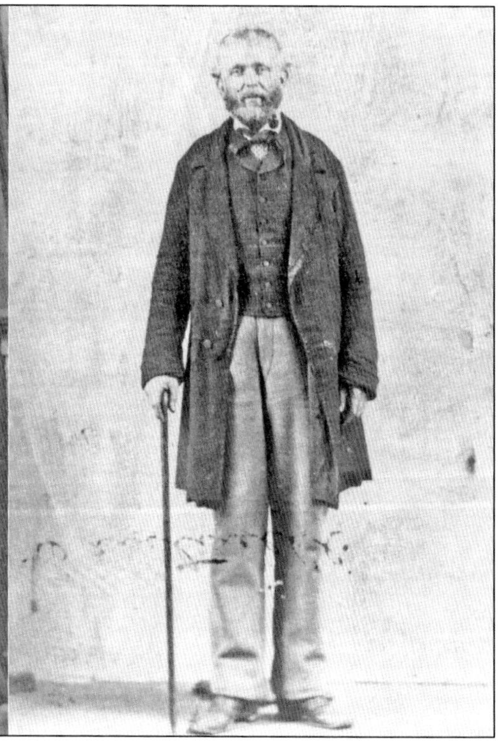

Elizabeth Kindred Simmons (left) came from Missouri by oxcart in 1844 in a party that included her husband, Michael T. Simmons (right), their four children, her parents, and assorted in-laws and cousins. Pregnant for part of the journey, Elizabeth gave birth to her fifth child near Washougal, in what is now the state of Washington, while the group decided where to settle. Michael T. Simmons was a member of the scouting party that ultimately chose Tumwater Falls as the place they should try their luck. (Left, courtesy of Henderson House Museum, No. 401; right, courtesy of Washington State Library.)

George Bush was a free man of mixed race who traveled west from Missouri in the same party as the Simmons family, along with his wife, Isabella (a white woman), and their five sons. Arriving at the end of the trail, the family discovered that the "anti-Negro" laws of Oregon Country potentially subjected George Bush to public whippings. The Simmons-Bush party headed north into what is now Washington, in hopes that the law would not be enforced north of the Columbia River. No known photograph of George Bush survives. (Timothy Patrick drawing courtesy of Henderson House Museum, No. 1033.)

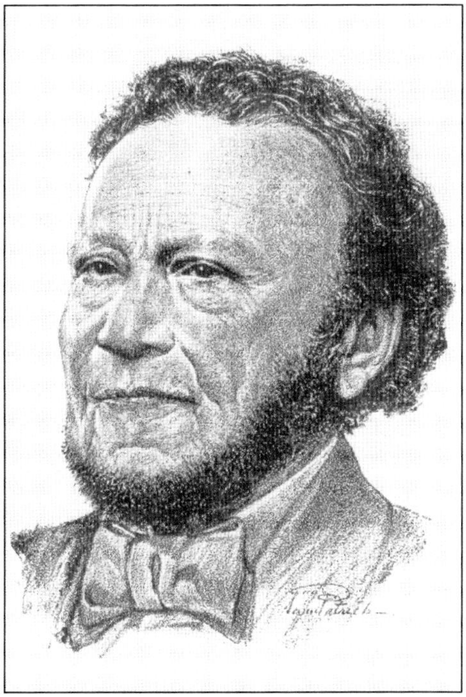

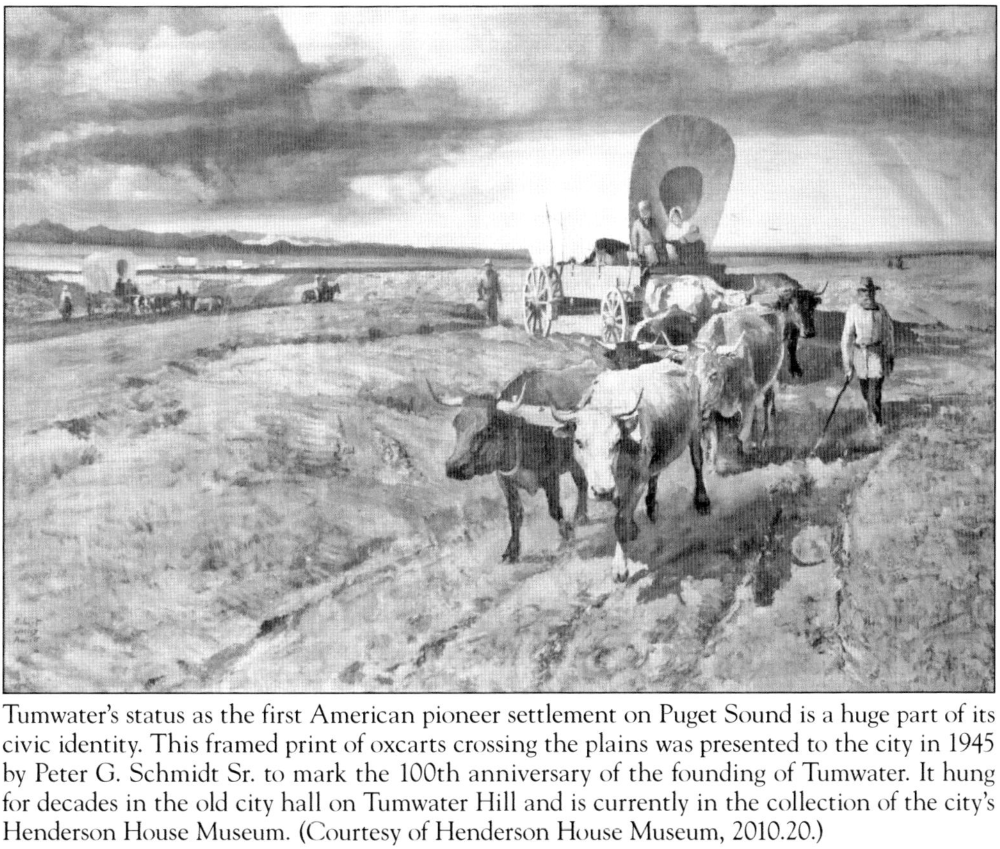

Tumwater's status as the first American pioneer settlement on Puget Sound is a huge part of its civic identity. This framed print of oxcarts crossing the plains was presented to the city in 1945 by Peter G. Schmidt Sr. to mark the 100th anniversary of the founding of Tumwater. It hung for decades in the old city hall on Tumwater Hill and is currently in the collection of the city's Henderson House Museum. (Courtesy of Henderson House Museum, 2010.20.)

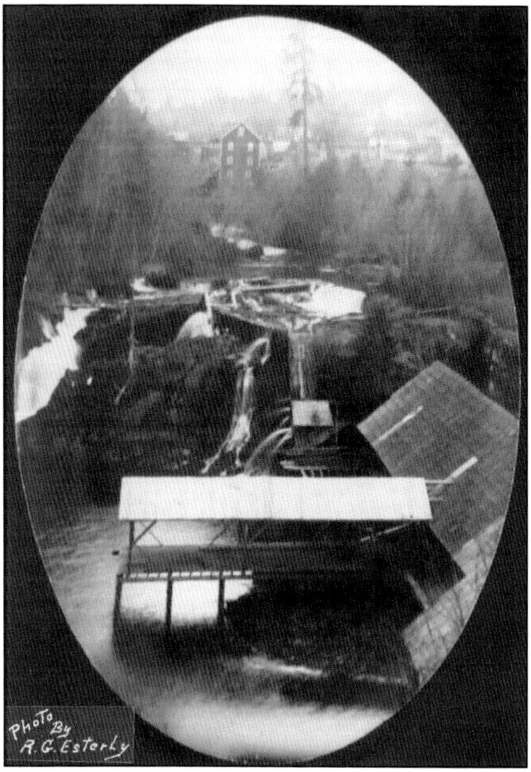

Michael T. Simmons and seven other investors formed the Puget Sound Milling Company and built a water-powered sawmill at the Lower Falls in 1847, buying a crank and other irons from the Hudson's Bay Company. The small square structure at the center of this photograph is often identified as the original Simmons sawmill but may instead be the tiny gristmill built by Simmons and his neighbors on the same stretch of riverbank in 1946. It was clearly abandoned by the time this picture was taken in the 1890s; note the water spewing uselessly from its side. (Courtesy of Henderson House Museum, No. 036.)

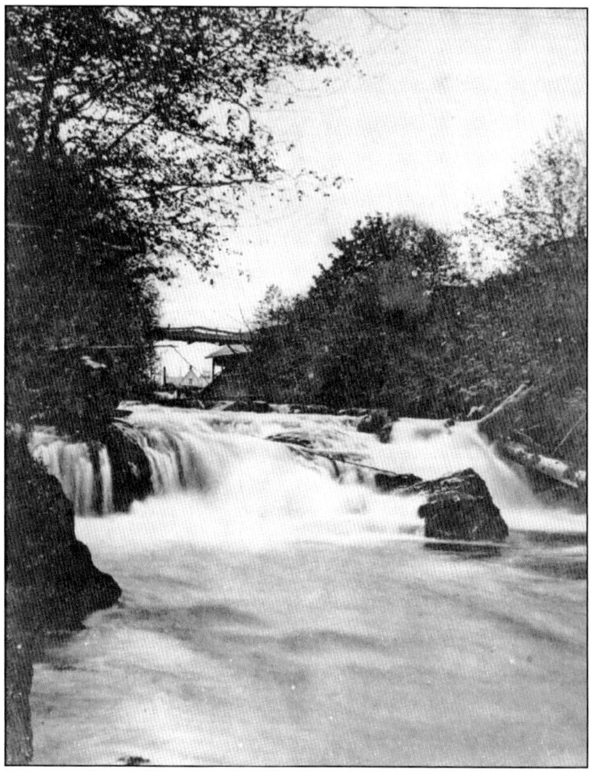

In January 1853, the *Washington Pioneer* newspaper in neighboring Olympia reported that a wagon bridge was being built at Tumwater "over Shute's River, between the two falls, and near the grist mill" (where the Boston Street Bridge stands today). With a wagon bridge in place, travel between the two towns was greatly improved. (Courtesy of Henderson House Museum, No. 945.)

Clanrick Crosby was one of two seafaring brothers from Maine who brought a sailing ship full of Crosby relations to the Pacific Northwest. Arriving in Tumwater in 1851, Clanrick and his wife, Phebe, filed a land claim for 524 acres that included virtually all the land on both sides of Tumwater Falls. Crosby apparently purchased the early Tumwater sawmill from Michael T. Simmons, although a lawsuit brought by Simmons suggests that he may never have finished paying the bill. (Courtesy of Thurston Regional Planning Commission.)

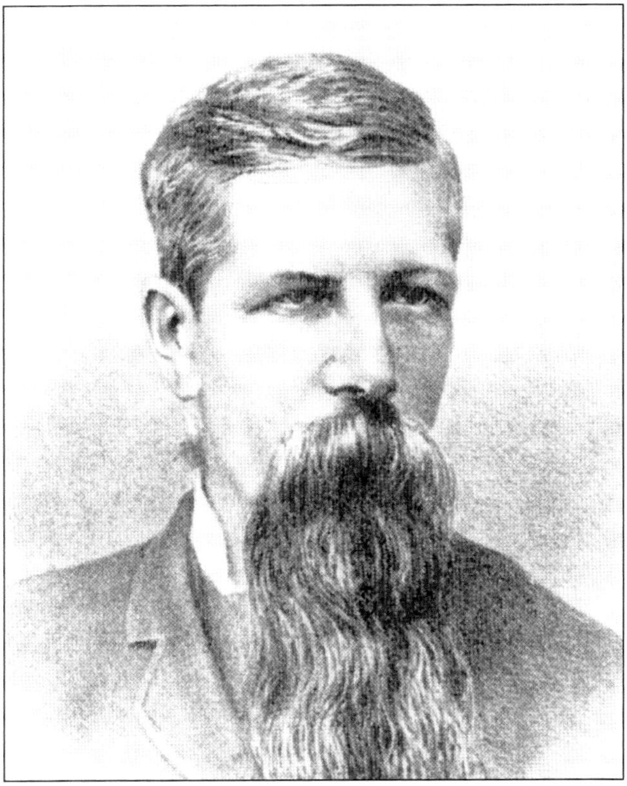

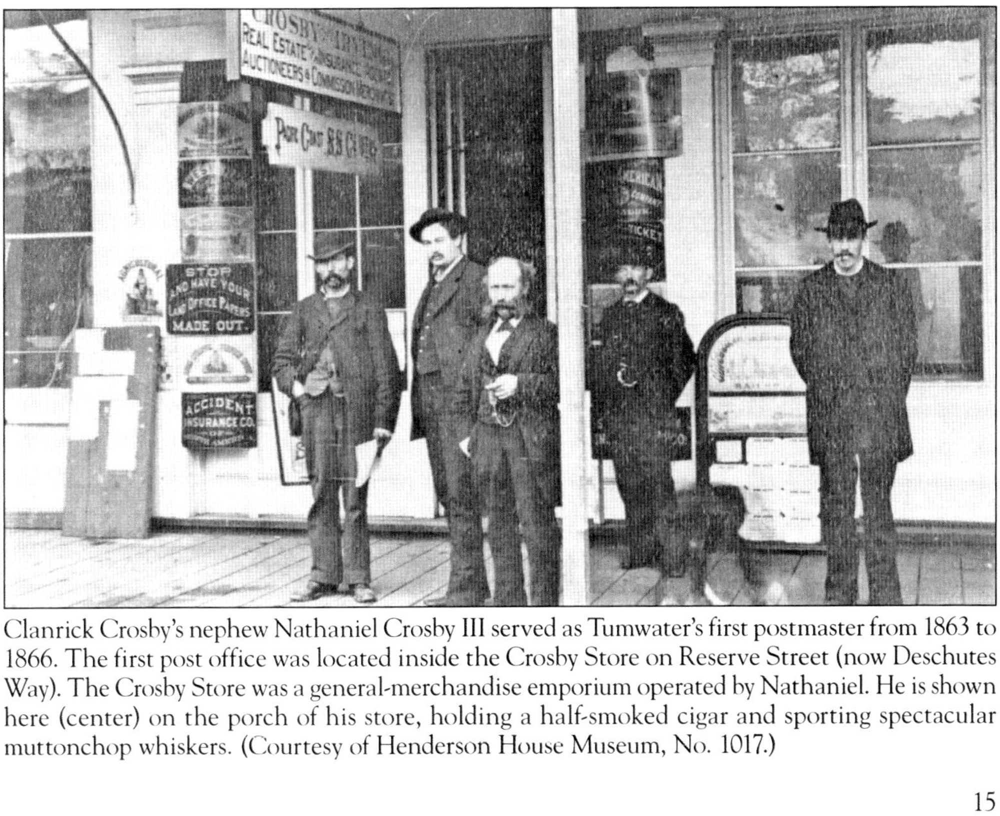

Clanrick Crosby's nephew Nathaniel Crosby III served as Tumwater's first postmaster from 1863 to 1866. The first post office was located inside the Crosby Store on Reserve Street (now Deschutes Way). The Crosby Store was a general-merchandise emporium operated by Nathaniel. He is shown here (center) on the porch of his store, holding a half-smoked cigar and sporting spectacular muttonchop whiskers. (Courtesy of Henderson House Museum, No. 1017.)

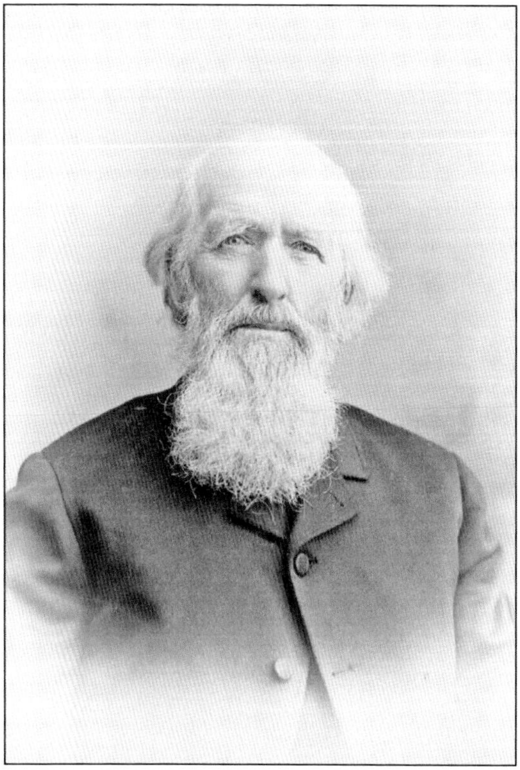

James Biles, originally from Kentucky, came west across the Oregon Trail with his wife, Nancy Merry Biles, and their seven children in 1853. The family settled first near Grand Mound but later moved to Tumwater—"the children having school advantages" according to Susan Biles Drew. With a partner, James built the Lee and Biles general store on Deschutes Way, just above the Lower Falls. When he was appointed postmaster of Tumwater in 1866, the post office moved down the street to his store. (Courtesy of Henderson House Museum, No. 361.)

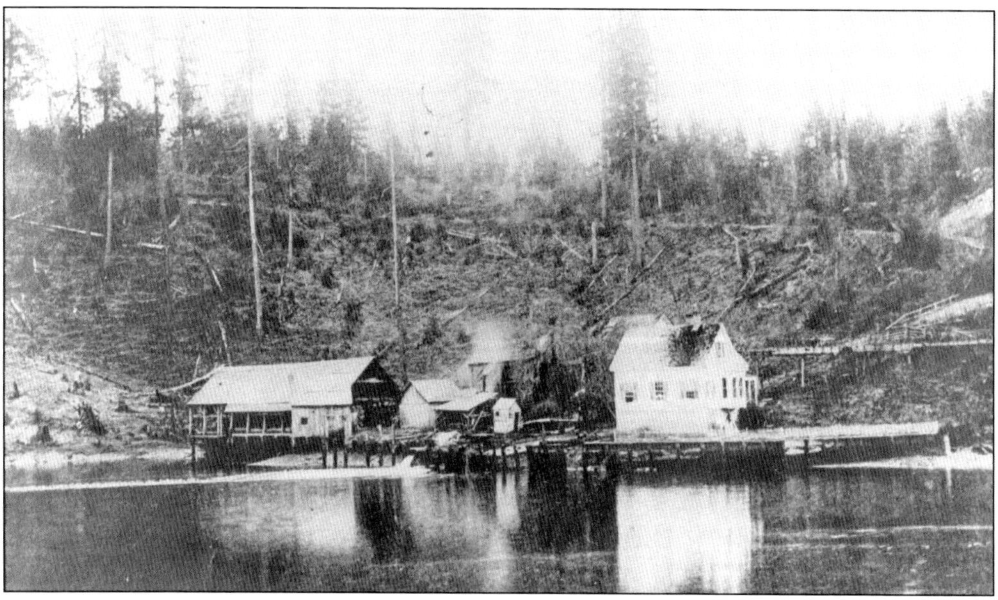

James Biles and a partner purchased land from Clanrick Crosby in 1859 and built a successful tannery on the east bank of the river below the Lower Falls. Originally known as the Biles and Carter Tannery, it eventually became James Biles and Sons. The Biles clan built two homes on their land next to their tannery operation. The neat white house seen above on the right is a recognizable landmark in many early photographs of the Tumwater waterfront. (Courtesy of Henderson House Museum, No. 1322.)

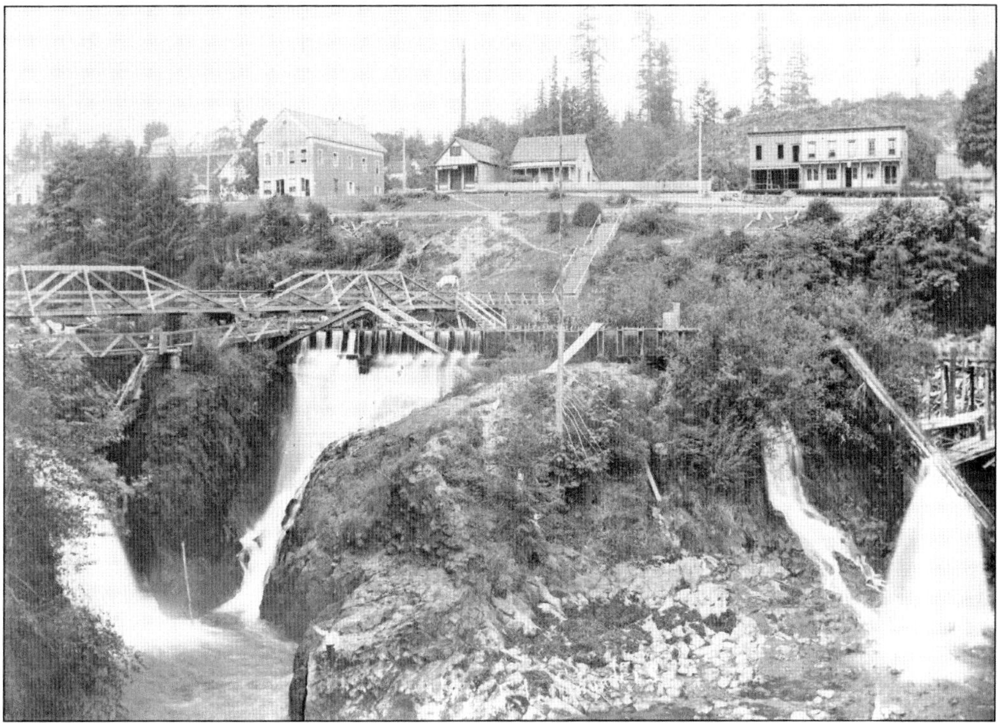

While industries grew at the river's edge, a town sprang up on the west bank above. In this view from 1891 looking west across the Lower Falls, the two-story Lee and Biles store stands head and shoulders above everything else on the street. (Courtesy of Henderson House Museum, No. 585.)

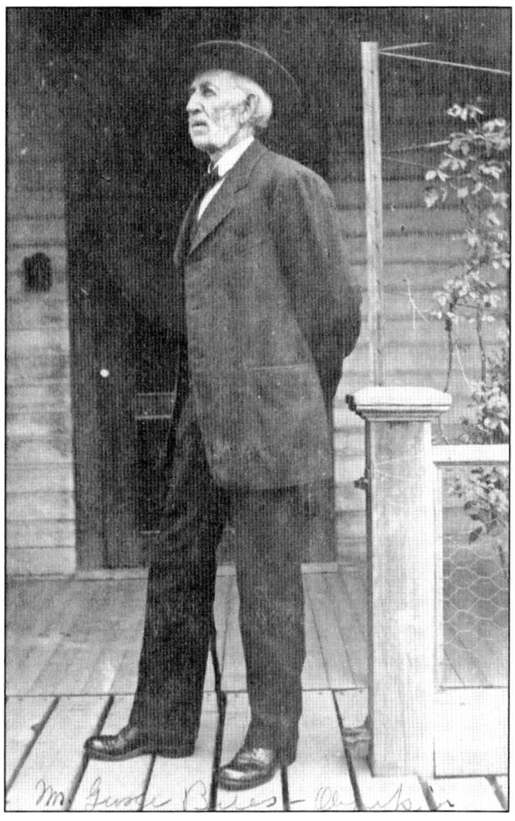

James Biles's son George became postmaster after his father. He was Tumwater's first marshal when the town was incorporated in 1869, and he served as mayor twice. Elected office was clearly a family tradition. His brother Clark Biles was mayor, too; their father served both on the city council and in the Washington Territorial Legislature. (Courtesy of Henderson House Museum, No. 362.)

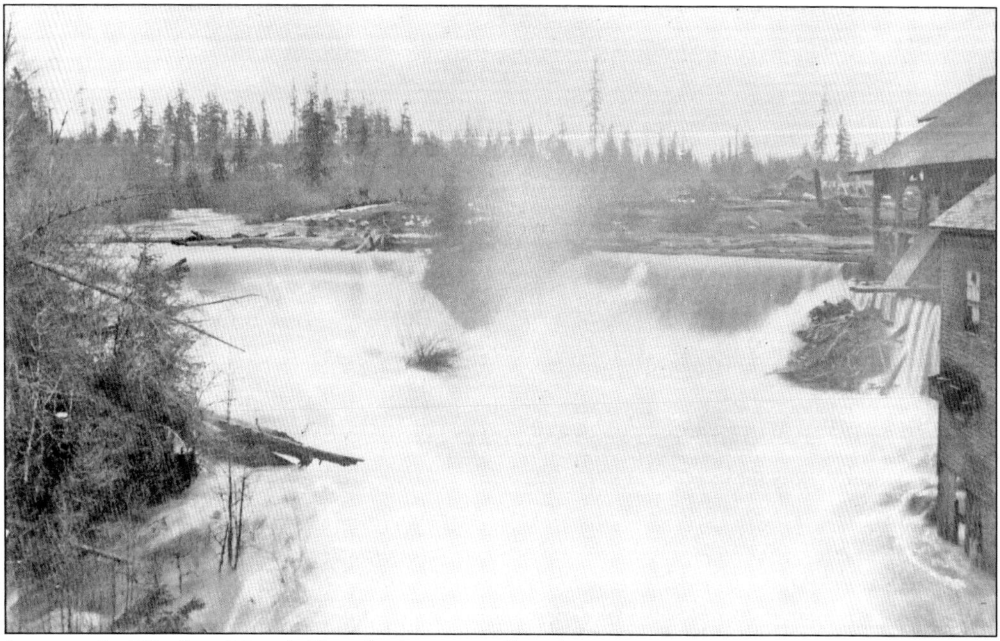

Pioneers Ira Ward and Smith Hays built a sawmill at the Upper Falls in 1852 (upper far right) on land they purchased from Clanrick Crosby. Two years later, they added a gristmill (lower right). "Most all of the farmers from Puget Sound to [the] Columbia [River] raised their own wheat in those days," remembered Henry Harrison Tilley, whose family owned a hotel south of town, "and would take it to Tumwater Mill to be ground into flour and feed." (Courtesy of Olympia Tumwater Foundation.)

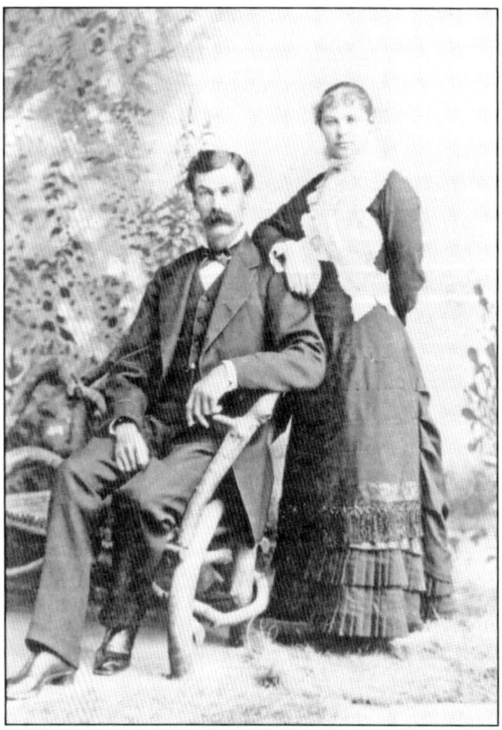

George Gelbach came to Tumwater in 1870, dabbling in business and real estate and serving a stint as postmaster in 1872. He may have leased space in the Ward and Hayes gristmill before building his own mill at the Middle Falls. He is pictured here with his wife, Etta Sprague, whose family came to the Tumwater area from Idaho in 1869. (Courtesy of Henderson House Museum, No. 379.)

Wagons and horses wait outside George Gelbach's mill in the late 1870s. Officially known as the Washington Mill, the building stood three stories tall from the road in front and four stories high from the river below. Notice the sacks of flour on the porch. (Courtesy of Henderson House Museum, No. 033.)

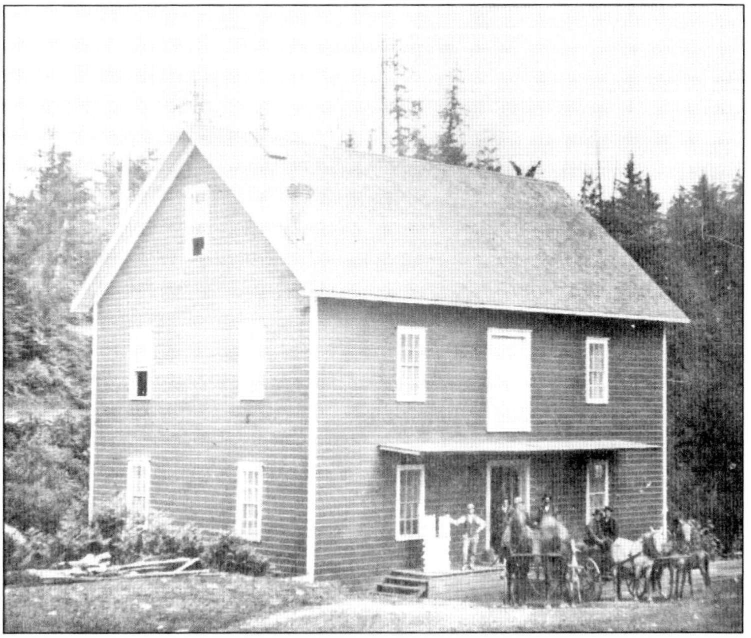

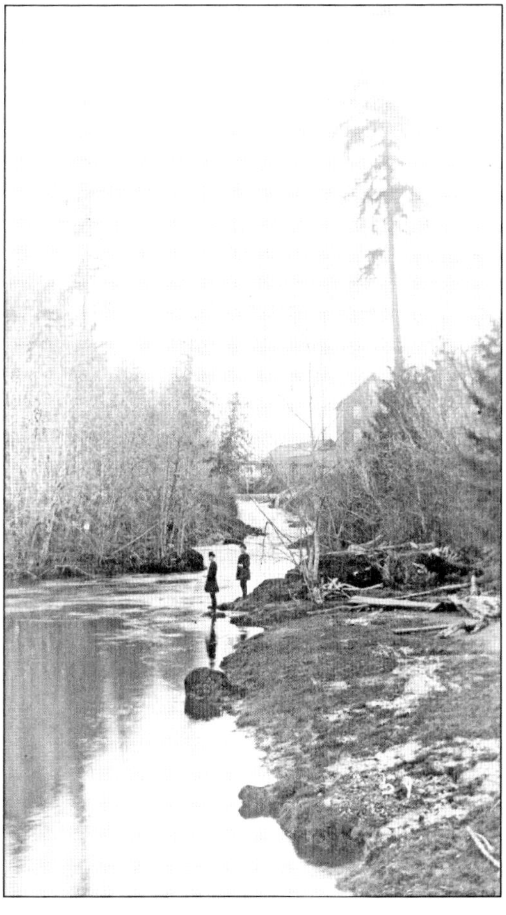

Two dapper gentlemen pose below the Middle Falls with Gelbach's mill in the background. The towering profile of the flour mill is easily identified in many Tumwater photographs from the late 1800s. (Courtesy of Henderson House Museum, No. 1301.)

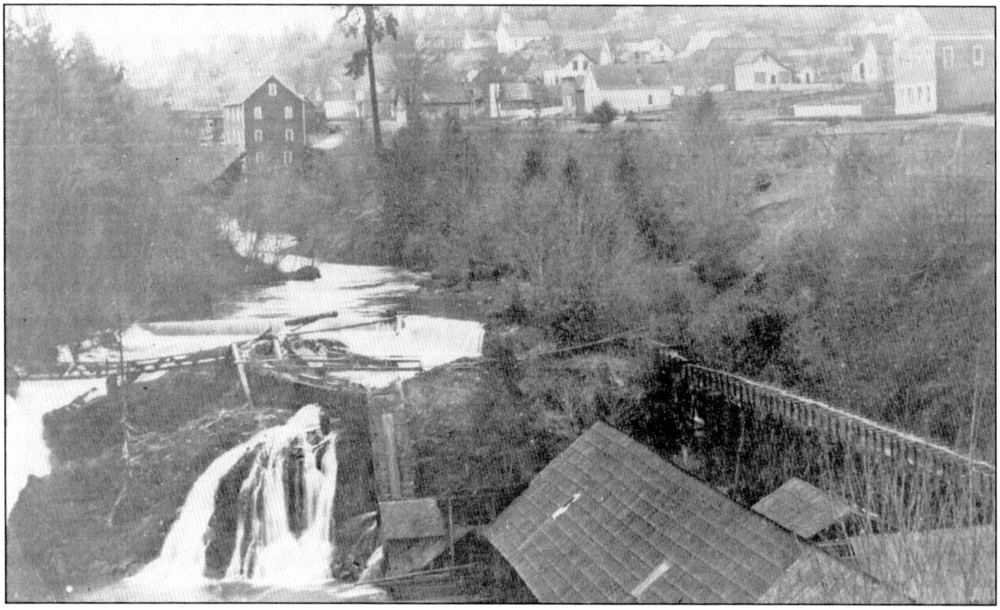

Wooden flumes carry the power of falling water to mills and factories on both banks of the Lower Falls. The shingled roof in the foreground belongs to the Horton Pipe Factory, where logs were turned into wooden water pipe. Gelbach's mill stands in the background. (Courtesy of Henderson House Museum, No. 582.)

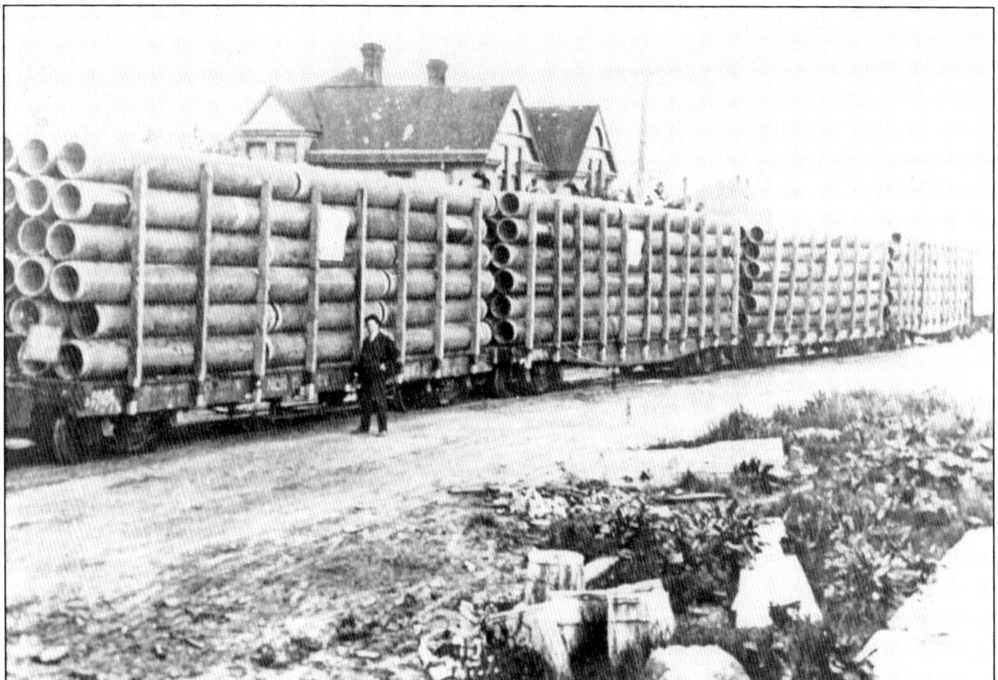

An order of Horton wooden pipe stands loaded on railcars, ready for shipping. This photograph was taken after 1878, when William Horton moved his factory to the neighboring town of Olympia. The large pipe pictured here was a style the company manufactured after leaving Tumwater Falls. (Courtesy of Olympia Tumwater Foundation.)

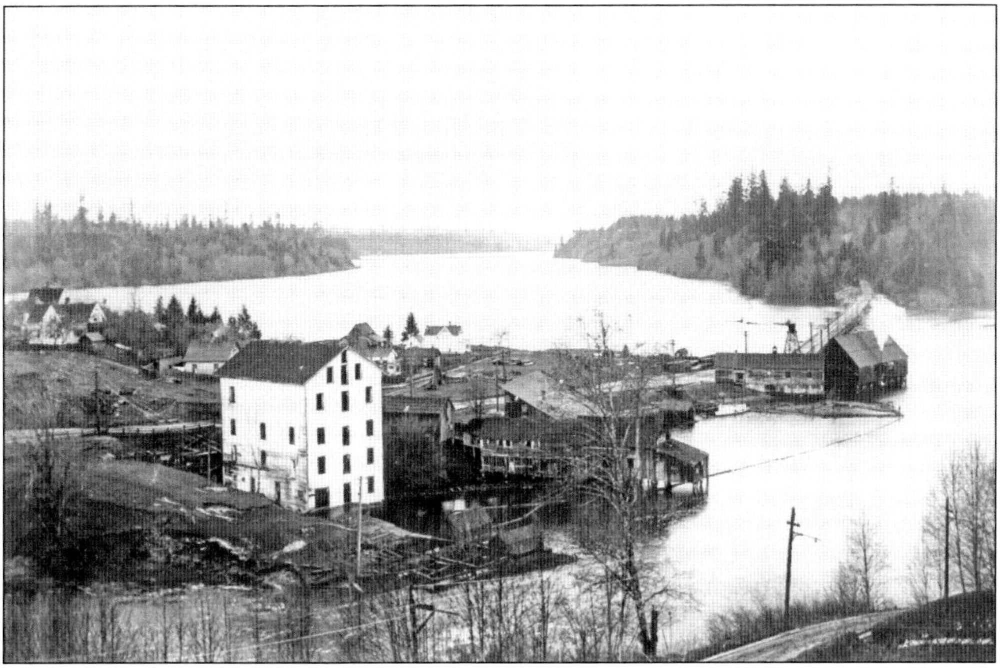

Until the mid-20th century, the mouth of the Deschutes River was a marine estuary that flooded and ebbed with the tide. In this view from the 1890s, looking north from the Lower Falls, the tide is clearly in. The long wooden wagon bridge on the right leads from the Tumwater waterfront to what is now the South Capitol neighborhood of Olympia. The big white structure in the foreground is the Lincoln Flour Mill, built by Clanrick Crosby in 1866. (Courtesy of Henderson House Museum, No. 009.)

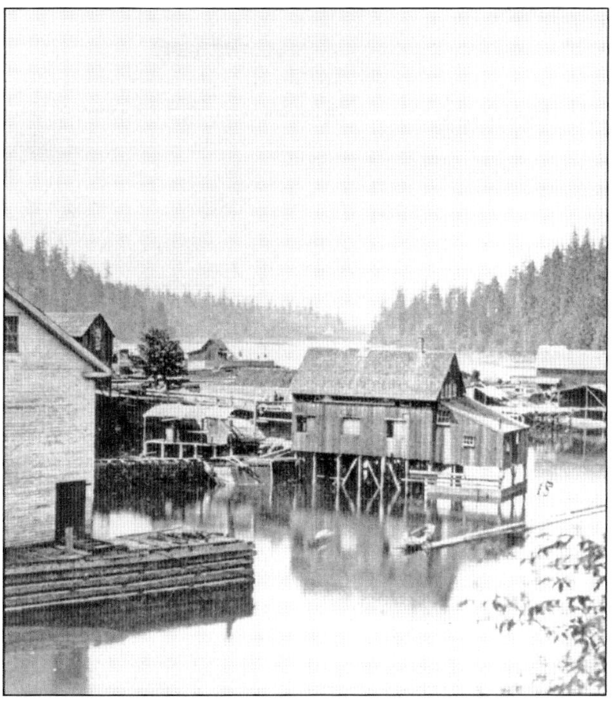

Waterfront businesses, many built up on pilings over the mudflats, crowded the shoreline of the Deschutes waterway, below the falls, where Tumwater Historical Park stands today. (Courtesy of Henderson House Museum, No. 051.)

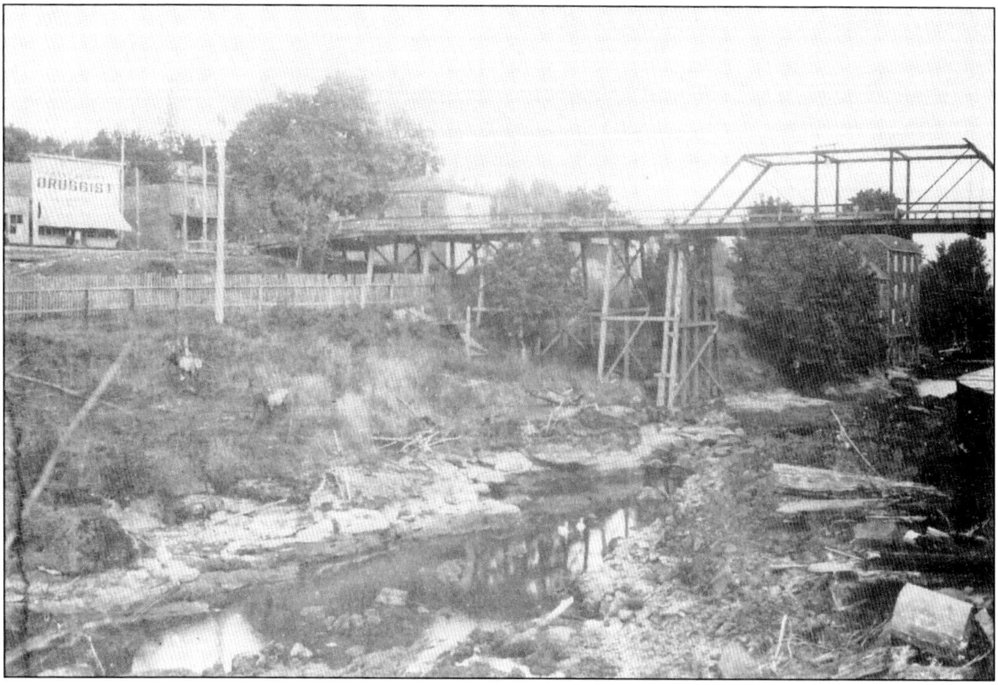

The heart of Tumwater's business district stood on Reserve Street (Deschutes Way) near the Upper Falls, at the end of the wagon bridge. The Hewitt Drugstore (left) was a fixture at this location for more than 50 years. (Courtesy of Henderson House Museum, No. 012.)

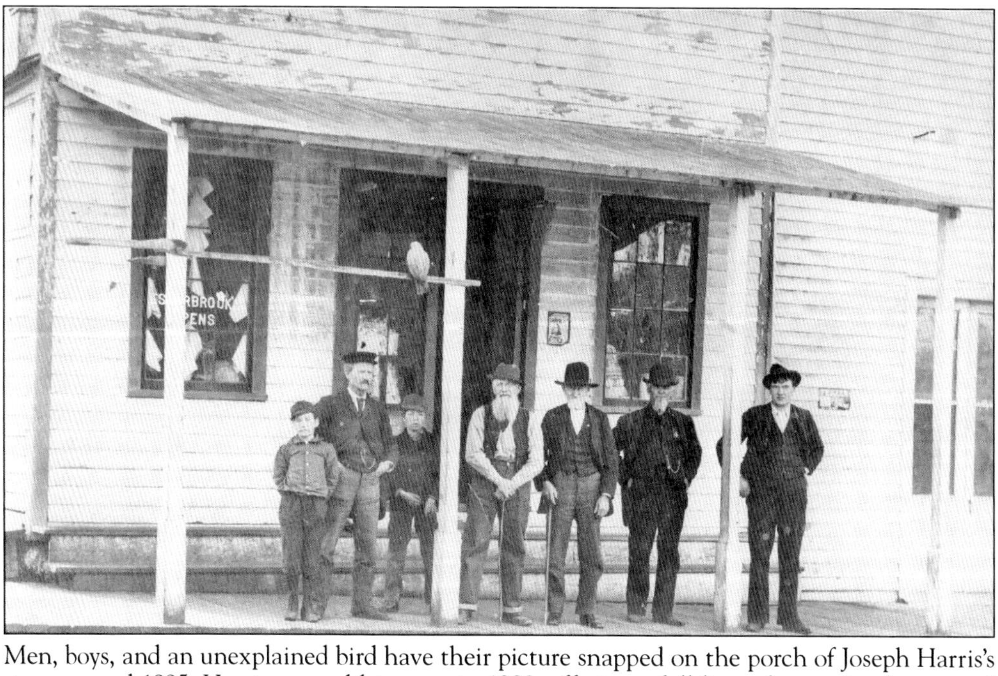

Men, boys, and an unexplained bird have their picture snapped on the porch of Joseph Harris's store around 1895. Harris opened his store in 1889, offering a full line of groceries, boots, and shoes, "including . . . such articles as are in demand by loggers and woodmen." (Courtesy of Henderson House Museum, No. 018.)

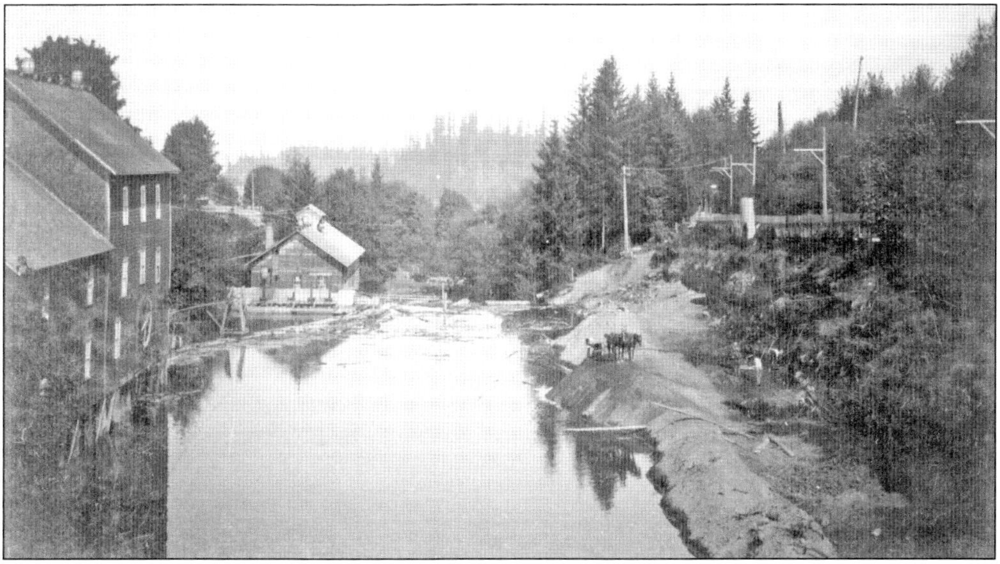

As early as 1882, local businessmen attempted to produce electricity at Tumwater Falls. In 1890, the Olympia Light and Power Company built a dam and a wooden powerhouse at the Middle Falls, just below Gelbach's mill (left). Electricity from the plant powered streetlights in downtown Olympia and a fleet of electric streetcars that ran between Olympia and Tumwater. (Courtesy of Henderson House Museum, No. 593.)

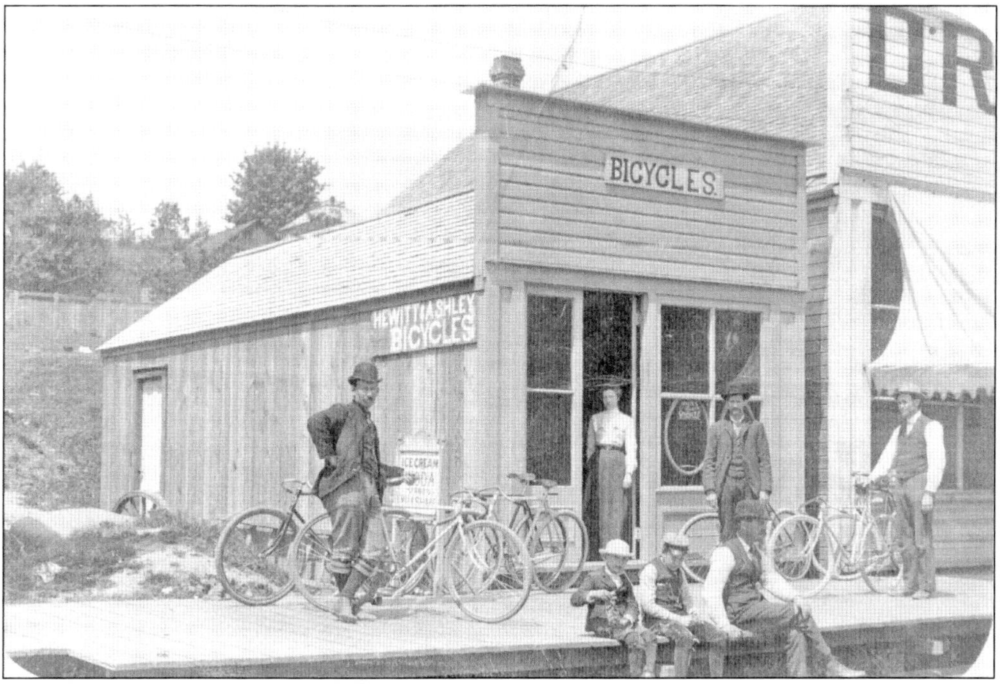

Bicycles were all the rage in the 1890s. Bicycle shop proprietors Wilbur Ashley (far left) and Charles Hewitt (second from right) pose with their wares in front of their establishment on Reserve Street (Deschutes Way). Wilbur's wife, Gertrude Ashley, stands in the doorway. The sign near the sidewalk, promising ice cream as well as bikes, probably pertains to the Hewitt Drugstore next door. (Courtesy of Henderson House Museum, No. 956.)

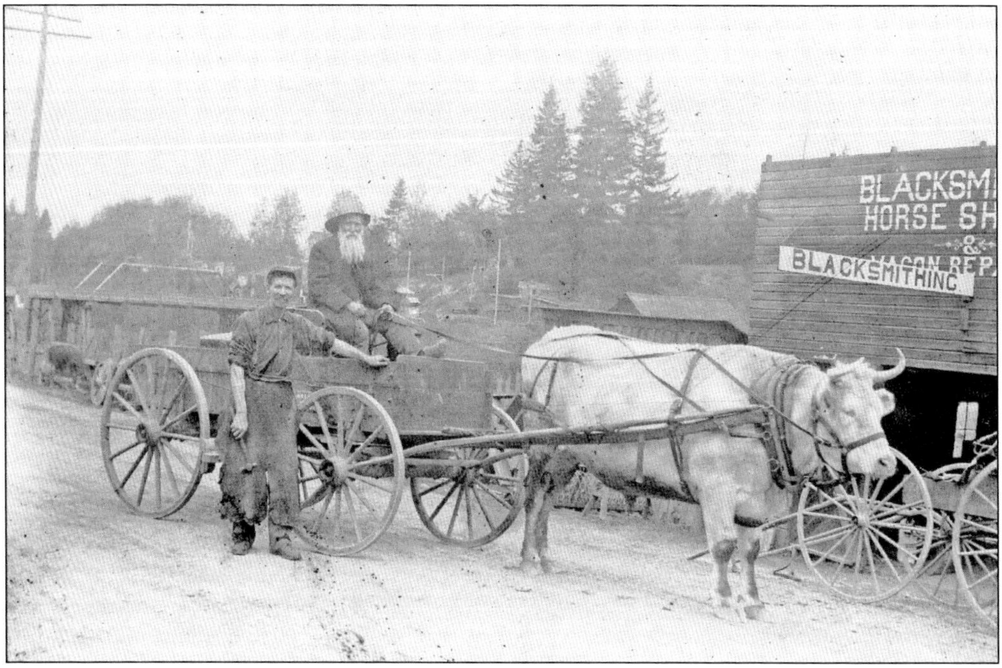

The blacksmith shop owned by Frank Eastman (left) stood near the Upper Falls, on the west side of the river, from 1876 until his death in 1910. This *c.* 1900 photograph captures both an old-fashioned oxcart and modern electrical power poles marching along the river. (Courtesy of Henderson House Museum, No. 005.)

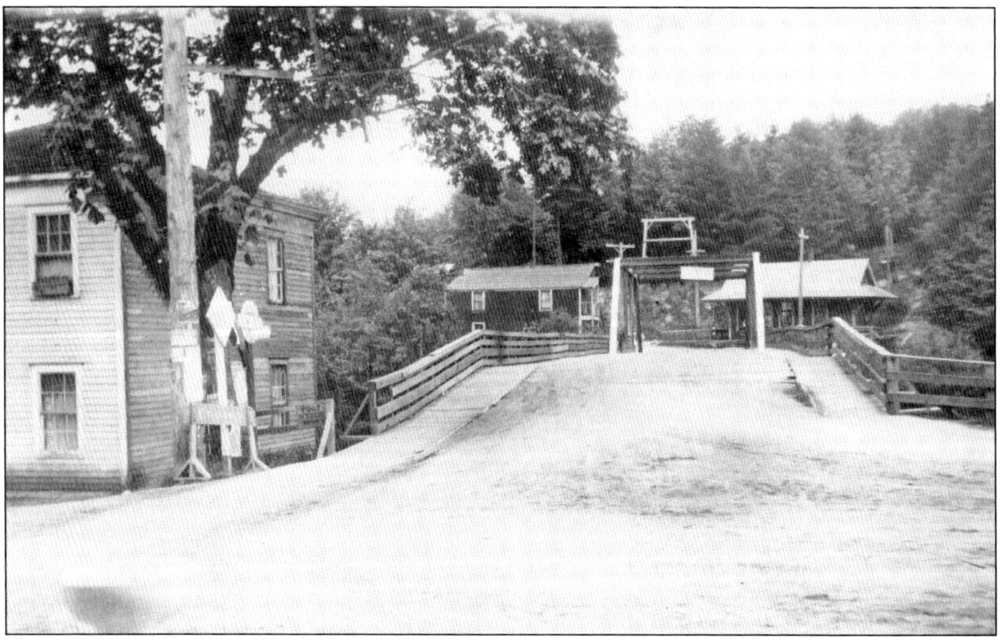
A second wagon bridge replaced the original pioneer bridge across the Deschutes River (at what is now Boston Street) in 1880. It was built as a single wooden span, 300 feet from end to end, with a dirt surface over its wooden planks to match the city streets. This view looks east across the bridge from Reserve Street (Deschutes Way). (Courtesy of Henderson House Museum, No. 640.)

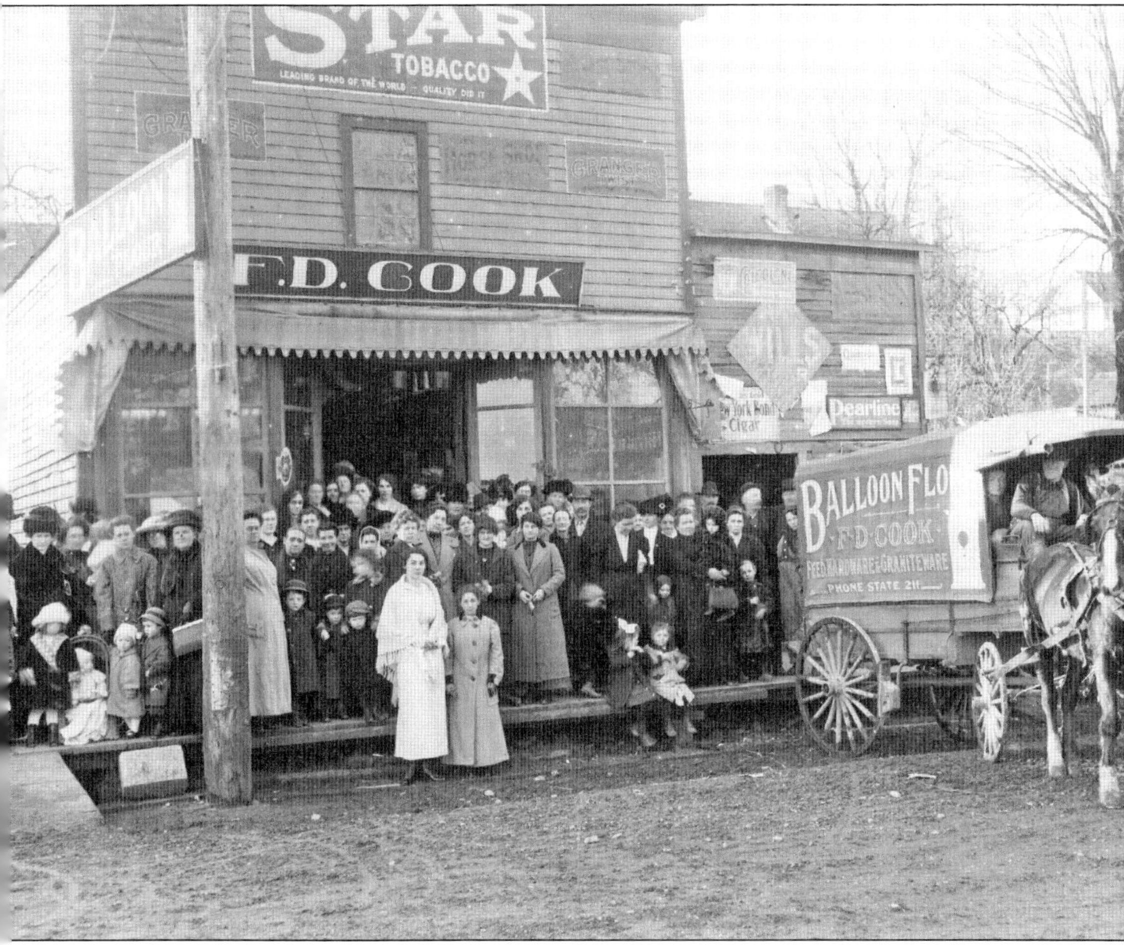

A crowd gathers for an unidentified occasion outside the F. D. Cook store, located on Reserve Street (Deschutes Way) near the Boston Street Bridge. Frank Cook, who operated the store from 1905 to 1919, was mayor of Tumwater twice. At the time this picture was taken, deliveries were still being made by horse-drawn vehicle—but a telephone number for the store appears on the side of the wagon. Times are changing fast. (Courtesy of Henderson House Museum, No. 1034.)

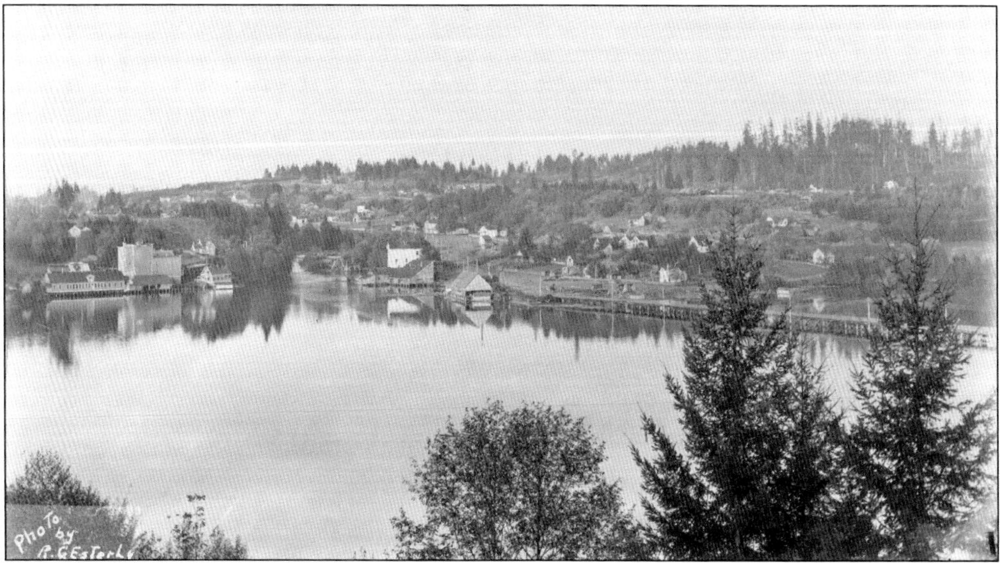

In this view of Tumwater from around 1902, looking upstream from neighboring Olympia, the white Lincoln Flour Mill—though idle—still commands center stage. To the left, the first wooden buildings of the Olympia Brewing Company occupy the former site of the Biles tannery, where the original Biles home still stands at the water's edge. The long wooden bridge to Olympia, built in 1860 and rebuilt around 1900, crosses the waterway on the right. (Courtesy of Henderson House Museum, No. 749.)

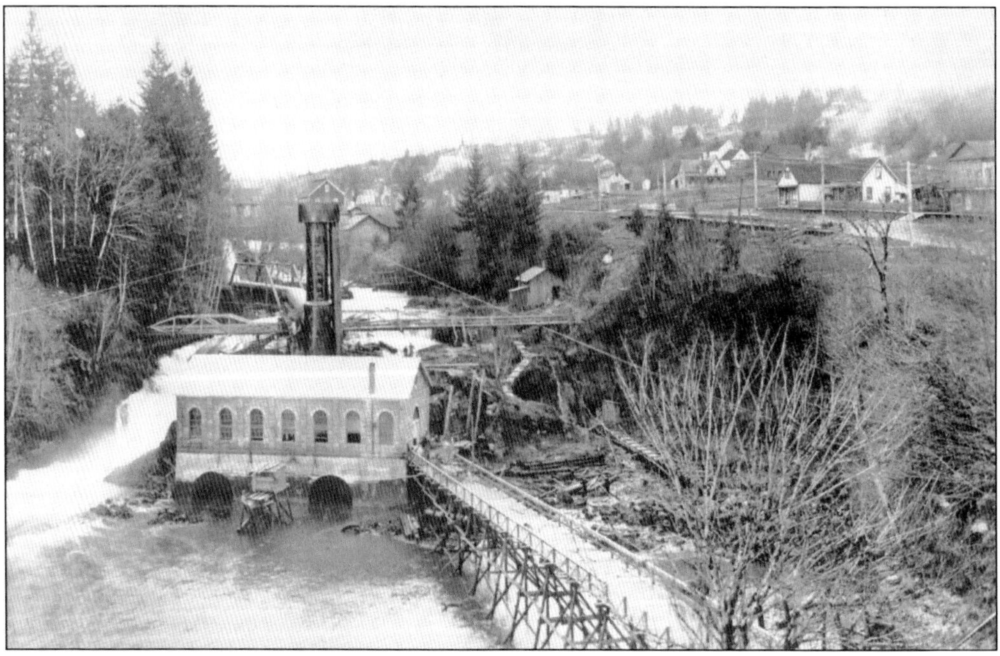

In 1904, the Olympia Light and Power Company built Powerhouse No. 2 at the foot of the Lower Falls. Water from the Upper Falls was piped down the river canyon to the new power plant at the bottom, taking full advantage of the river's 82-foot descent. The huge metal pipe, or penstock, can be seen on the left bank, just as it crosses the footbridge and enters the power plant. (Courtesy of Henderson House Museum, No. 038.)

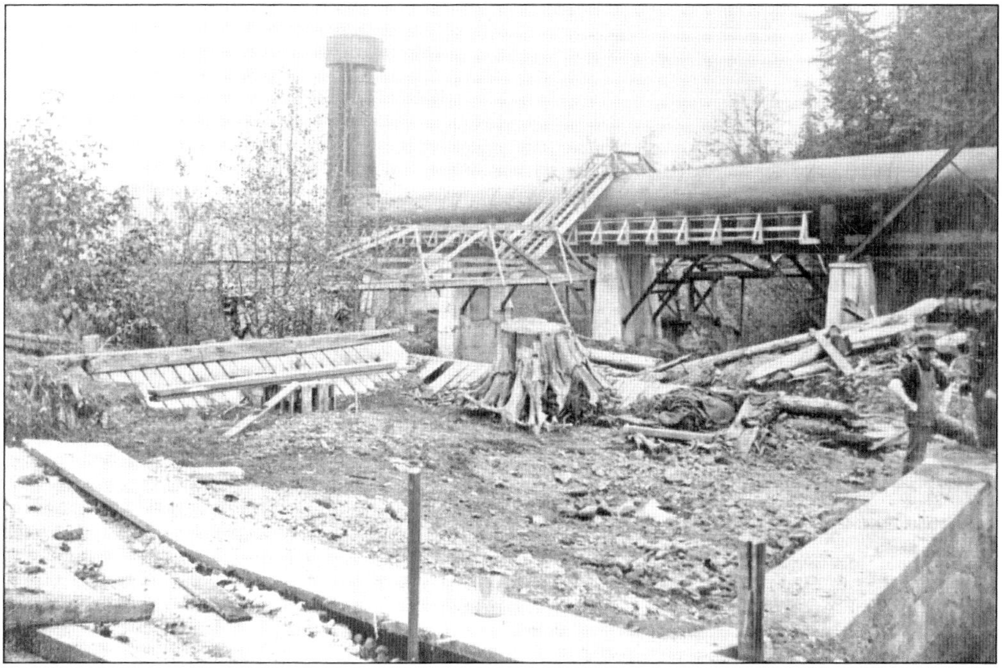

When Powerhouse No. 2 was built, the pedestrian bridge at the Lower Falls—visible in so many photographs of pioneer Tumwater— had to be rerouted up and over the giant penstock. (Courtesy of Henderson House Museum, No. 599.)

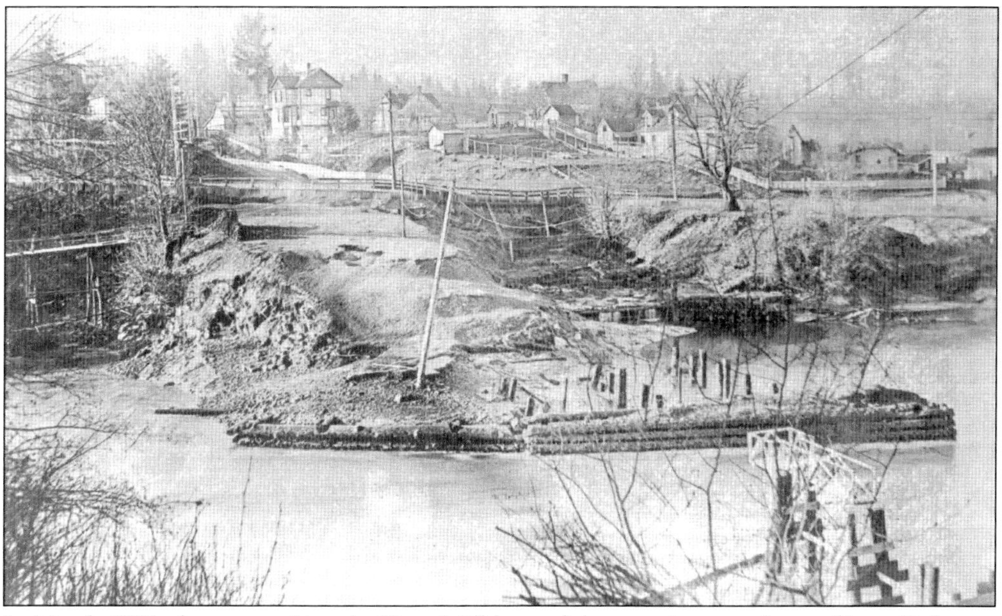

In March 1905, the vacant Lincoln Flour Mill burned down to its waterfront pilings. Only two months earlier, the adjacent Kendall Sash and Door Factory had burned to the ground as well. Yet even as the old waterfront industries disappeared, new signs of life were emerging. In this view from the early 20th century, the 1905 Naumann home, now the Henderson House Museum (tall structure, left of center), rises above the charred timbers of the burned-out Lincoln Mill. (Courtesy of Henderson House Museum, No. 1279.)

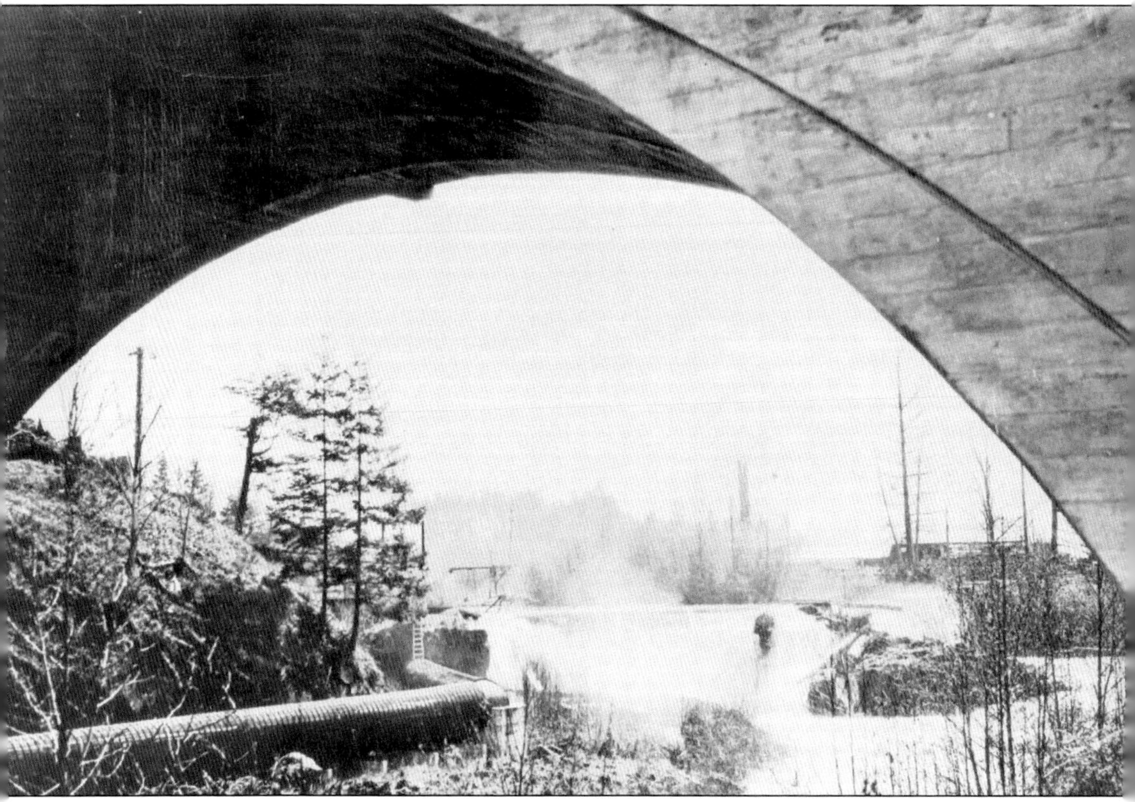

In 1915–1916, the wagon bridge "between the two falls" was replaced with the concrete structure of the current Boston Street Bridge. In this view, looking south around 1920, the Upper Falls are nicely framed through one of the bridge's three arches. The penstock for Powerhouse No. 2 can be seen on the left. (Courtesy of Henderson House Museum, No. 590.)

Two

The Best Beer on the West Coast

The Olympia Brewing Company got its start with a shave and a haircut. German immigrant Leopold Schmidt—already a successful brewer of beer in Montana—was visiting the state capital of Olympia in 1894 when a local barber tipped him off to the presence of artesian springs a few miles away. Schmidt made a detour to neighboring Tumwater and liked the water he found there. He collected some samples, shipped them off to Chicago for testing, and got the results he had hoped for: Tumwater's artesian springs were ideal for brewing beer.

Schmidt sold his Montana brewery and purchased 5 acres, complete with springs, at the foot of Tumwater Falls. By October 1896, his tiny, new Tumwater brewery was marketing its first batch of Olympia Pale Export lager. "It is unqualifiedly the best beer made on the West Coast," one local newspaper editor wrote emphatically, "and that is saying much."

In 1906, having outgrown its original wooden buildings, the Olympia Brewing Company expanded into a handsome six-story brick brewhouse—an unmistakable symbol of prosperity and success. But in 1914, the citizens of Washington voted to outlaw alcohol, forcing Olympia Brewing to suspend all beer production. After trying unsuccessfully to convert the brewery to other uses, the Schmidt family was forced to close the plant and sell the land and buildings below the Lower Falls.

By 1933, America was fed up with Prohibition. When the laws against brewing were lifted, the sons of Leopold Schmidt decided to build another Tumwater brewery just upstream from the old one. On January 14, 1934, workers cheered as the first brown bottle of Olympia beer rolled out of the new brewing plant.

Family-owned Olympia Brewing was sold to the Pabst Brewing Company in 1983, sold again to the Miller Brewing Company 16 years later, and acquired by South African Breweries Limited (SAB Ltd.) in 2002. The following year, more than a century after Leopold Schmidt first came to town, the brewery beside the river sounded its whistle a final time and closed its doors for good.

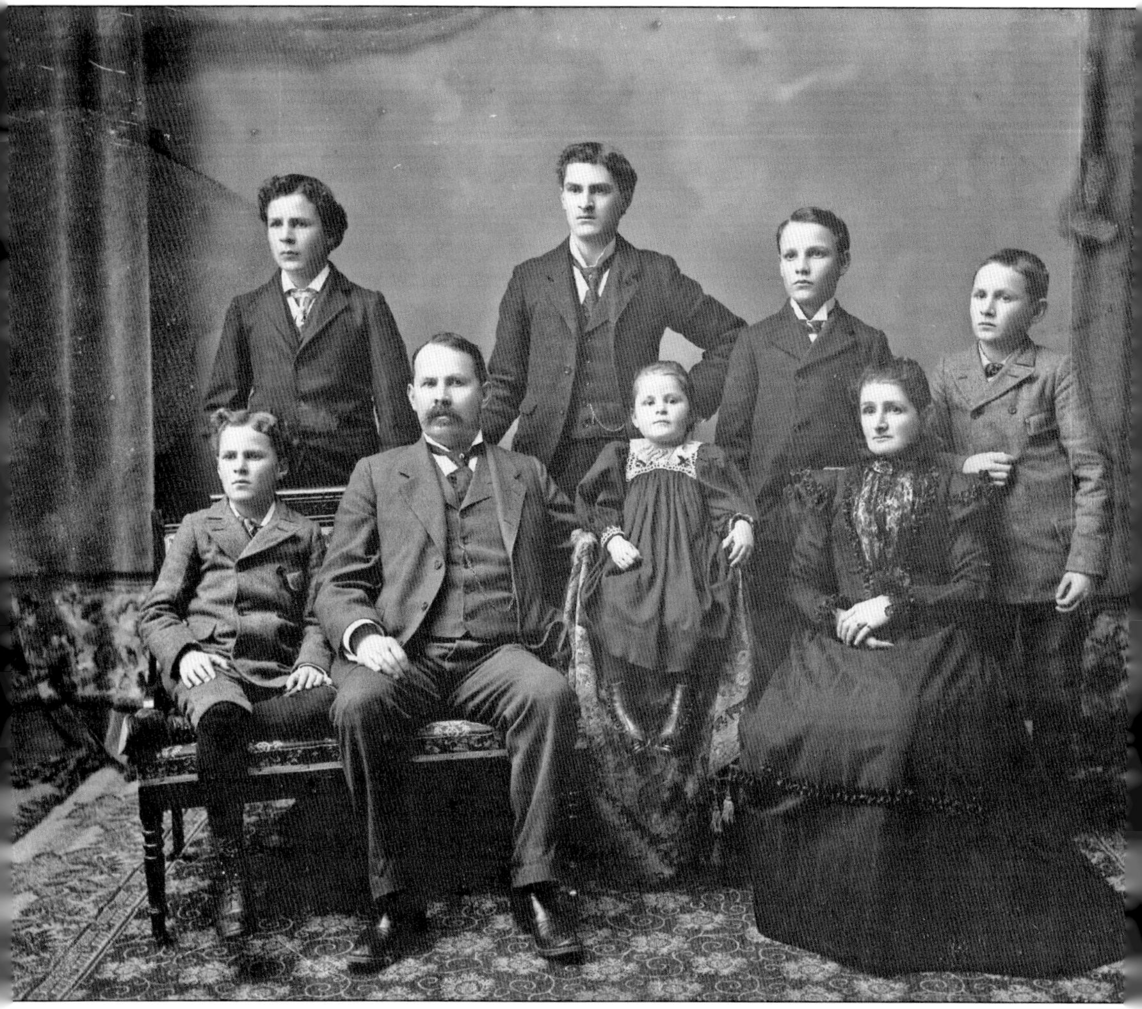

German-born Leopold Schmidt came to America when he was 20, made his way to the goldfields of Montana, and found a job in a frontier brewery. In 1878, at the age of 32, he returned to his native country to study the science of brewing beer. He met and married his wife, Johanna Steiner, while attending the brewing academy in her hometown of Worms and brought her back to Montana with him. This portrait of the Schmidts and their six children was taken in the late 1890s, shortly after they moved to Tumwater. They are, from left to right, (first row) Frederick, Leopold, Philippine, and Johanna; (second row) Frank, Peter G., Leopold II, and Adolph. (Courtesy of Olympia Tumwater Foundation.)

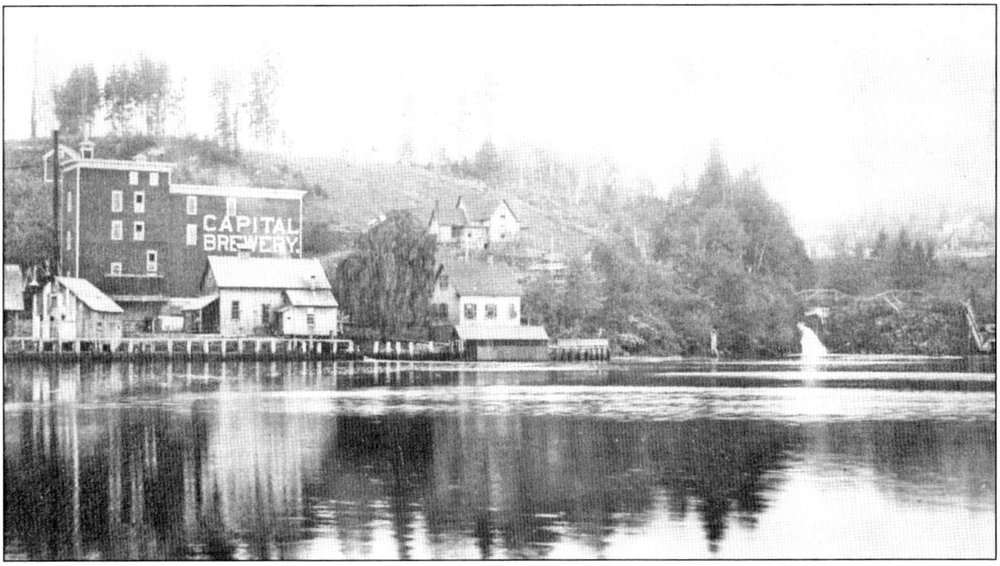

Leopold Schmidt bought the former Biles and Sons Tannery site from Clark Biles's widow, Fannie, in 1895. In addition to artesian springs, the site had potential for docks and shipping (at least when the tide was in). In this photograph, the original name of Schmidt's company, the Capital Brewing Company, appears on the side of his first wooden brewhouse. The pioneer Biles family home still stands at the water's edge. (Courtesy of Henderson House Museum, No. 1321.)

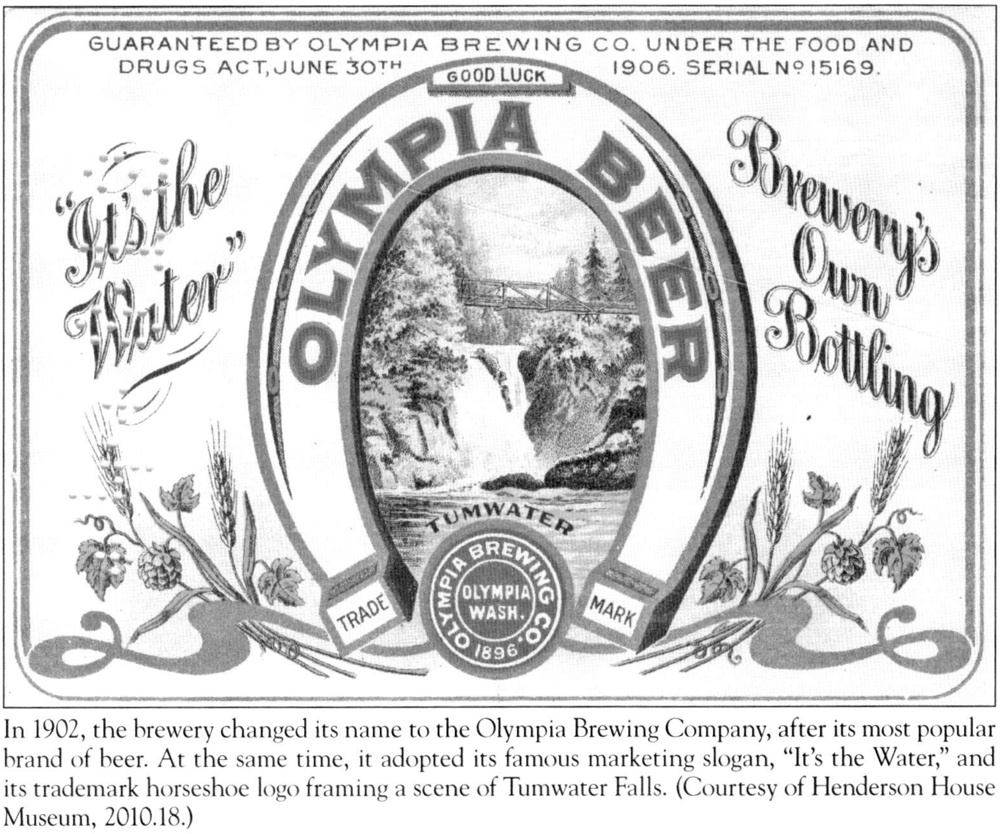

In 1902, the brewery changed its name to the Olympia Brewing Company, after its most popular brand of beer. At the same time, it adopted its famous marketing slogan, "It's the Water," and its trademark horseshoe logo framing a scene of Tumwater Falls. (Courtesy of Henderson House Museum, 2010.18.)

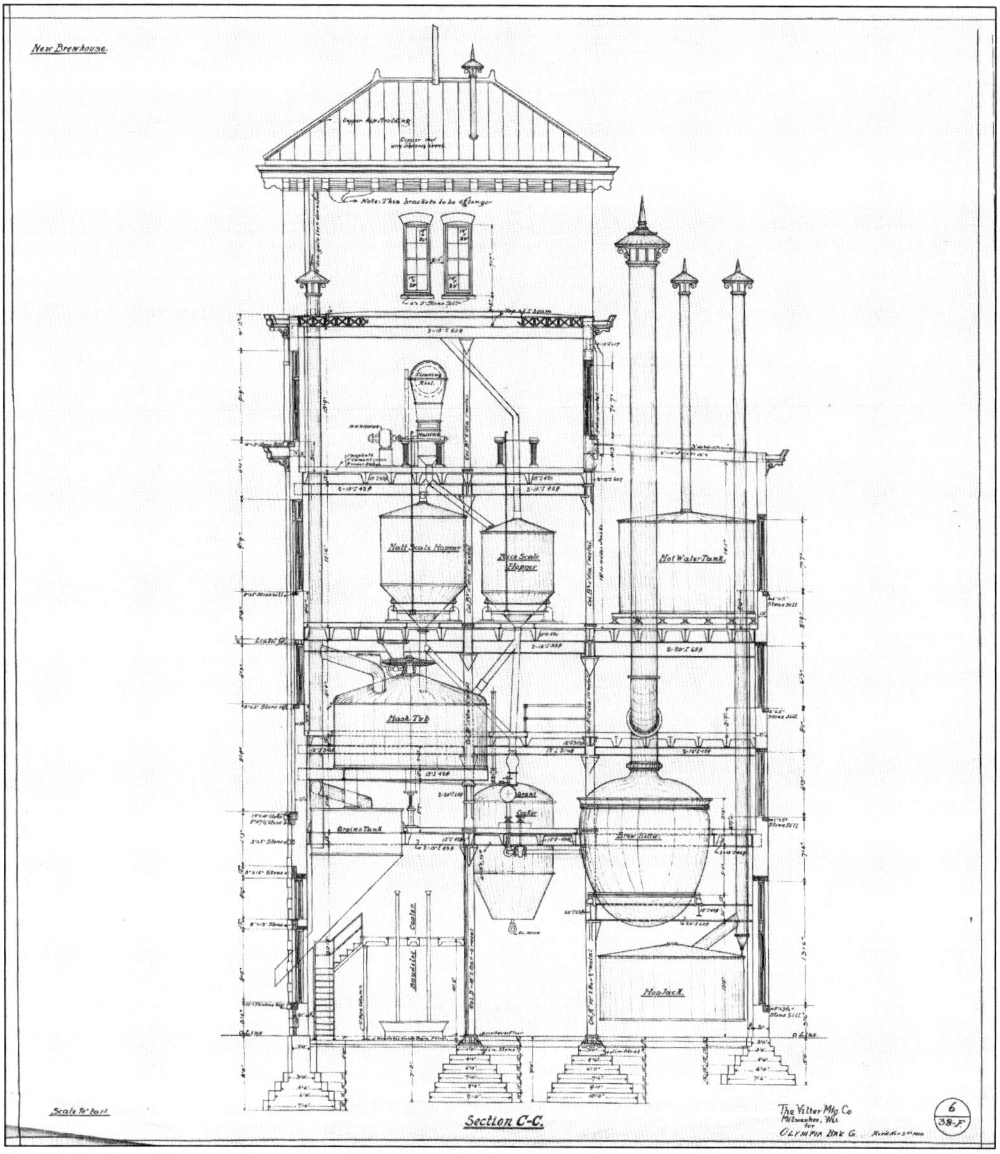

In 1905, the Olympia Brewing Company broke ground on a new six-story brick brewhouse. Hidden behind its splendid facade was a gravity-brewing system that began with the grinding of roasted malt barley upstairs and ended down at the bottom with kettles of hop-flavored brew. (Architectural drawing by the Vilter Manufacturing Company, section C-C; courtesy of Henderson House Museum Collection.)

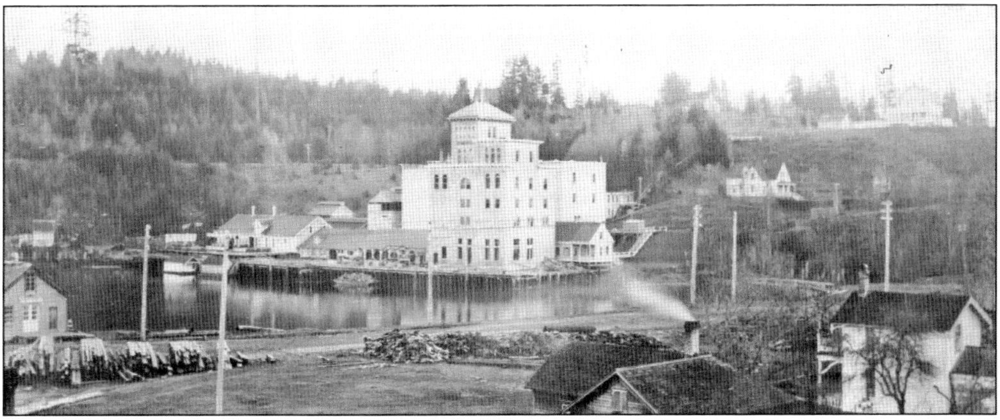

The new redbrick brewhouse towered over the lower buildings of the Olympia Brewing Company in 1906, completely dwarfing the waterfront Biles house. The grand home on top of the hill is Schmidt's own, built in 1904 and still standing today. Before moving into the big house, the Schmidts lived in the steep-roofed house located halfway up the slope. (Courtesy of Henderson House Museum, No. 1057.)

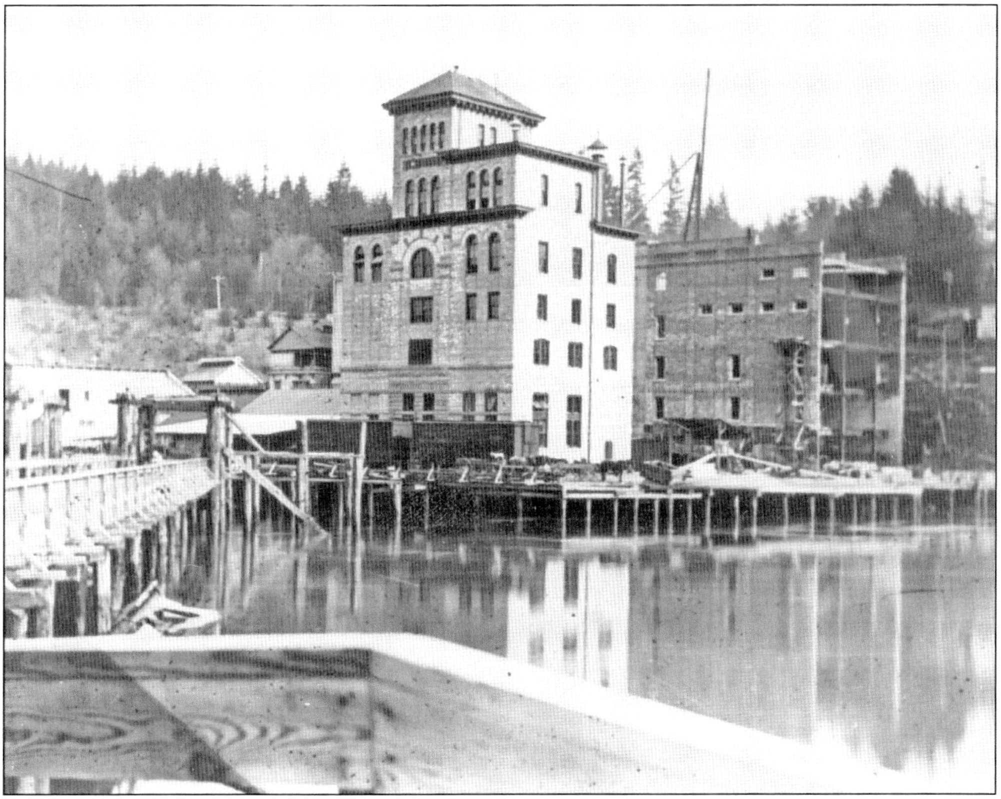

Two additional structures appeared on the scene by 1907. One was a railroad bridge across the river (left), allowing Northern Pacific trains to reach the brewery complex. The other was a brick warehouse (under construction, right), where beer would be stored in enormous tanks while fermentation took place. The Biles house was gone—but it hadn't gone far. It was moved by barge to the residential neighborhood on the opposite bank of the river. (Courtesy of Henderson House Museum, No. 1302.)

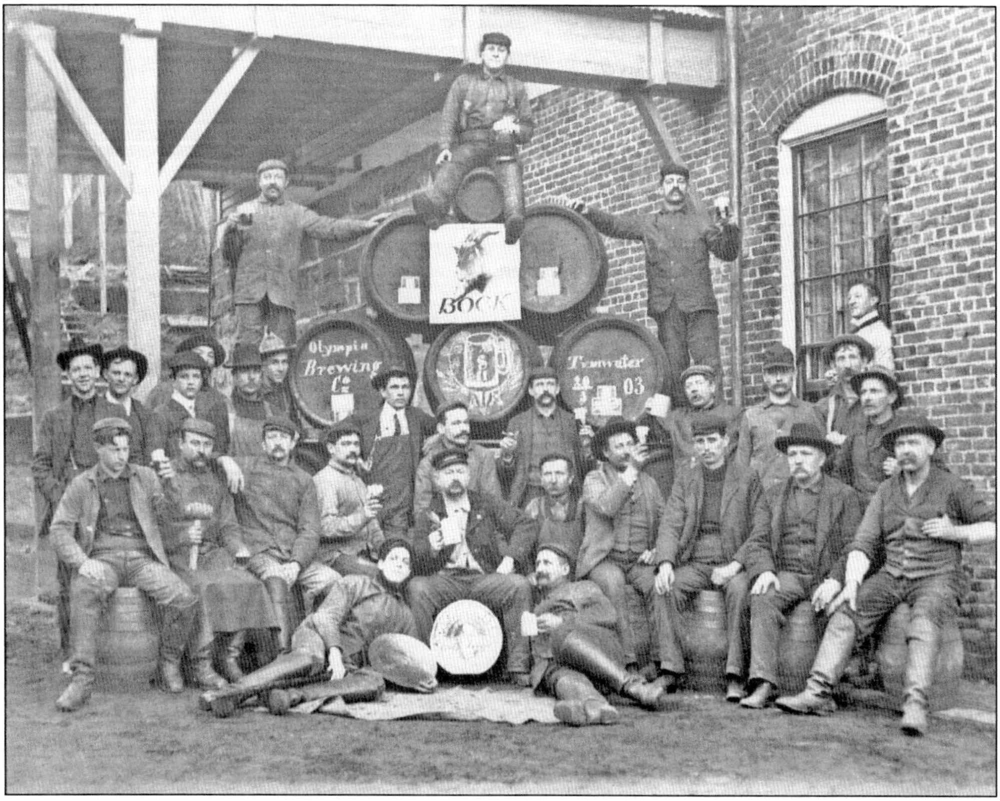

Brewery workers raise a glass with brewmaster William Naumann (seated at center, with beard), the original owner of the home now known as the Henderson House Museum. The 1903–1905 Brewers Union contract guaranteed workers free beer "four times a day during working hours, at the noon hour, and at quitting time," provided that no more than five minutes each time was spent at the tap. (Courtesy of Olympia Tumwater Foundation.)

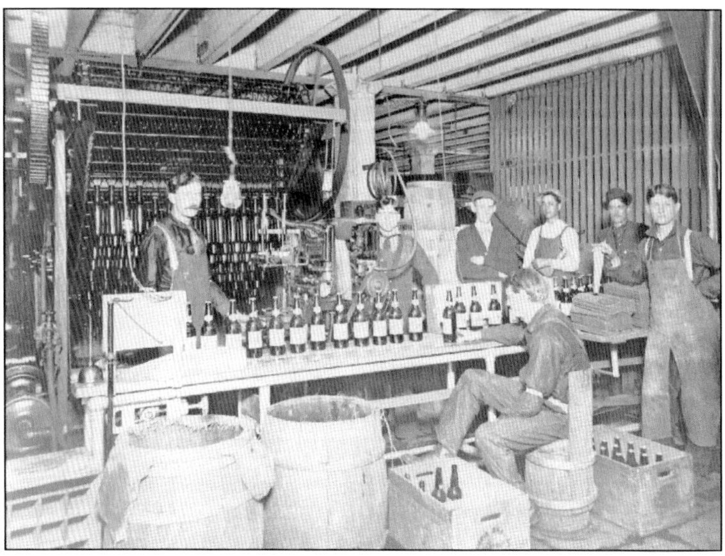

Schmidt adopted the use of metal bottle caps early, which improved pasteurization and allowed him to ship beyond local markets. Here the packaging crew inspects bottles as they come off the pasteurizer. Workers will next wrap each one in brown paper and pack them in barrels for shipping. (Courtesy of Olympia Tumwater Foundation.)

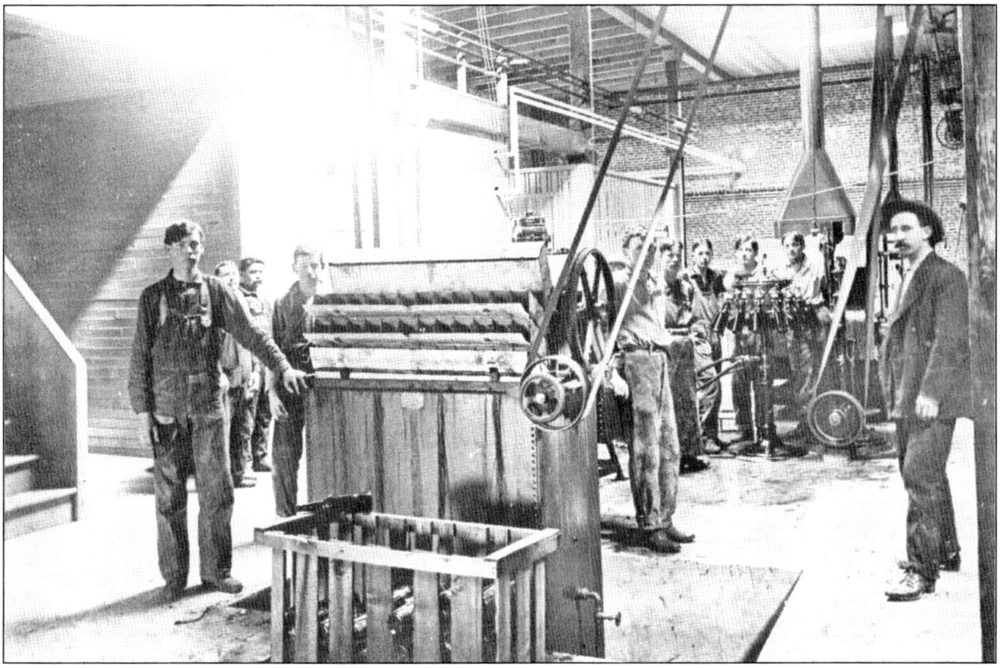

Empty beer bottles were returned to the brewery where they were cleaned up and reused. This contraption was used to soak the labels from bottles so they could be filled again. (Courtesy of Olympia Tumwater Foundation.)

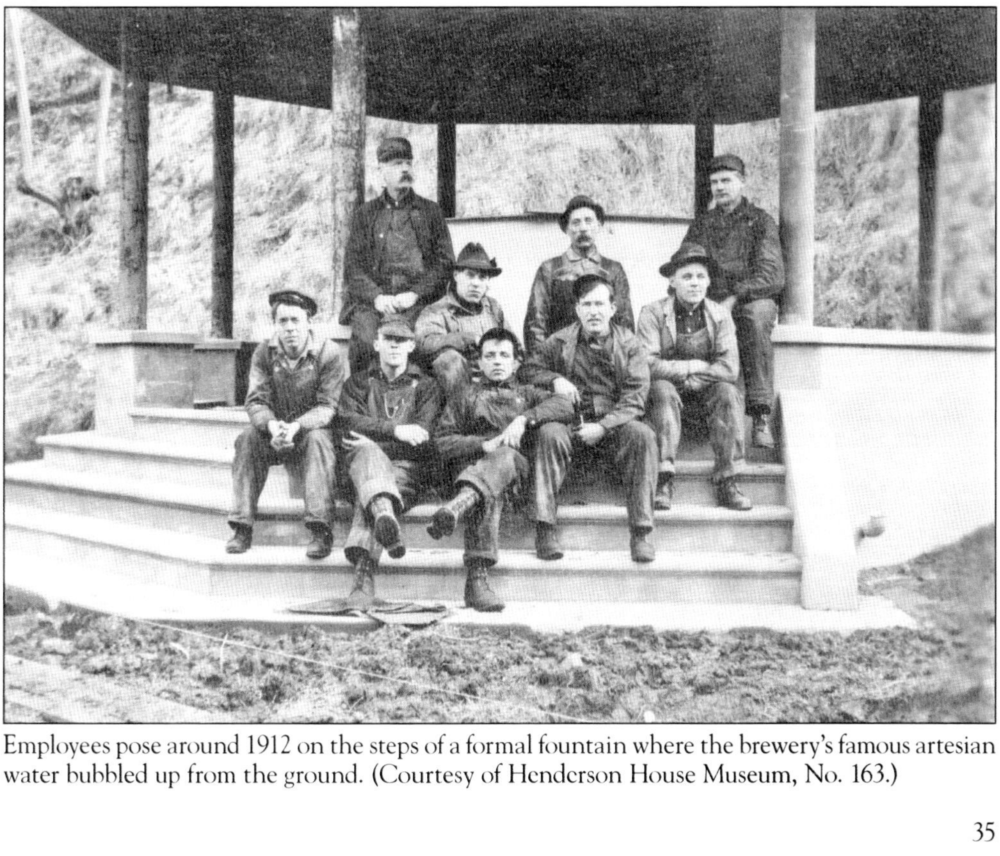

Employees pose around 1912 on the steps of a formal fountain where the brewery's famous artesian water bubbled up from the ground. (Courtesy of Henderson House Museum, No. 163.)

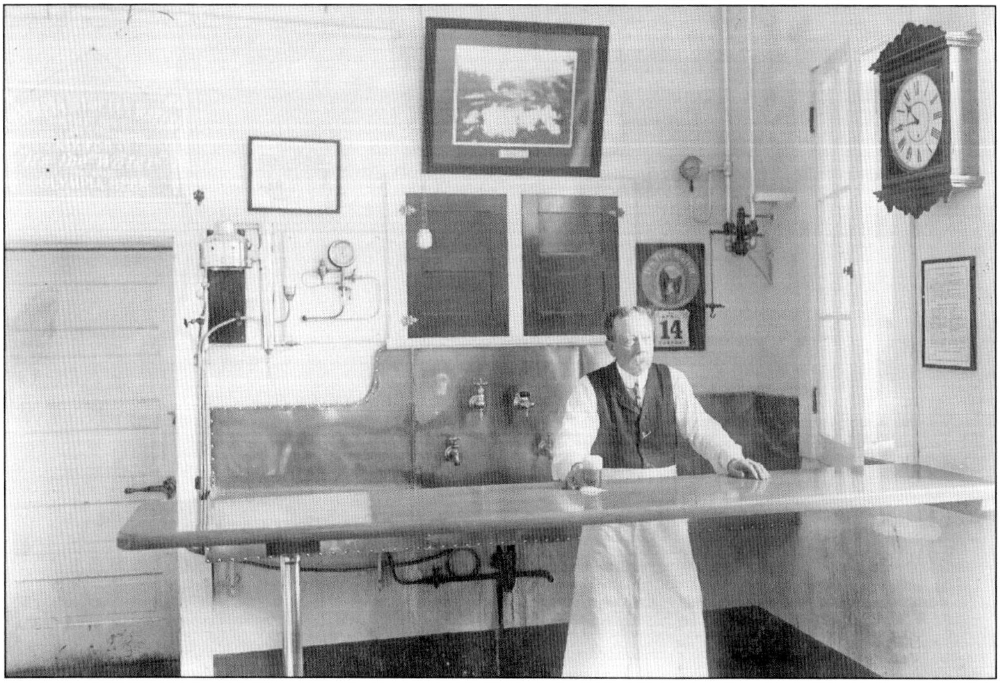

Harry B. Cusack enjoys a pint in the brewery's tap room. Cusack was mayor of Tumwater in 1898. The photograph was taken in 1903 before the brick brewhouse was built. (Courtesy of Henderson House Museum, No. 160.)

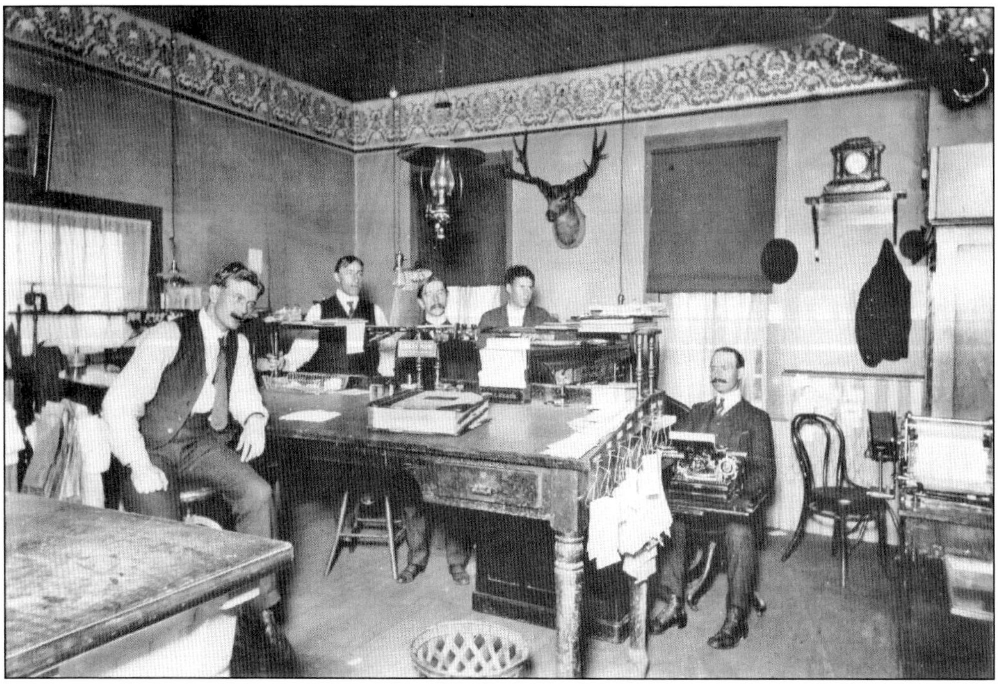

Accountant John Rohrbeck (second from left) rose to the position of assistant secretary of the Olympia Brewing Company in the 1930s. He is pictured here around 1905 with the rest of the brewery's accounting staff. (Courtesy of the Mildred Rohrbeck Hotop family.)

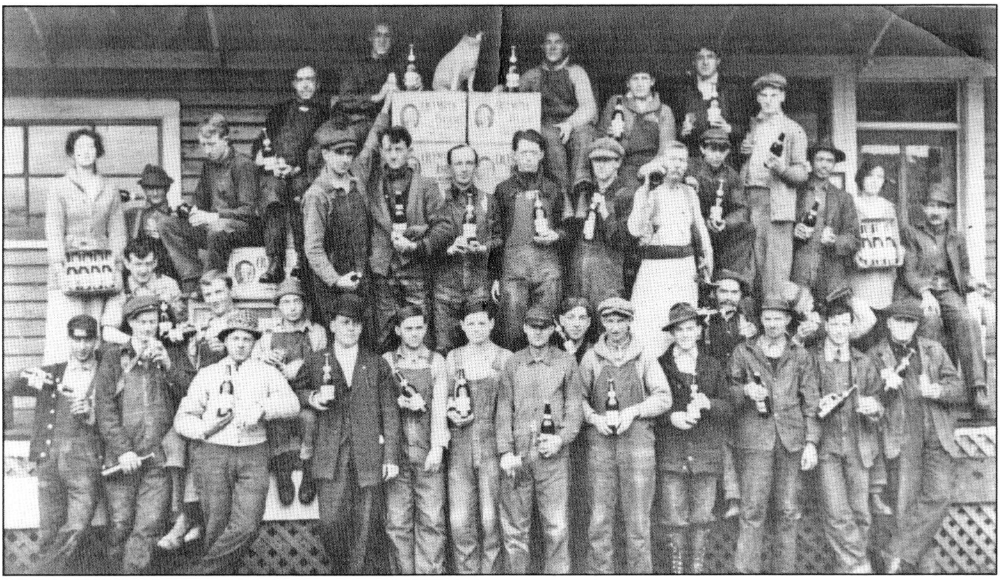

The bottling crew shows off the big bottles known as "jumbos." The bottle house dog (on top of the crates) was called Jumbo, too. (Courtesy of Olympia Tumwater Foundation.)

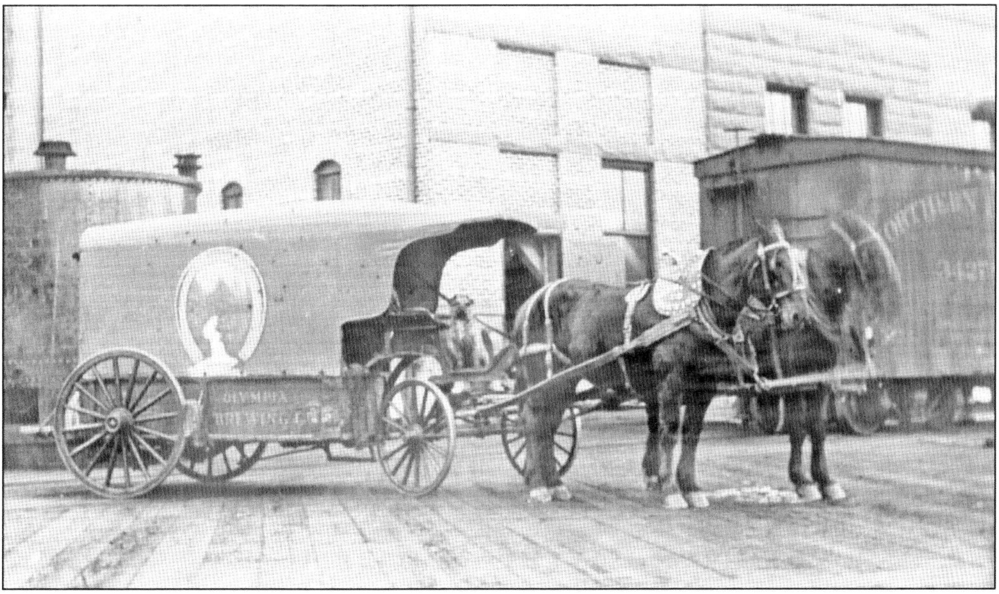

A horse-drawn brewery wagon waits on the dock outside the brick brewhouse. Note the railroad car on the right and the company's horseshoe logo on the side of the van. (Courtesy of Olympia Tumwater Foundation.)

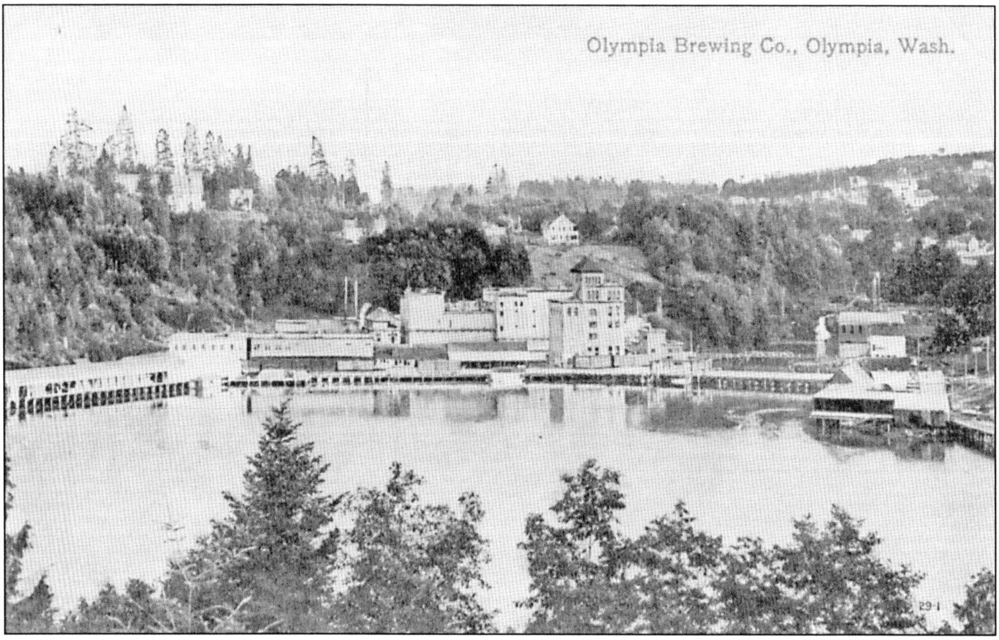

Although Leopold Schmidt eventually owned five West Coast breweries, he brewed the Olympia brand exclusively at his flagship plant in Tumwater. He considered it his best line of beer and believed its taste could not be duplicated without water from Tumwater's springs. (Courtesy of Henderson House Museum, No. 1536.)

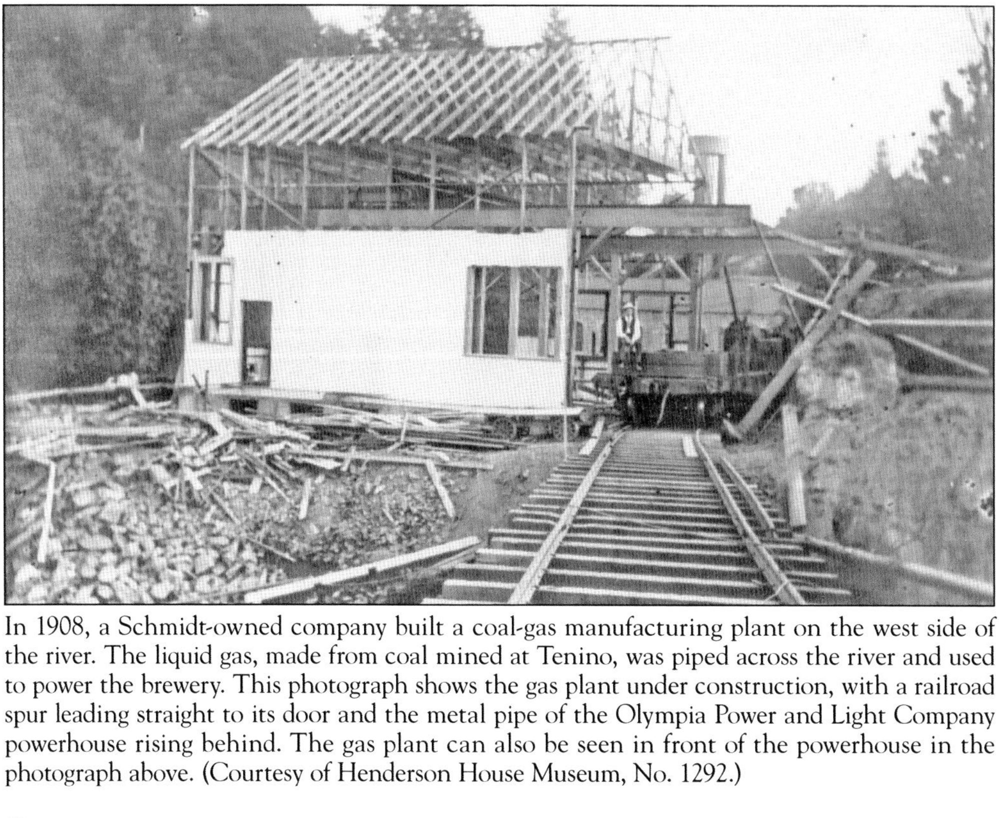

In 1908, a Schmidt-owned company built a coal-gas manufacturing plant on the west side of the river. The liquid gas, made from coal mined at Tenino, was piped across the river and used to power the brewery. This photograph shows the gas plant under construction, with a railroad spur leading straight to its door and the metal pipe of the Olympia Power and Light Company powerhouse rising behind. The gas plant can also be seen in front of the powerhouse in the photograph above. (Courtesy of Henderson House Museum, No. 1292.)

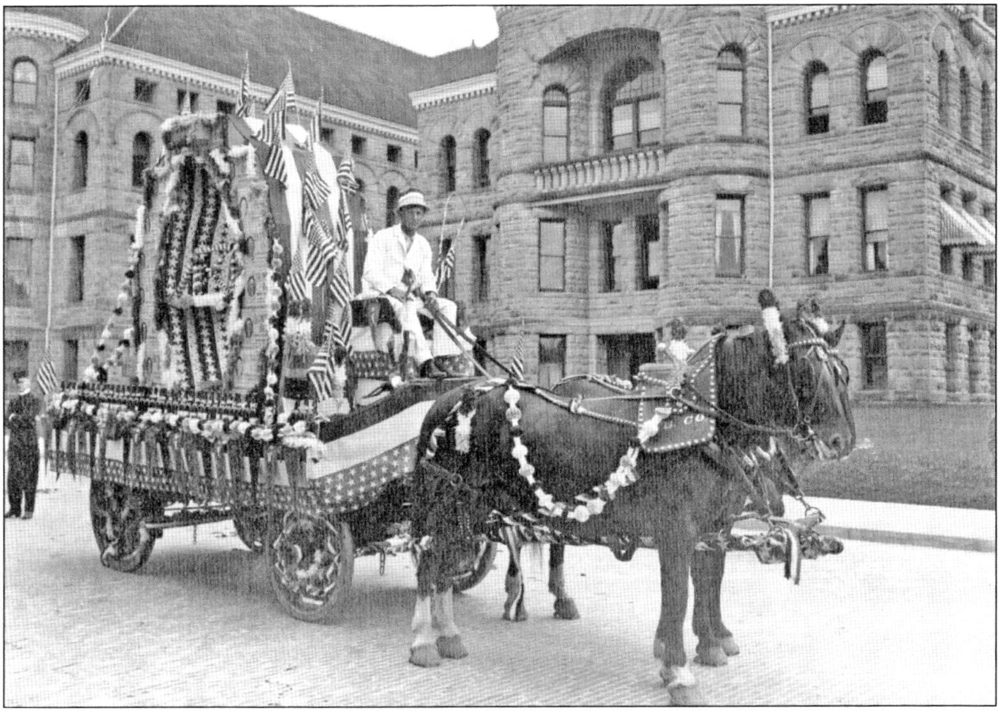

The brewery, though located in Tumwater, maintained a close relationship with the adjacent city of Olympia. This is the brewing company's patriotic entry—complete with bunting, pom-poms, and flags—in Olympia's Fourth of July Parade around 1910. (Courtesy of Henderson House Museum, No. 299.)

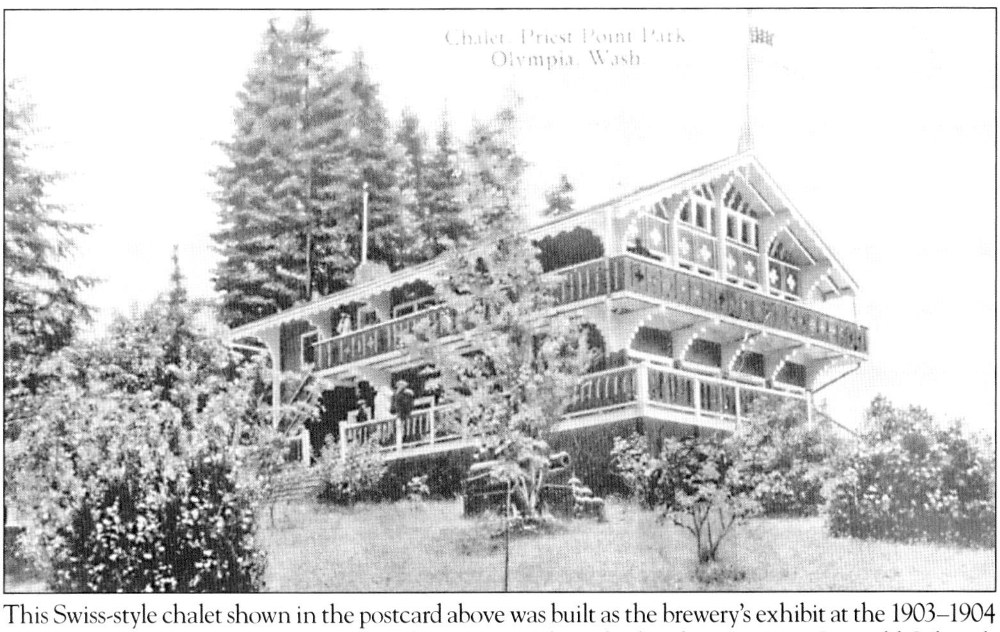

This Swiss-style chalet shown in the postcard above was built as the brewery's exhibit at the 1903–1904 Lewis and Clark Exposition in Portland, Oregon. When the big fair was over, Leopold Schmidt donated the chalet to the City of Olympia for use in its new Priest Point Park. The chalet was reassembled at Priest Point in 1905 and survived into the 1960s. (Courtesy of private collection.)

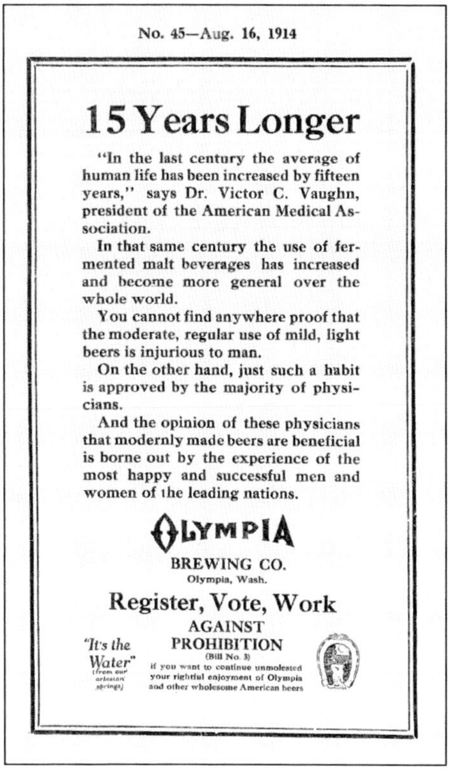

Leopold Schmidt, alarmed by the growing influence of antialcohol crusaders, tried to fight the temperance movement of the early 20th century, but Prohibition came anyway. Schmidt died in 1914—six weeks before the citizens of Washington, Oregon, and Idaho voted to "go dry." National Prohibition followed in 1920. (Both, courtesy of Olympia Tumwater Foundation.)

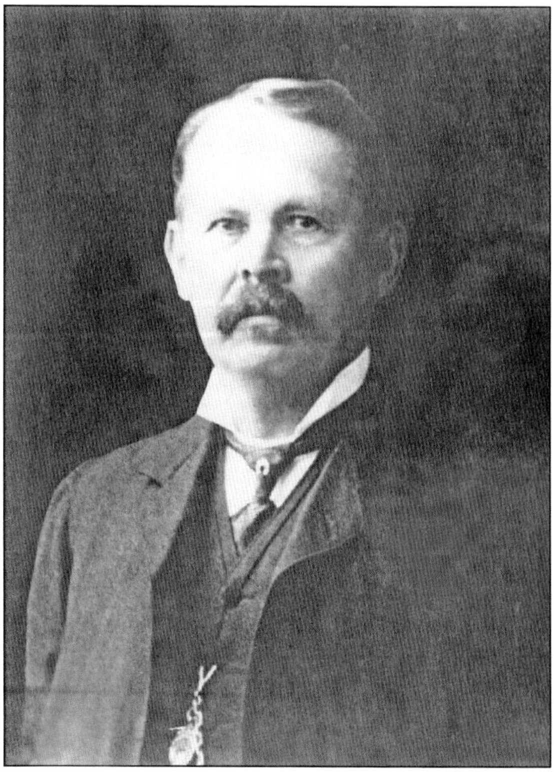

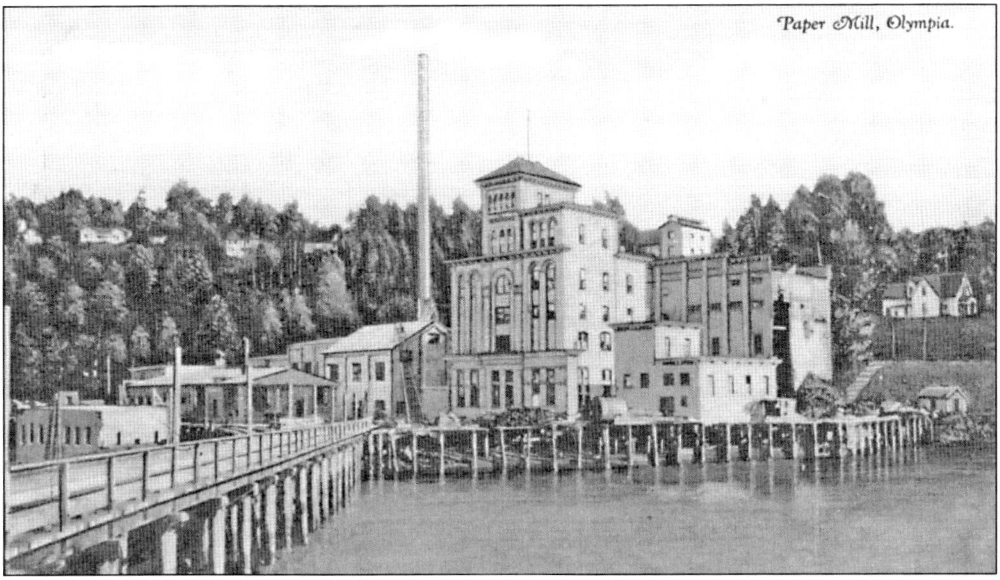

On January 1, 1916, all Northwest breweries were forced to stop brewing beer. After an unsuccessful effort to produce nonalcoholic fruit juice instead, Schmidt's heirs closed down operations in 1921 and sold off the land and buildings at the foot of Tumwater Falls. For a brief time in the late 1920s, a pulp and paper mill occupied the old brewery site. (Courtesy of private collection.)

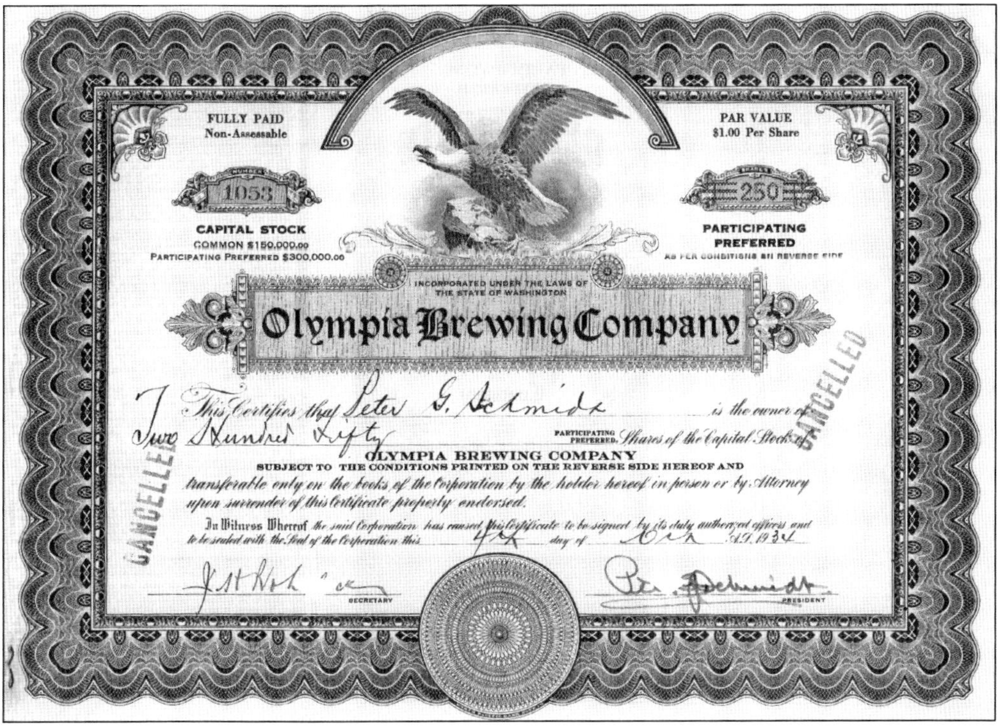

FULLY PAID
Non-Assessable

PAR VALUE
$1.00 Per Share

1053

250

CAPITAL STOCK
COMMON $150,000.00
PARTICIPATING PREFERRED $300,000.00

PARTICIPATING
PREFERRED
AS PER CONDITIONS ON REVERSE SIDE

INCORPORATED UNDER THE LAWS OF THE STATE OF WASHINGTON

Olympia Brewing Company

This Certifies that Peter G. Schmidt is the owner of Two Hundred Fifty PARTICIPATING PREFERRED Shares of the Capital Stock of OLYMPIA BREWING COMPANY SUBJECT TO THE CONDITIONS PRINTED ON THE REVERSE SIDE HEREOF AND transferable only on the books of the Corporation by the holder hereof in person or by Attorney upon surrender of this Certificate properly endorsed.

In Witness Whereof the said Corporation has caused this Certificate to be signed by its duly authorized officers and to be sealed with the Seal of the Corporation this 4th day of Oct A.D. 1934

SECRETARY

PRESIDENT

CANCELLED

CANCELLED

When national Prohibition was repealed in 1933, the Olympia Brewing Company jumped right back into business. Schmidt's sons considered the cost of refitting the old brick brewhouse and decided to build a new facility on land near the Upper Falls. Stock was sold at $1 per share to finance quick construction. (Courtesy of Olympia Tumwater Foundation.)

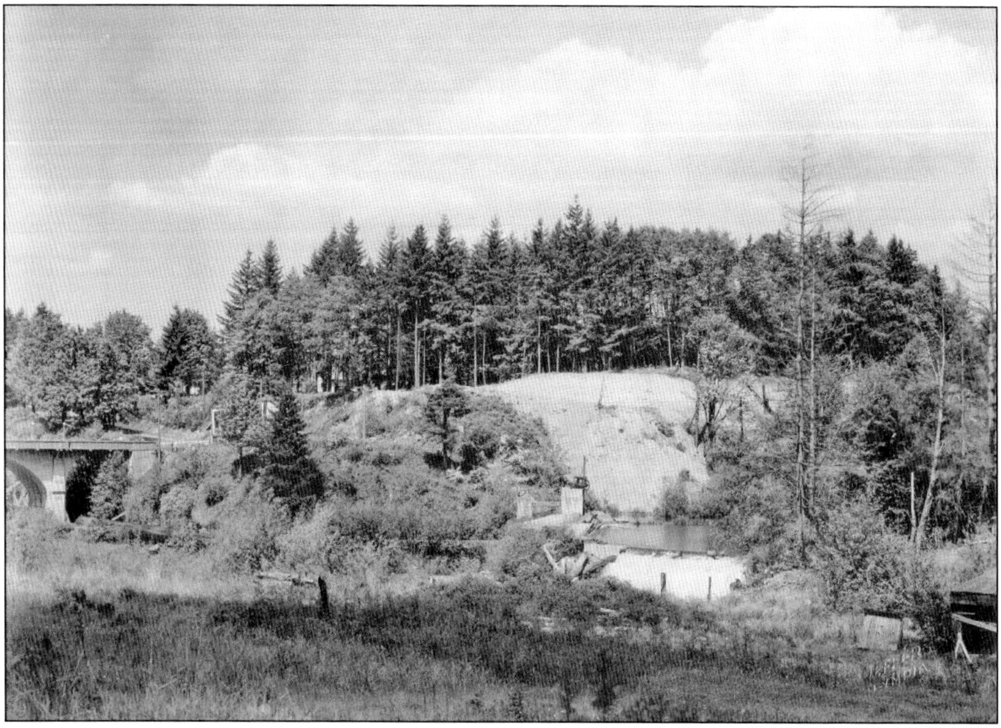

Construction of the new brewery began with clearing the site in the spring of 1933. The east end of the Boston Street Bridge is visible on the left. (Courtesy of Henderson House Museum, No. 071.)

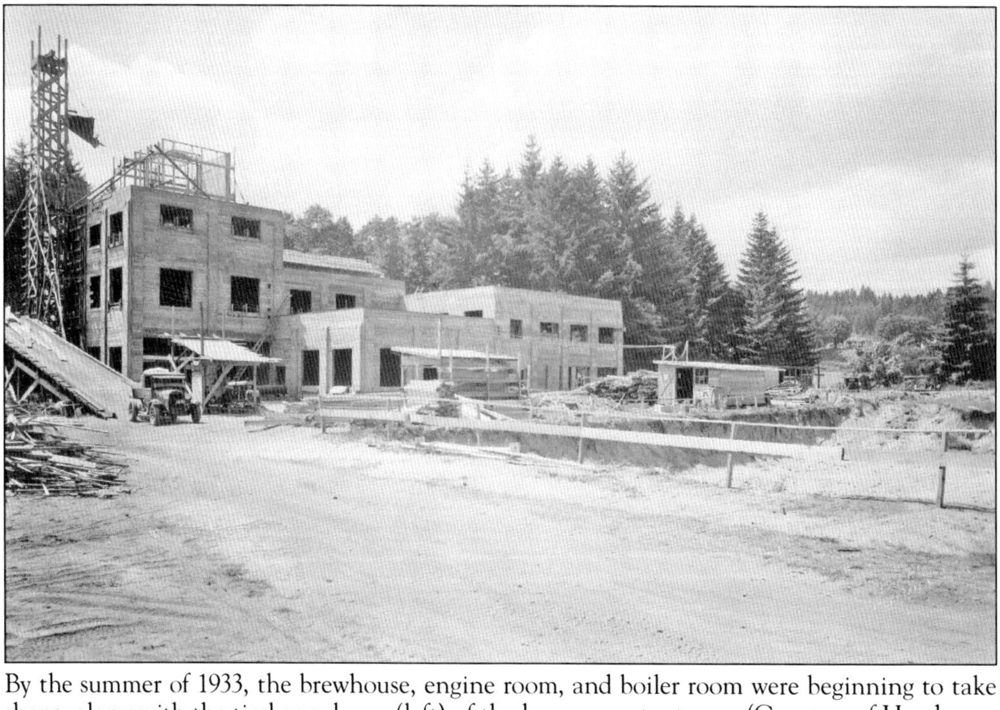

By the summer of 1933, the brewhouse, engine room, and boiler room were beginning to take shape, along with the timber column (left) of the brewery water tower. (Courtesy of Henderson House Museum, No. 070.)

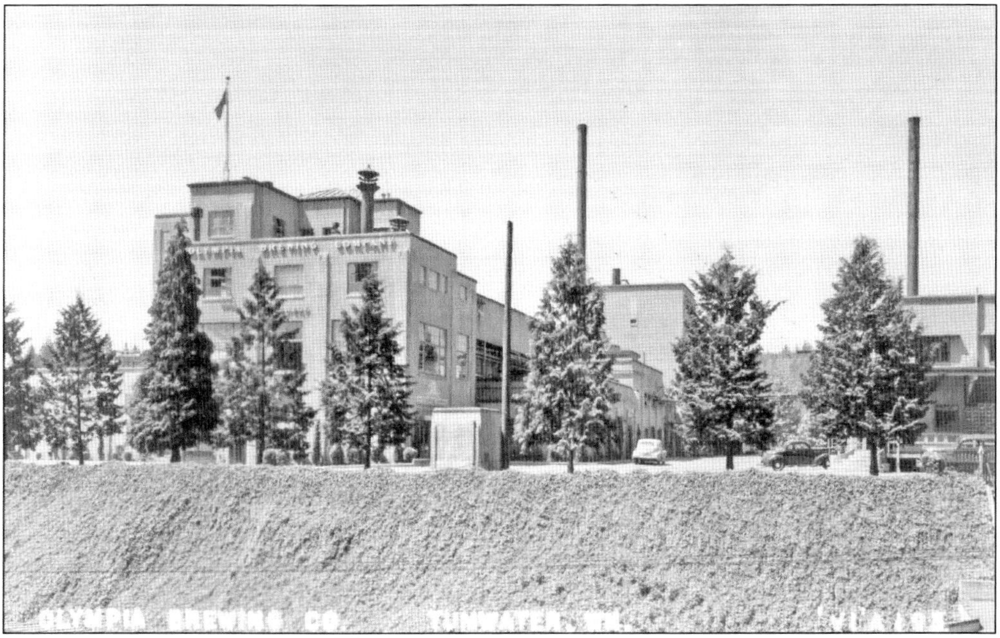

The second Olympia Brewing Company complex, designed by Olympia architect Joseph Wohleb and shown above in this postcard, started brewing beer in October 1933. The new facility hired 112 workers—nearly half of whom had worked at the old brewery before Prohibition. (Courtesy of private collection.)

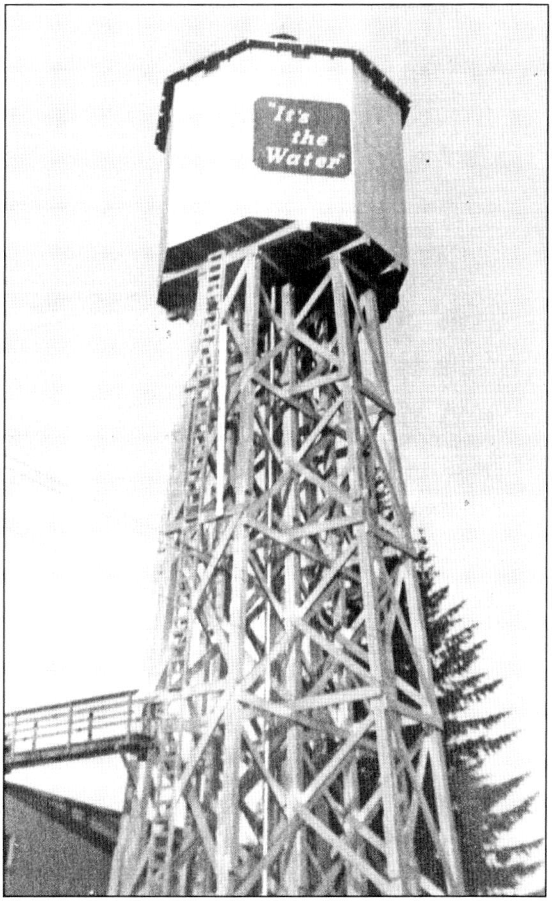

The company's famous artesian water, pumped from wells and springs in Tumwater Valley, was stored in the brewery's wooden water tower until the 1940s, when improved pumping techniques rendered the tank obsolete. (Courtesy of Henderson House Museum, No. 086.)

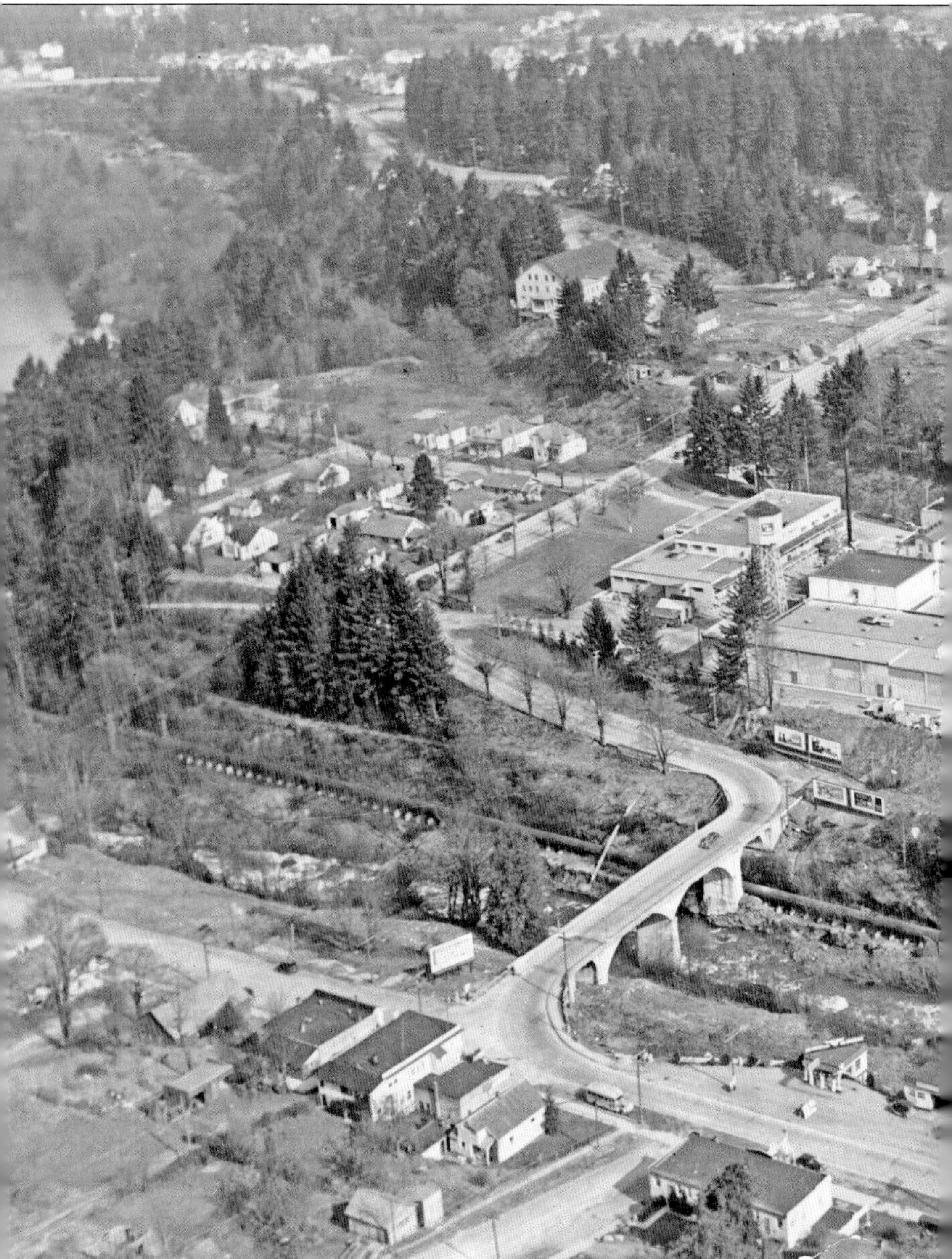

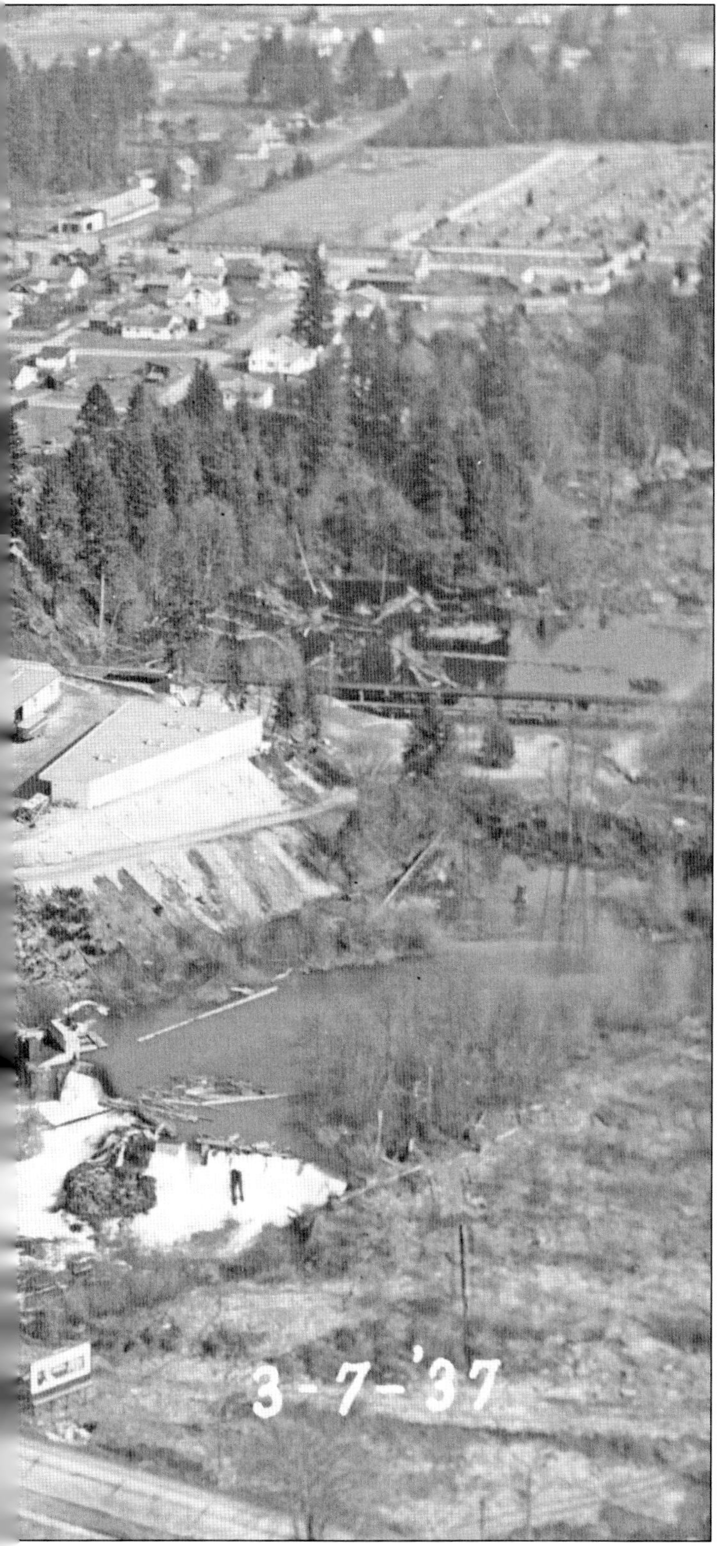

The brewery dominates this aerial view of Tumwater from the mid-1930s. Only a railroad trestle crosses the Deschutes River behind it; the Capitol Boulevard Bridge is not yet in place. At the upper left of the photograph is the three-story structure built by the Schmidts in 1908 as the Tumwater Club, a social gathering spot for brewery employees (see page 95). The Schmidt House stands at the far left, partly obscured by trees (see pages 63 and 64). The powerhouse at the Lower Falls—not visible here—is no longer in operation, but the metal pipe of its penstock still snakes down the east bank of the river from the Upper Falls. (Courtesy of Olympia Tumwater Foundation.)

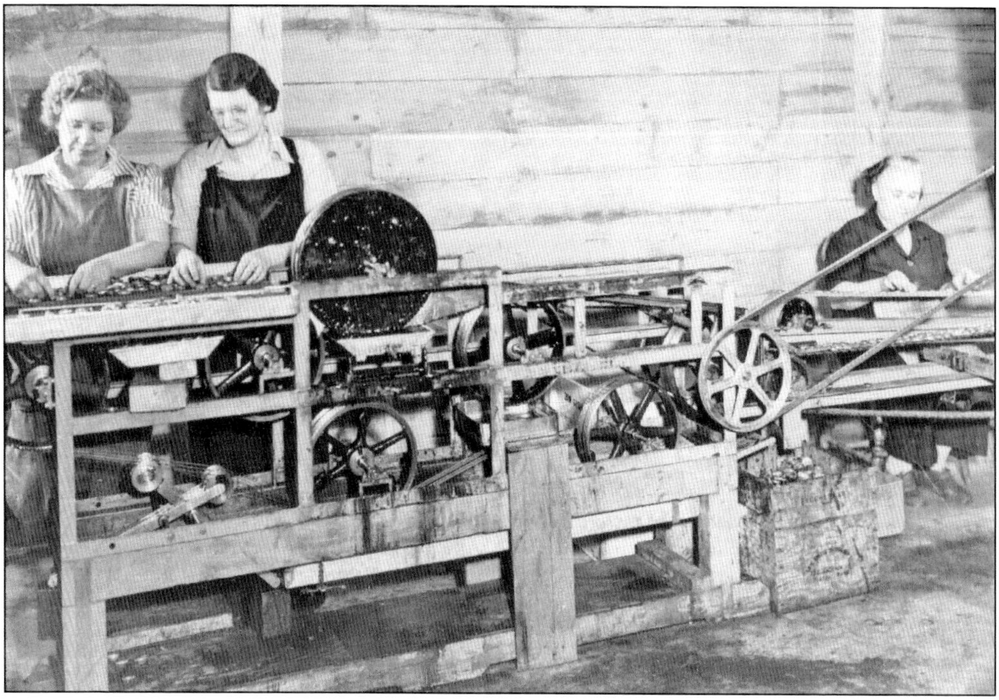

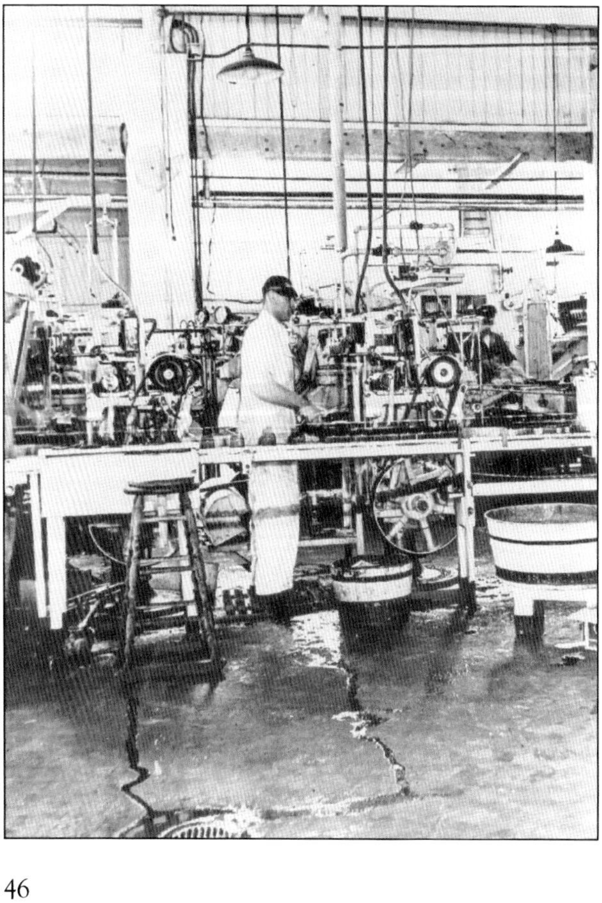

World War II brought shortages of both men and vital supplies. Above, female brewery employees, filling in for men serving in the armed forces, sort and reshape used bottle caps so they can be used again. (Courtesy of Henderson House Museum, No. 105.)

After the war ended in 1945, the Olympia Brewing Company entered a period of rapid growth and expansion. A new bottle house was completed in 1948, replacing the one pictured at left. (Courtesy of Henderson House Museum, No. 102.)

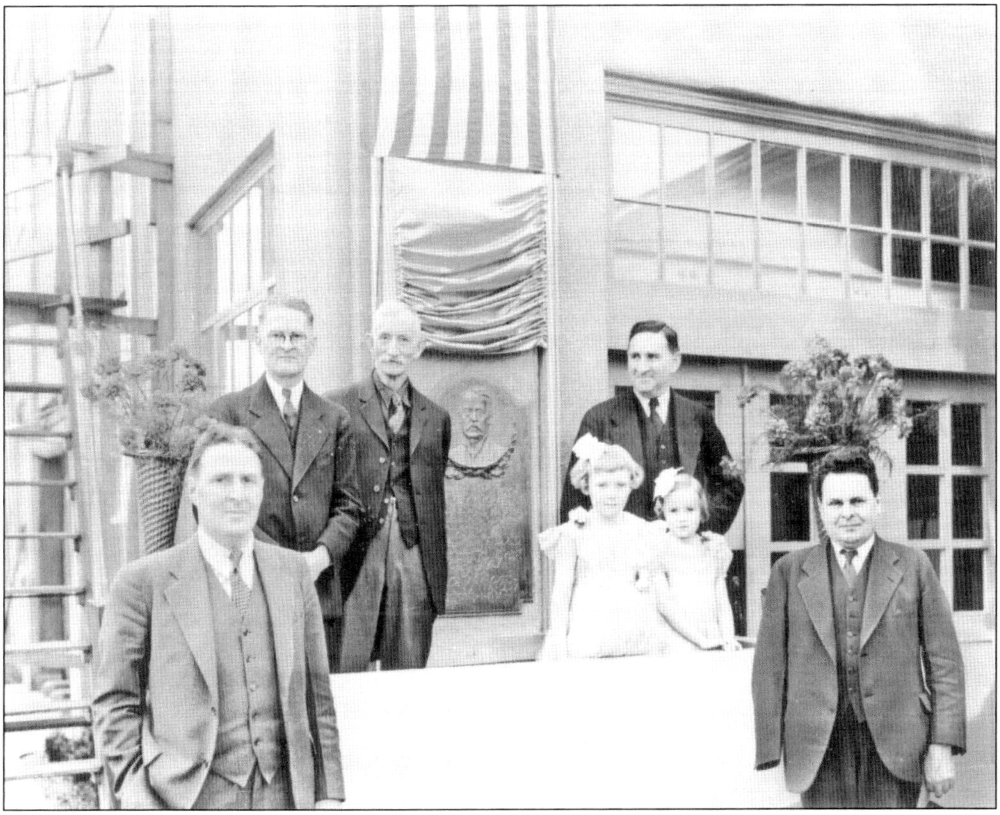

Leopold Schmidt's sons dedicate a bronze plaque in his honor during the company's 50th anniversary celebrations in 1946. From left to right are Frederick Schmidt, Peter G. Schmidt Sr., longtime brewery worker Marion Canby, Adolph Schmidt Sr., and Frank Schmidt. The two little girls are Norma Jean Simila (left) and Lois Plamandon (Brouillet), daughters of brewery employees. A somewhat younger Marion Canby can also be spotted at the far right in the upper photograph on page 34. (Courtesy of Henderson House Museum, No. 121.)

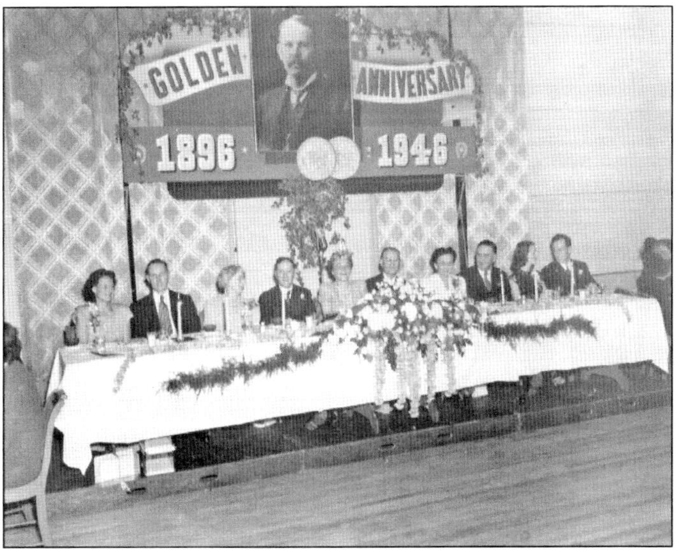

The spirit of Leopold Schmidt looks down on the head table at the golden anniversary banquet in 1946. From left to right are Clara "Nootchie" and Sherman Huffine, Elsa and Frederick Schmidt, Clara and Peter G. Schmidt Sr., Winnifred and Adolph Schmidt Sr., and Waynette and Adolph "Bump" Schmidt Jr. (Courtesy of Henderson House Museum, No. 112.)

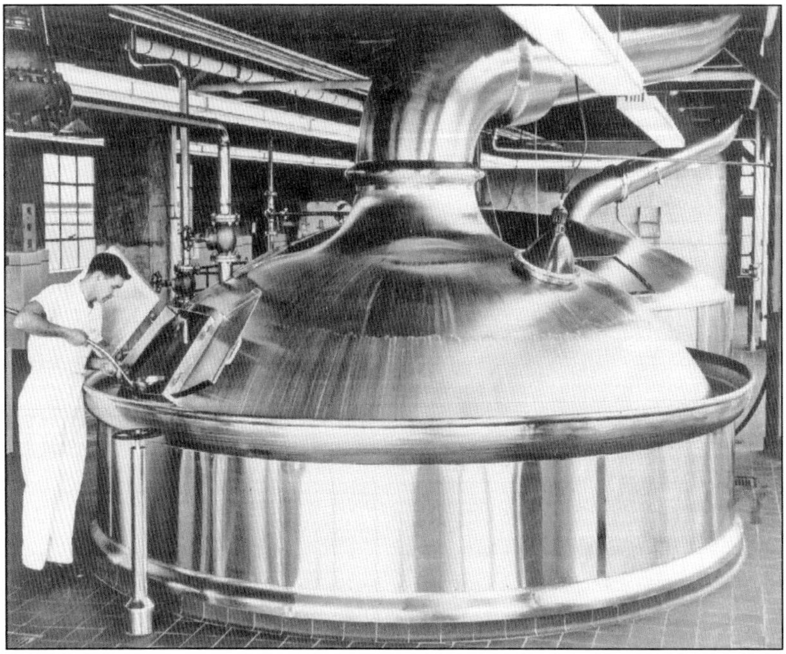

Dick Fant, in spotless white coveralls, dips a sample of beer for testing. Stainless steel brew kettles replaced traditional copper kettles in the late 1940s. (Courtesy of Henderson House Museum, No. 093.)

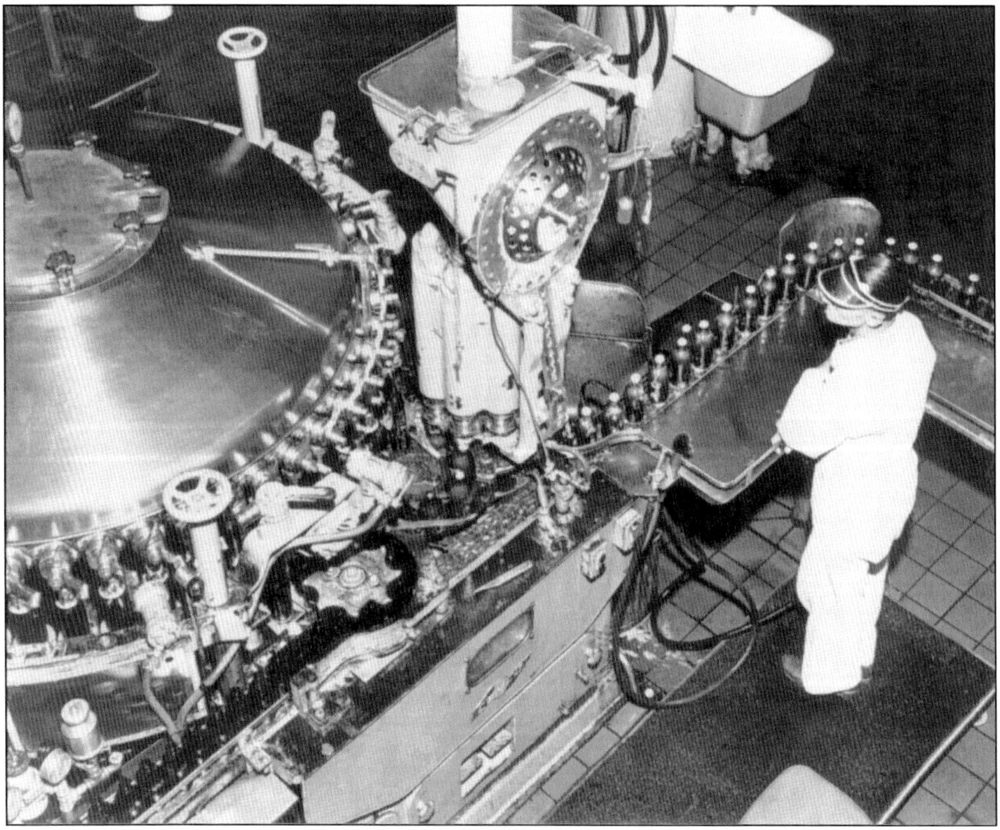

"Stubby" bottles file through the filler and crowner in 1948, each receiving 11 ounces of beer and a metal cap or crown. (Courtesy of Henderson House Museum, No. 095.)

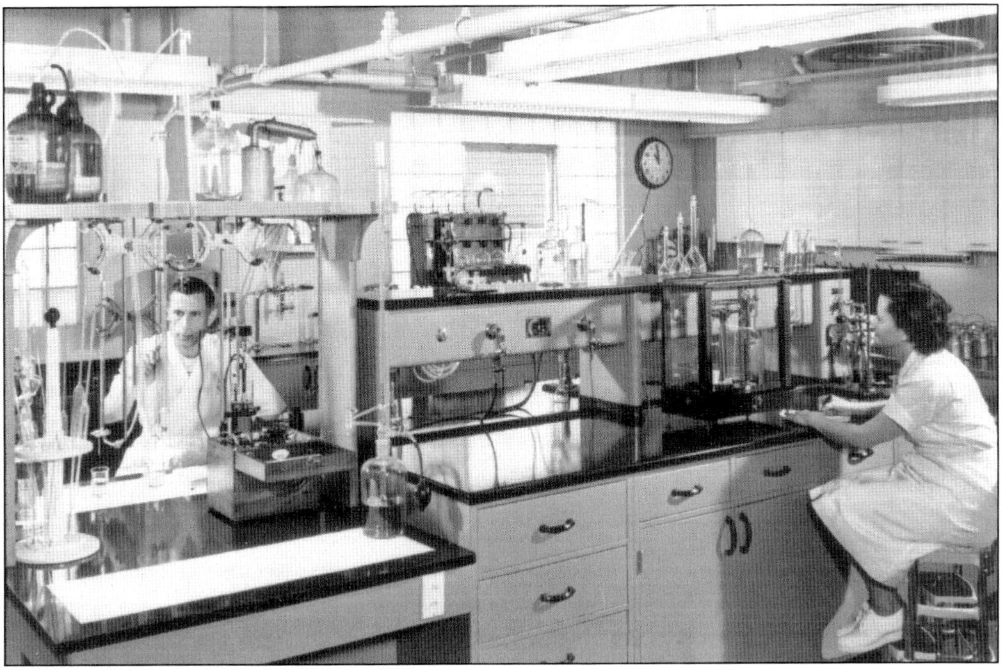

Laboratory employees Lee Gamer (left) and Margaret Keller test samples in the brand-new Olympia Brewing Company lab in June 1953. Beer was tested constantly for quality and content to make sure every batch was exactly right. (Courtesy of Henderson House Museum, No. 098.)

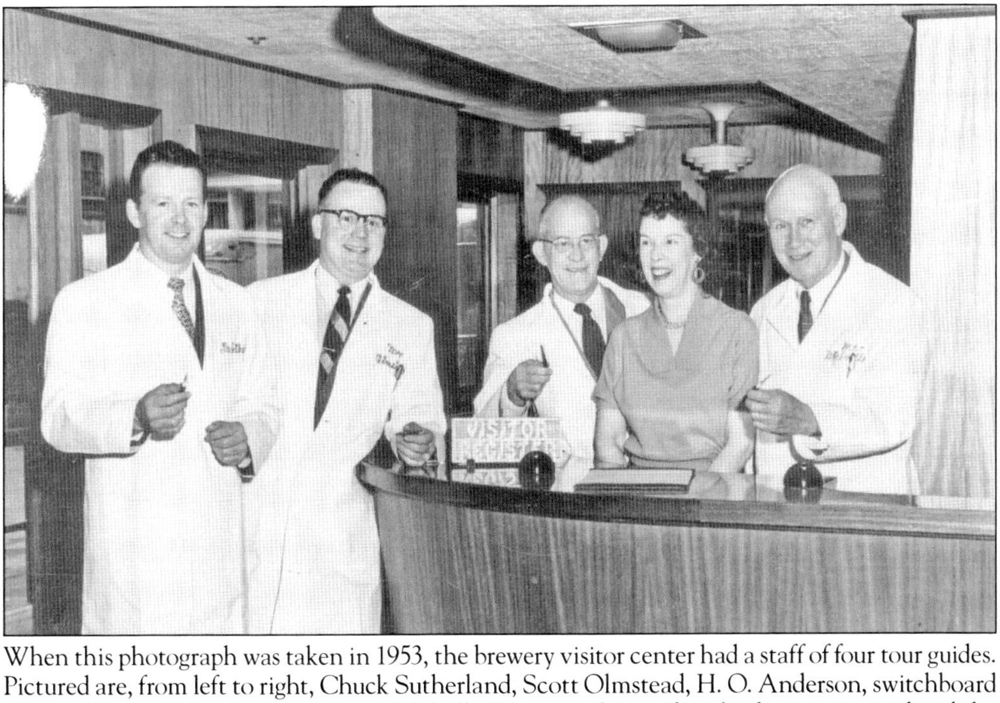

When this photograph was taken in 1953, the brewery visitor center had a staff of four tour guides. Pictured are, from left to right, Chuck Sutherland, Scott Olmstead, H. O. Anderson, switchboard operator Peggy Townsend, and Frank Melville. Ten years later, after the freeway opened and the 1962 Seattle World's Fair brought thousands of visitors to the Northwest, the visitor center staff numbered 21. (Courtesy of Henderson House Museum, No. 120.)

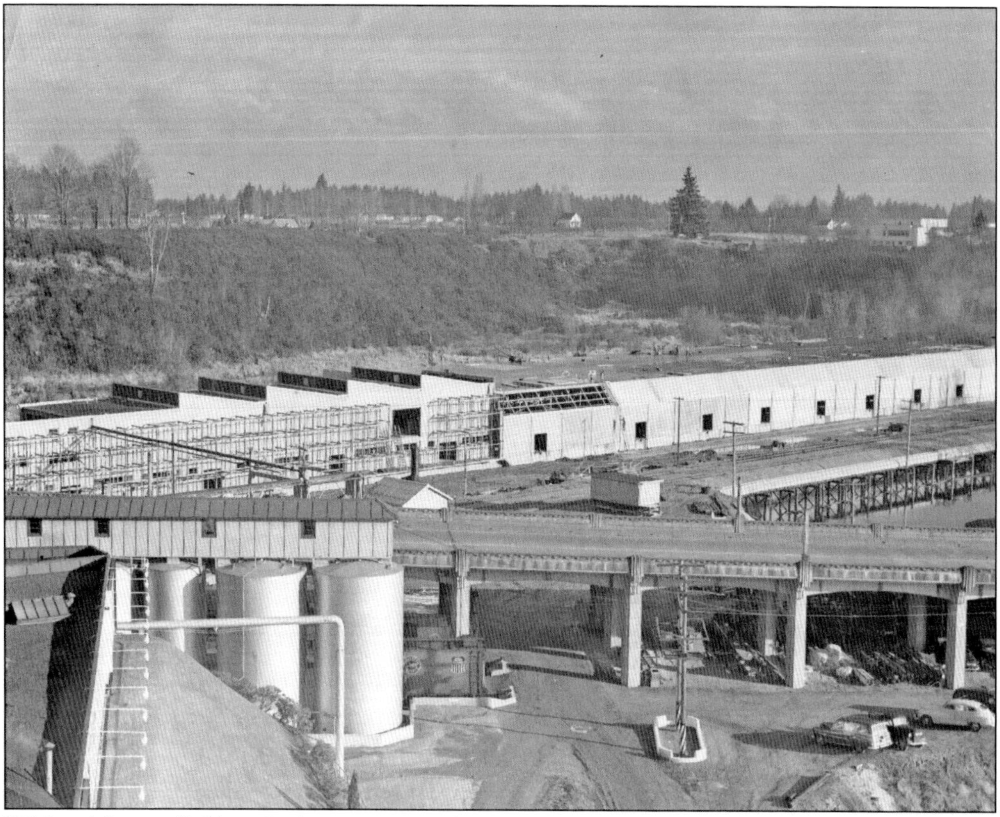

"B" bottlehouse (left) and a huge new warehouse were added in the mid-1950s on the east side of the Capitol Boulevard Bridge, on what had once been bog land. A massive filling project along the banks of the Deschutes River was needed to pull it off. (Courtesy of Henderson House Museum, No. 076.)

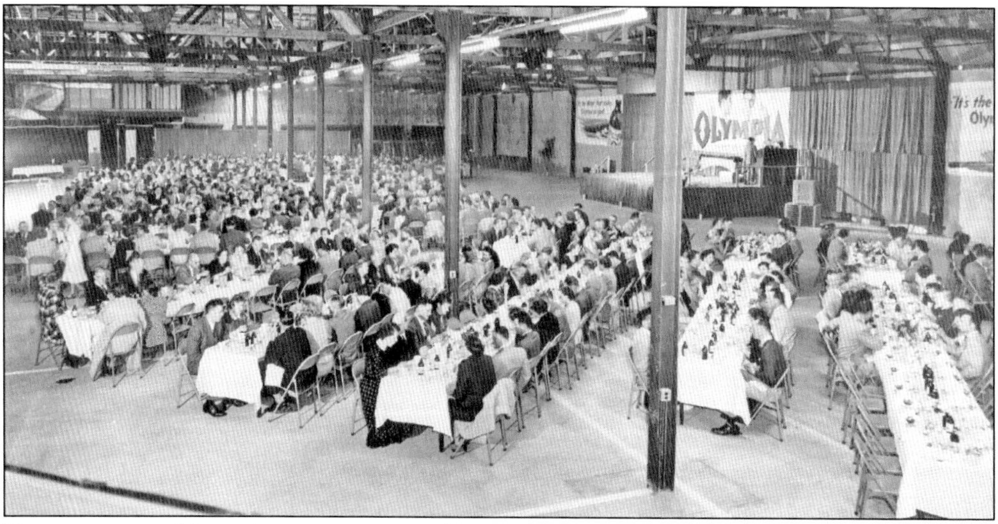

The company celebrated its expansion with a grand dinner and dance for employees and their spouses, held inside the newly completed warehouse in April 1955. (Courtesy of Henderson House Museum, No. 114.)

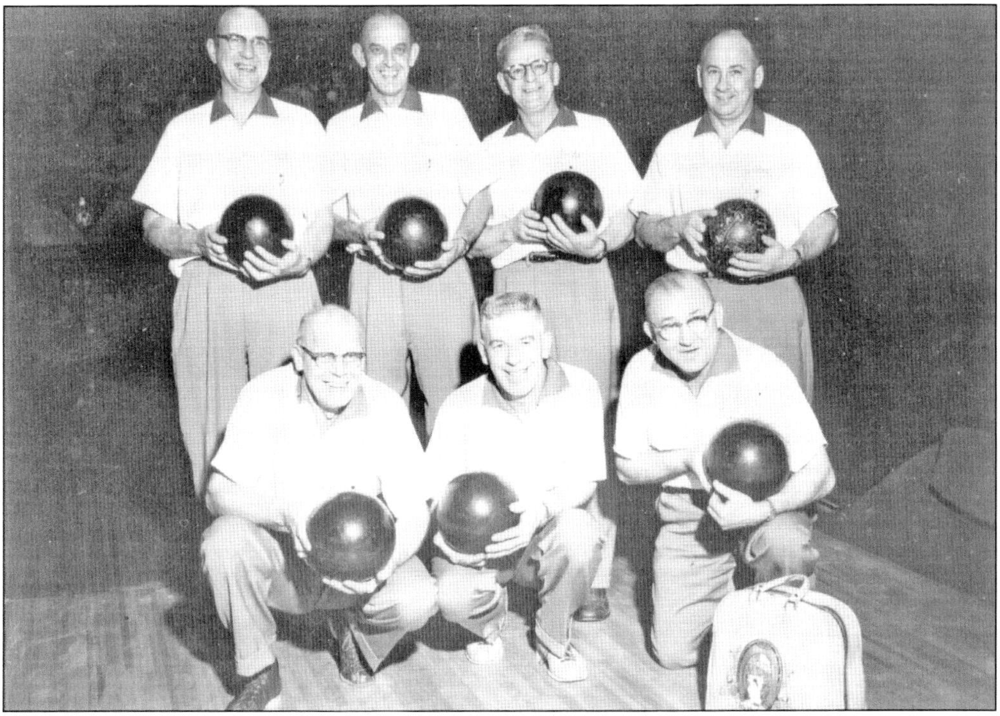

The brewery sponsored not only a community bowling team, but basketball and baseball teams, too. Note the logo of horseshoe and waterfalls on the side of the bowling bag. (Courtesy of Henderson House Museum, No. 1516.)

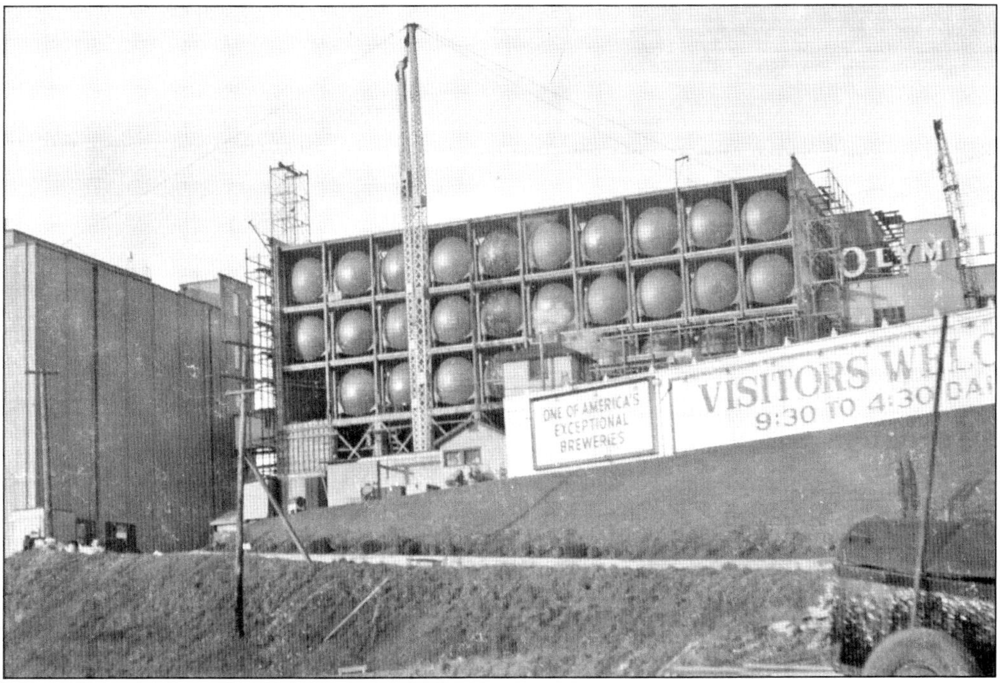

Construction of "K" cellar, on the south side of the complex, began in 1953. New fermentation cellars continued to be added until 1970. (Courtesy of Henderson House Museum, No. 083.)

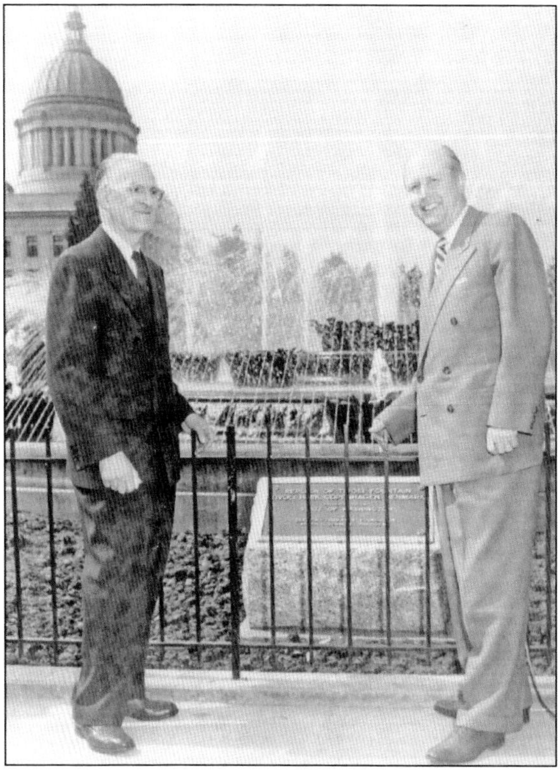

In 1950, company president Peter G. Schmidt Sr. established the charitable Olympia Tumwater Foundation. The new foundation's first project was the donation of the Tivoli Fountain, a replica of a fountain in the Danish brewing city of Copenhagen, for the Washington State Capitol Campus. Schmidt is pictured here (left) with Gov. Arthur Langlie in front of the fountain in 1953. (Courtesy of Olympia Tumwater Foundation.)

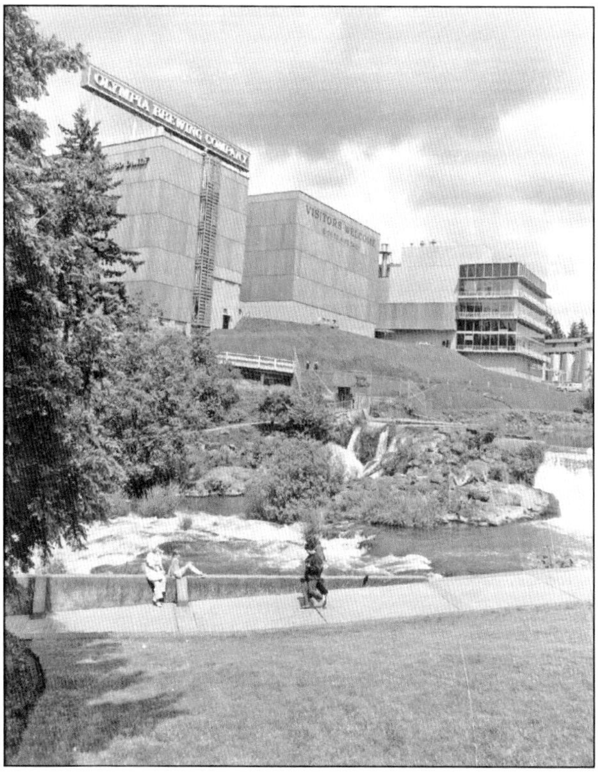

The buildings of the Olympia Brewing Company rise over the Upper Falls in this view from the 1960s. Visible in the foreground is Tumwater Falls Park, created in 1962 by the Olympia Tumwater Foundation and still owned and operated by the foundation today. (Courtesy of Olympia Tumwater Foundation.)

Three

Homes and Neighborhoods

For the American Indians who lived near Tumwater Falls, homes and neighborhoods changed with the seasons. In summer, bands moved together between established food-gathering sites where they fished or hunted, picked berries, and dug camas root from the prairie. They carried their summer homes with them, erecting clusters of pole-and-mat shelters in each different location. In winter, they returned to permanent village sites, where communal cedar lodges housed up to eight families at once.

Like Native people before them, most American settlers chose to live where they worked. Farm families lived near their fields and barns, away from their nearest neighbors. Merchants and mill workers lived in town, close to their factories and shops. Tumwater's first residential neighborhood developed around the pioneer business district on the west bank of the river, gradually creeping up Tumwater Hill and down toward the waterfront. Some of the finest homes of the pioneer period stood near the shore at the north end of town, where the freeway now skirts the edge of Tumwater Historical Park.

In the early 20th century, when streetcars ran east of the river on Capitol Boulevard and Leopold Schmidt built his own grand home on the bluff above the old brewery, houses spread to the east along Custer Way and Log Cabin Road (now North Street). The official city limits of Tumwater fluctuated repeatedly in this area, resulting in the ragged Tumwater-Olympia boundary that twists through the North Street neighborhood today.

Construction of Interstate 5 in the mid-1950s essentially obliterated the houses, streets, and small storefronts in the oldest section of town. While some buildings were salvaged and moved to other parts of Tumwater, only two historic downtown homes—the Crosby House (around 1860) and the Naumann House/Henderson House Museum (1905)—survive today in their original locations. Though their surroundings have changed dramatically, these two authentic houses remain charmingly intact.

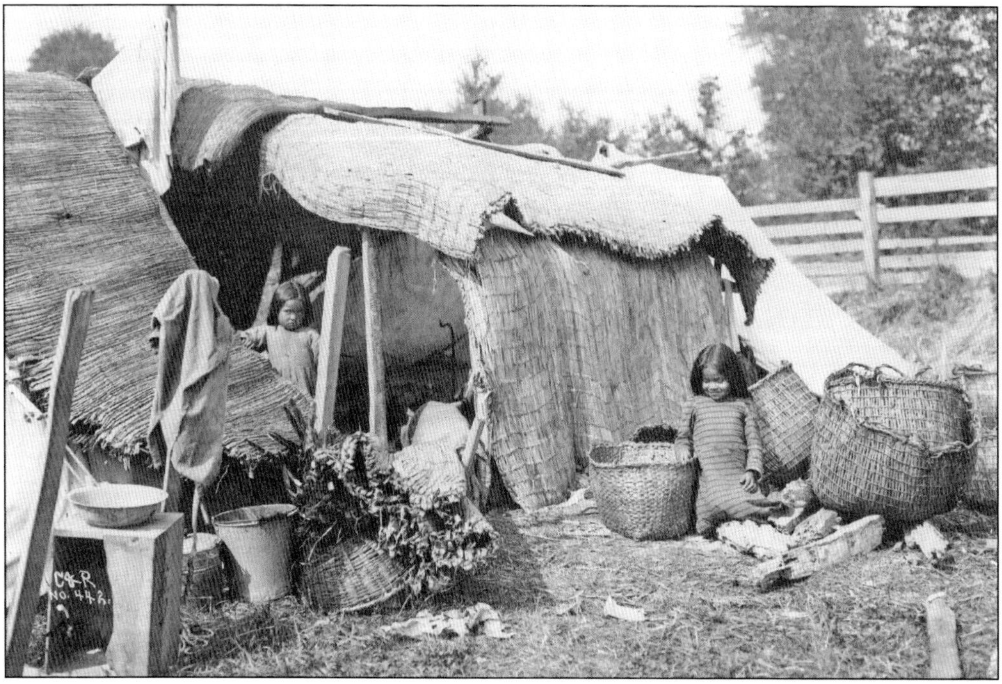

American Indians of Puget Sound carried portable houses with them as they moved between traditional food-gathering camps in summer. Pole frames were covered with versatile matting woven by American Indian women out of cedar bark, cattails, or reeds. (Courtesy of University of Washington Libraries, No. NA690.)

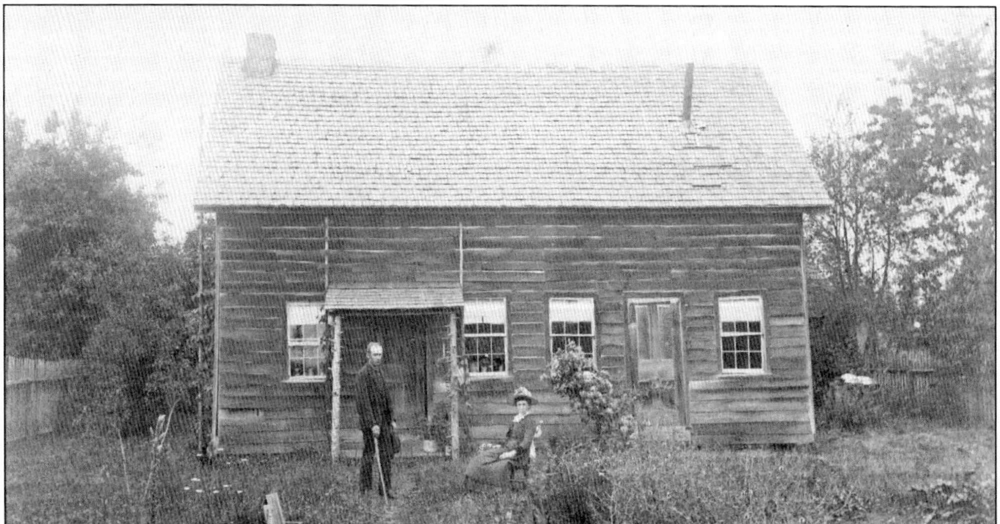

Pioneer homestead cabins were basic, often consisting of just one or two rooms. The roughest were built out of whole, round logs, but the presence of early sawmills made it possible for many Tumwater settlers to build with planked lumber instead. This photograph, probably taken in the 1870s, shows pioneer Jesse Ferguson (a member of the original Simmons-Bush party of 1845) and his daughter Sarah on the Ferguson land claim near the north end of Littlerock Road. Note the porch columns made of stripped tree trunks. (Courtesy of Henderson House Museum, No. 472.)

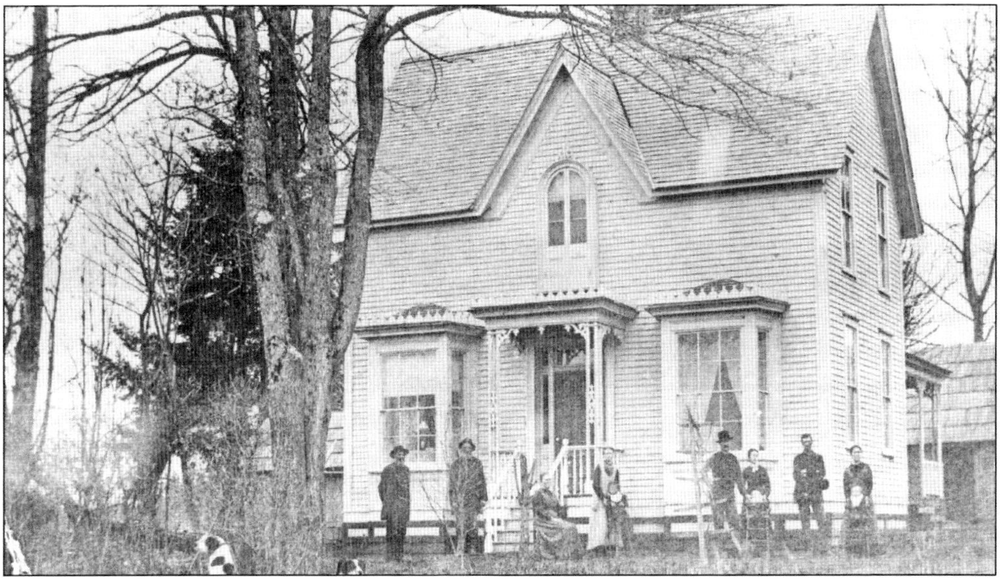

As sawmills became more sophisticated, local homes grew more stylish. Here the second and third generations of the George and Isabella Bush family pose outside a house on the Bush farm in the area south of Tumwater still known as Bush Prairie (see page 9). Son William Owen Bush (second from left) was an accomplished farmer, a promoter of Washington agriculture, and an advocate for the farming college in Pullman that later became Washington State University. He was also elected to the first Washington State legislature in 1889. (Courtesy of Henderson House Museum, No. 441.)

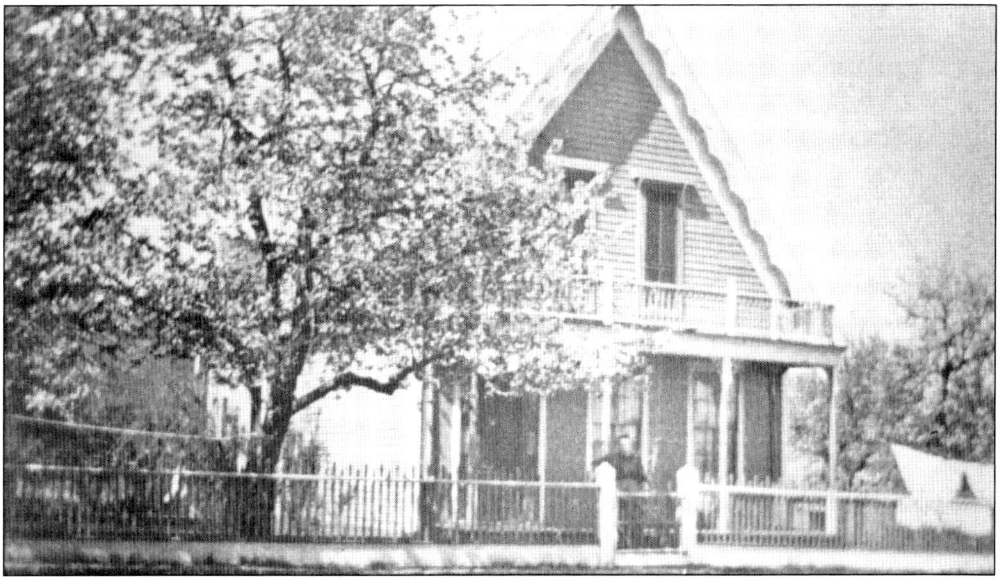

The Crosby House was built for Nathaniel Crosby III and his new bride, Cordelia Jane Smith, around the time of their marriage in 1860 (see page 15). The house combines two building styles—Greek Revival and Gothic Revival—that were common in New England at the time the Crosbys left Maine. The woman at the gate is Fannie Ostrander Moore, whose parents bought the house from the Crosbys in 1872. The Crosby House is listed on both the National and Washington State Registers of Historic Places and on the Tumwater Historical Register. (Courtesy of Henderson House Museum, No. 453.)

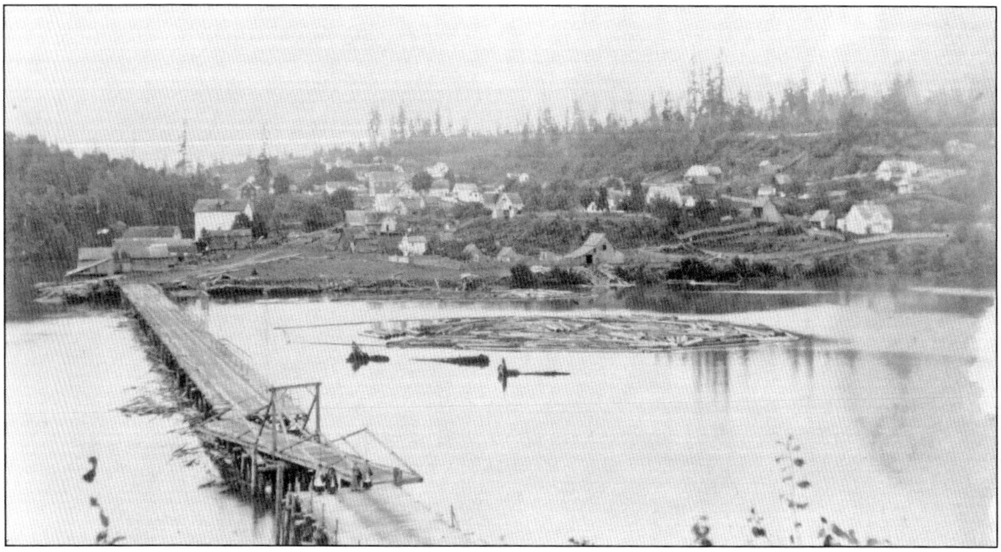

Tumwater was still just a village when this photograph was taken around 1890. This view, looking across to Tumwater from the south end of Olympia, shows the bridge between the two cities with its swing section partially open. A rotating platform in the bridge deck allowed ships through at high tide. The roof of the Crosby house can be seen, right of center, partly obscured by trees. Note the logs in the waterway, waiting to be milled. (Courtesy of Henderson House Museum, No. 632.)

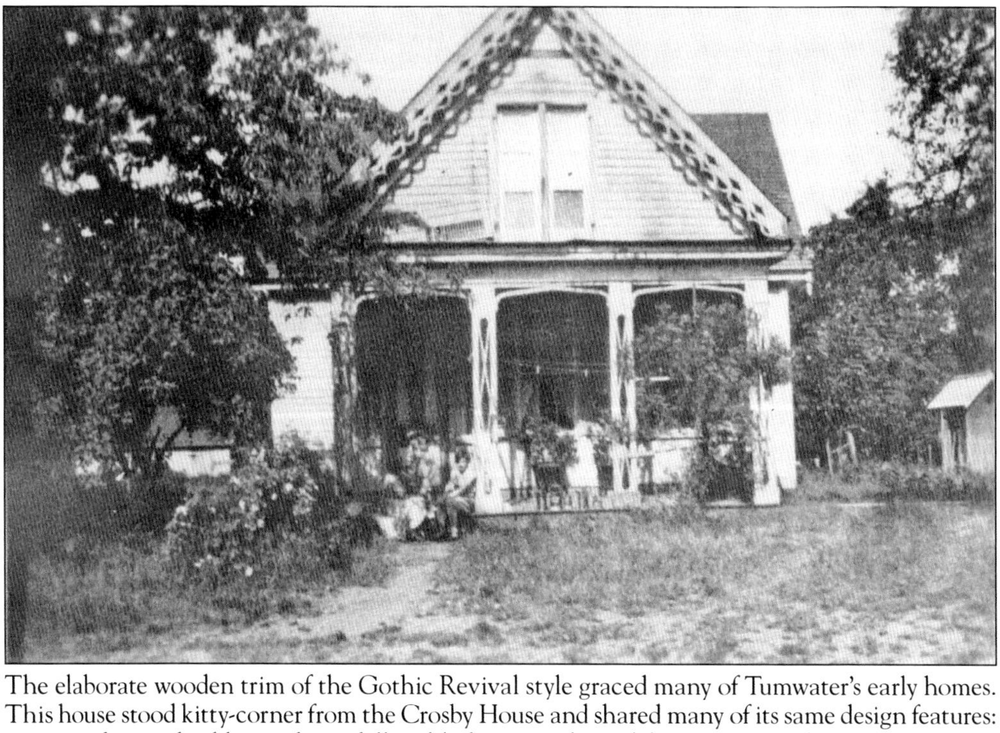

The elaborate wooden trim of the Gothic Revival style graced many of Tumwater's early homes. This house stood kitty-corner from the Crosby House and shared many of its same design features: steep roof, paired gable windows, full-width front porch, and fancy trim on the eaves. Believed to have been built for pioneer settler Clark Biles, it was owned by the Beigh family when this photograph was taken in 1927. It survived the construction of Interstate 5 but was demolished in the 1960s. (Courtesy of Henderson House Museum, No. 433.)

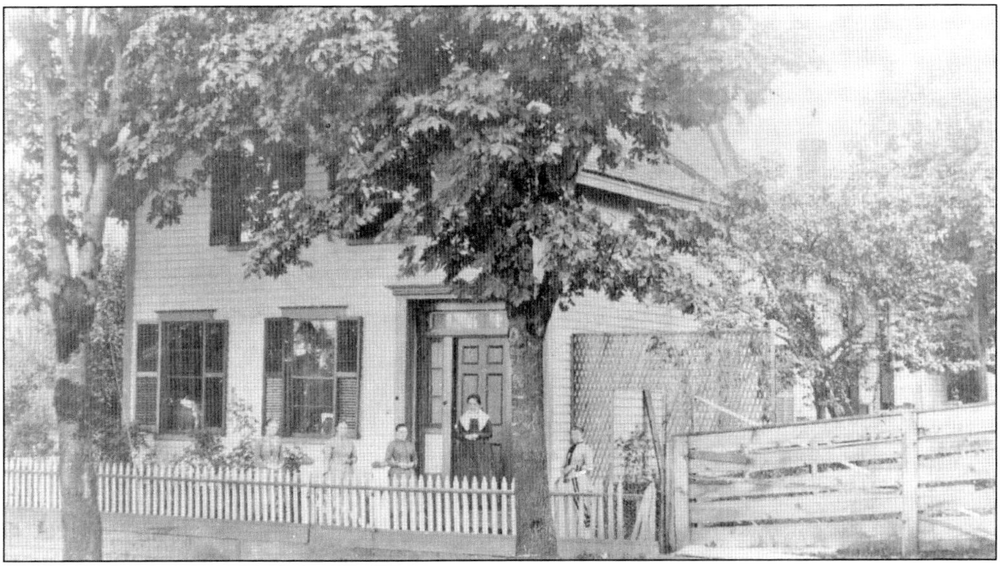

According to a scribbled note, the Eastman house was known as "Maple Cottage"—presumably for the two large maple trees in front. The house and trees were located on Bates Street, below Second Avenue. Blacksmith Ebenezer Eastman and his wife, thrice-married Rebecca Shute Shattuck Draper Eastman, arrived in Tumwater in 1863. Their son C. F. (Frank) Eastman followed his father into the blacksmithing trade. (Courtesy of Henderson House Museum, No. 464.)

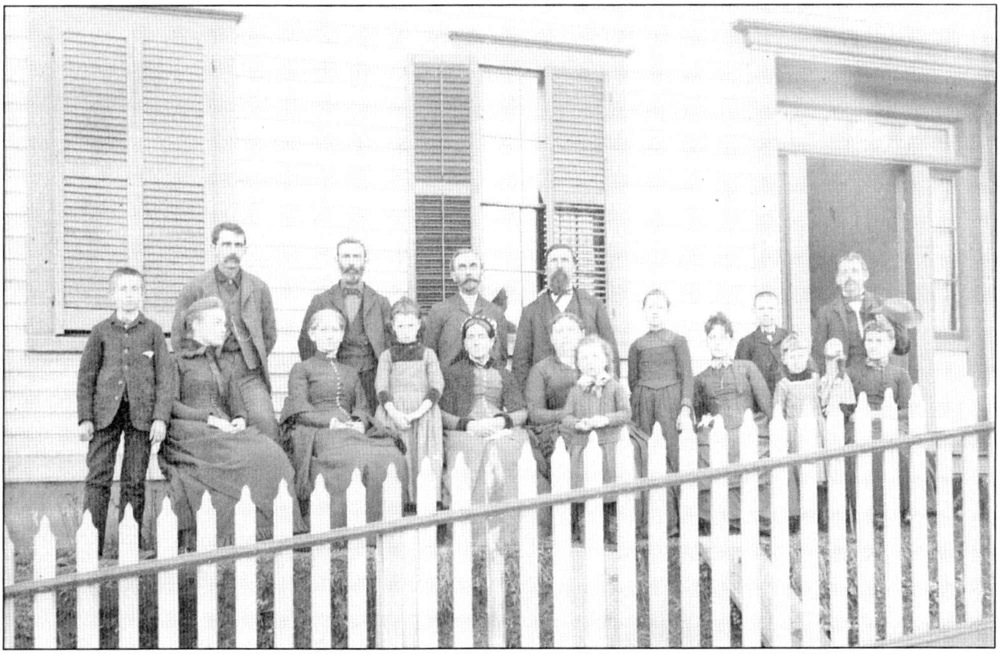

Matriarch Rebecca Eastman sits, surrounded by family, on the porch of Maple Cottage around 1890. From left to right are (first row) May Ostrander Eastman, Hannah Chase Shattuck, Nellie Shattuck, Rebecca Eastman, Hattie Bolender, Charlie Bolender, Linnie Barnes, Helen Eastman, and Emma Manning Eastman; (second row) Ralph Eastman, Ellery Eastman, George Nelson Shattuck, Henry Shattuck, Jake Bolender, Amie Shattuck, George Henry Shattuck, and Frank Eastman. (Courtesy of Gary Hopkins.)

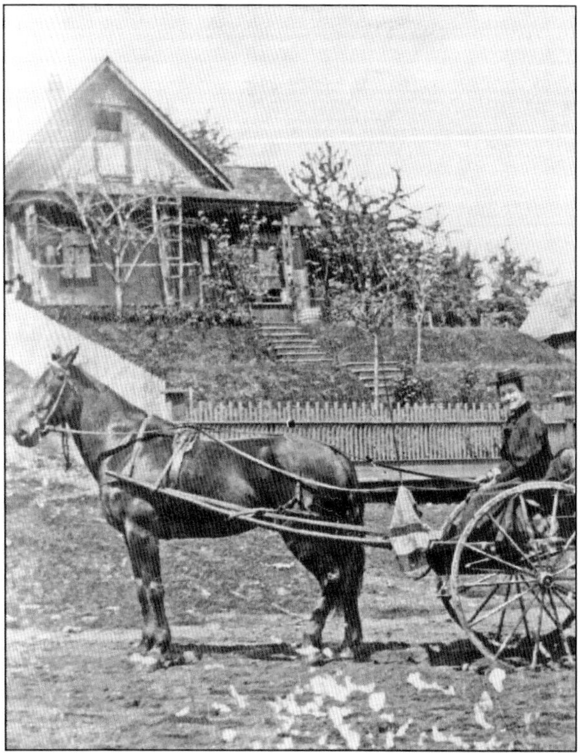

Nova Scotia natives Mary Jane Swan McIntosh (at left) and her husband, Robert (with Mary Jane, below), arrived in Tumwater in 1883 and purchased this house on Simmons Road. "The family home with yard occupied a block opposite the old brewery," their grandson remembered later. "The front yard was terraced and my grandmother, who loved dahlias, had many of them there. . . . There was a very large vegetable garden, many raspberry bushes, cherry and other fruit trees in the backyard, and a flock of chickens." Robert McIntosh worked in logging, first as an ox-team driver and then as a foreman in camps throughout Thurston and Mason Counties. He and brother-in-law James Swan ran their own logging operation at Deep Lake from 1907 to 1912. McIntosh was mayor of Tumwater from 1931 to 1934. (Both, courtesy of Henderson House Museum. Left, No. 497; below, No. 391.)

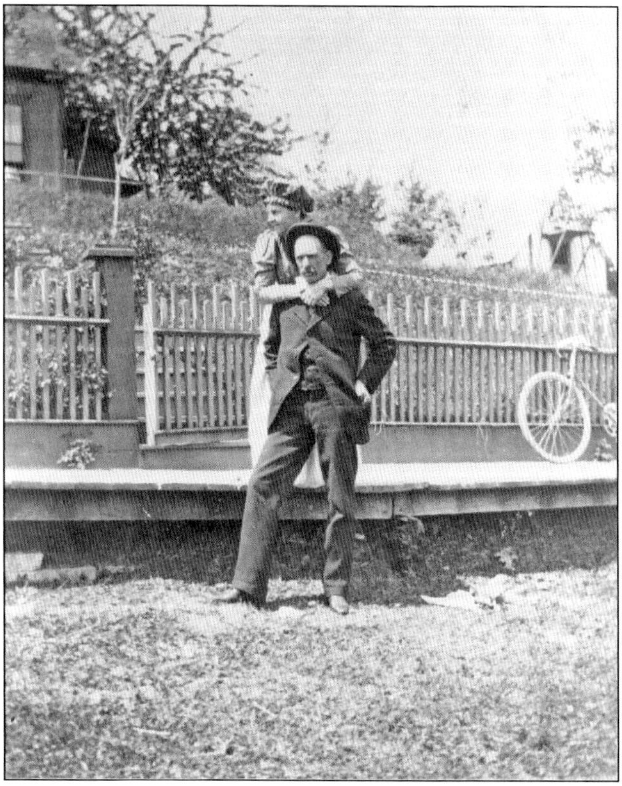

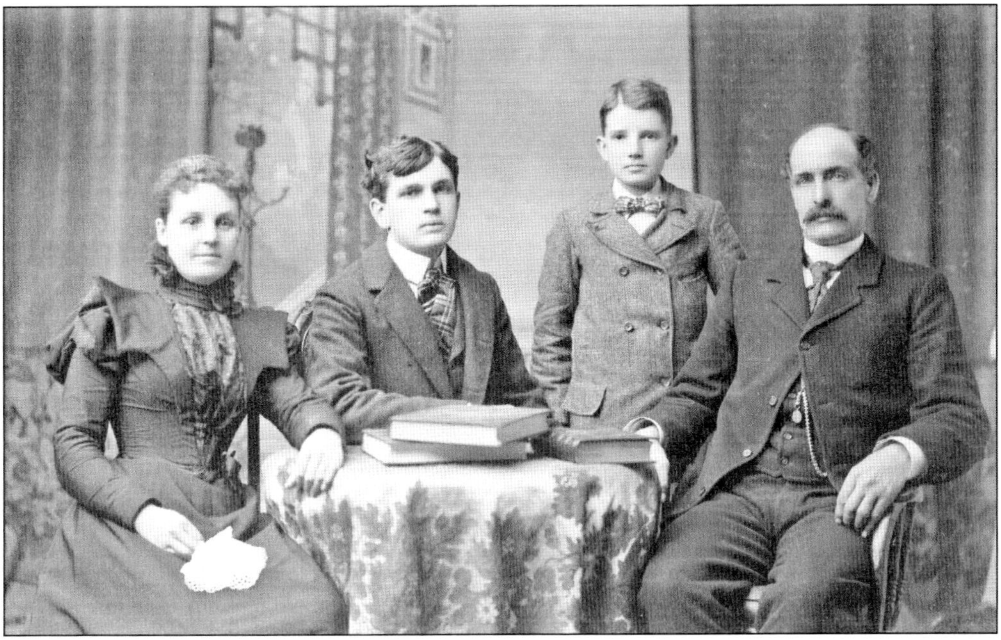

Mary Jane and Robert McIntosh had two sons, Albert (left) and Lawrence. Albert grew up to marry Helen Eastman, the little girl with the doll in the Eastman family portrait on page 57. He is credited as the builder of Three Meter, the 1904 home of brewery owner Leopold Schmidt. (Courtesy of Robert M. McIntosh.)

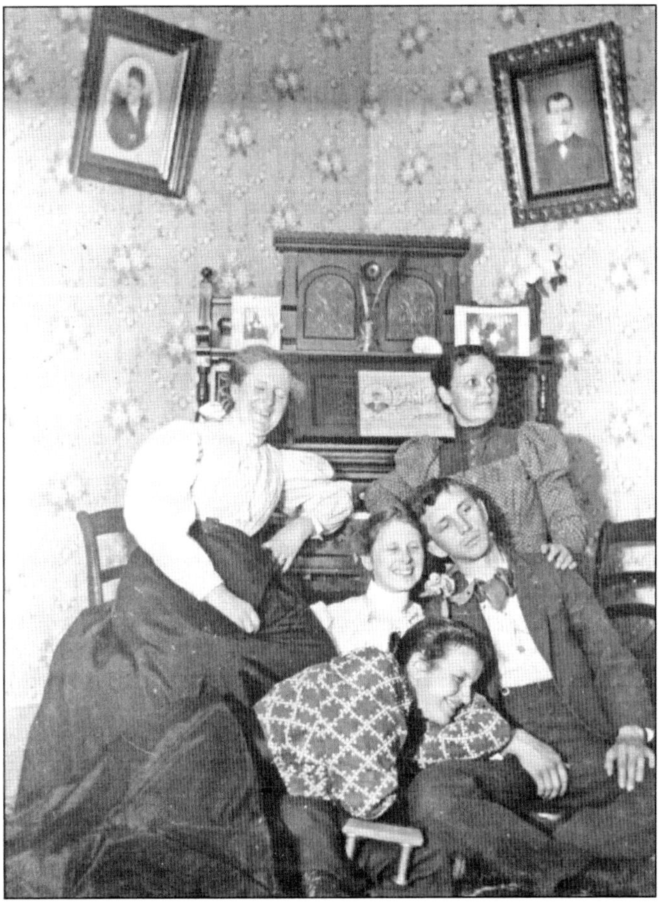

Framed portraits of Robert and Mary Jane McIntosh in the background suggest that this lighthearted scene took place inside the McIntosh house. Mary Jane herself is seated at top right, leaning against the pump organ. (Courtesy of Henderson House Museum, No. 425.)

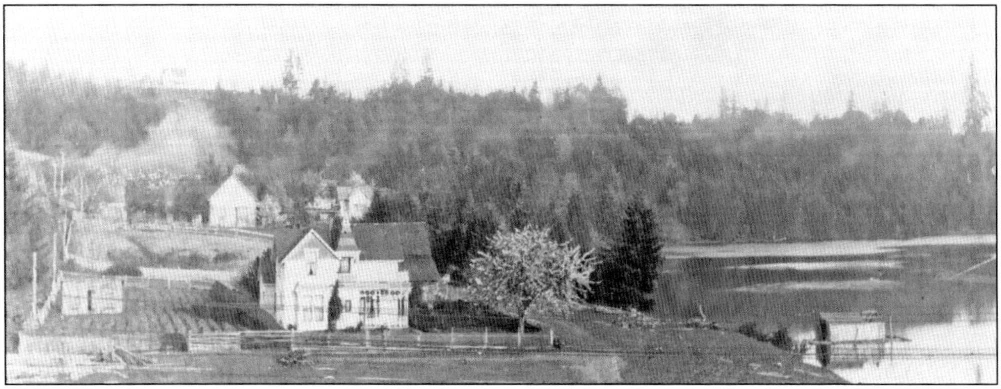

Tumwater businessman Robert Esterly built a spectacular home near the waterfront, close to his planing mill, in 1895. The Esterly property, like that of the nearby McIntosh house, originally included fruit trees and an ample vegetable garden. (Courtesy of Henderson House Museum, No. 971.)

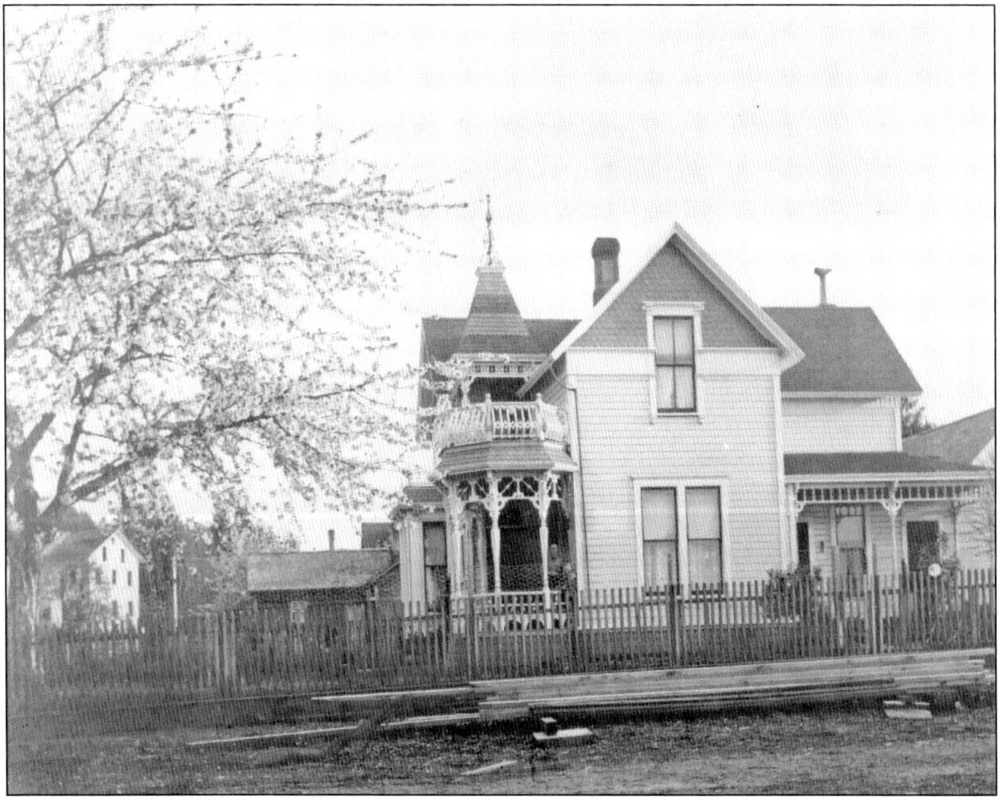

Built in the ornate Queen Anne style, the Esterly house was a showcase of fancy moldings, railings, turned posts, and trim—all of it manufactured at Robert Esterly's mill. A neighboring house had crowded into what once was a garden by the time this picture was taken around 1903. The four-story Lincoln Flour Mill can be seen in the background. (Courtesy of Henderson House Museum, No. 467.)

Robert Esterly came to San Francisco from Wisconsin by rail in 1869, then north to Thurston County the following year. "Mr. Esterly has resided in Tumwater, off and on, for twelve years," declared a Tumwater promotional booklet in 1890, "and is highly esteemed by his fellow townsmen." He was mayor in 1889 and served five years on the local school board. He was also an eager photographer and took many fine local photographs at the turn of the 20th century, including the two views of his own house on the opposite page. (Courtesy of Henderson House Museum, No. 374.)

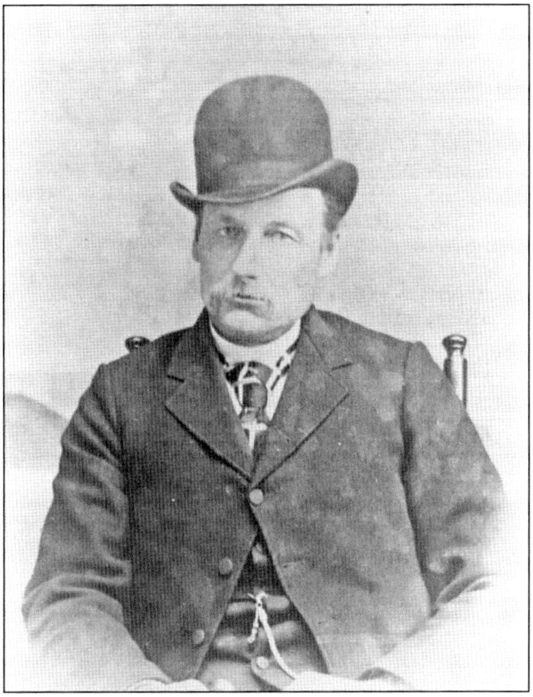

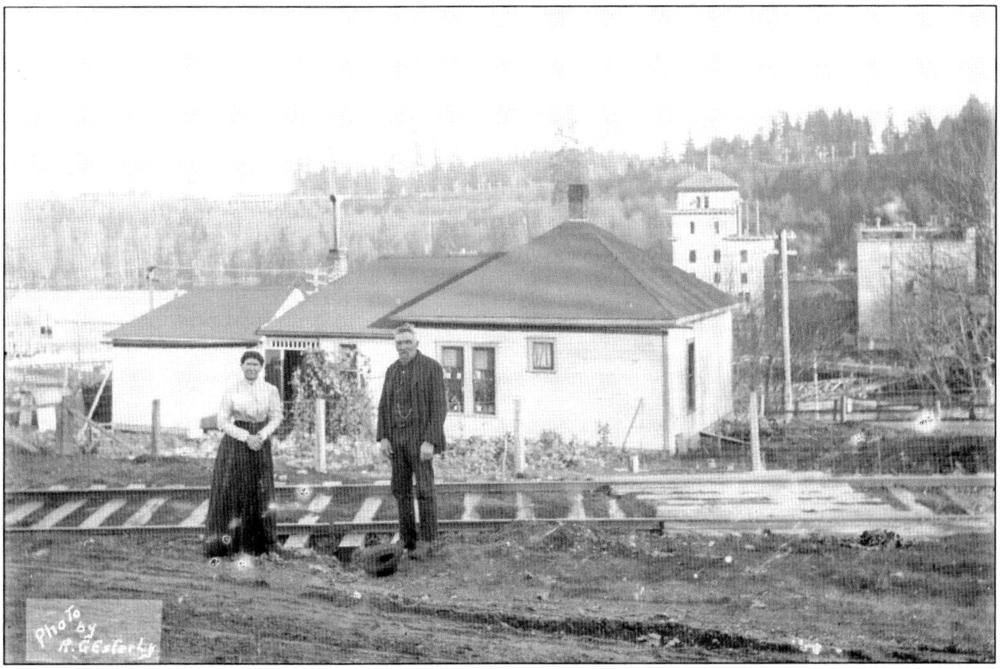

Robert Esterly took this photograph around 1910, looking east toward the river across the tracks of the Port Townsend Southern Railroad. Identification on the print reads, "Mr. and Mrs. Cannon in front of the Cannon (Franco) House." The man is likely James W. Cannon, manager of the Tumwater Shingle Company, which operated near the Upper Falls from about 1910–1917. The Cannon/Franco house survived freeway construction in the 1950s but was burned, for practice, by the Tumwater Fire Department in 2004. (Courtesy of Henderson House Museum, No. 446.)

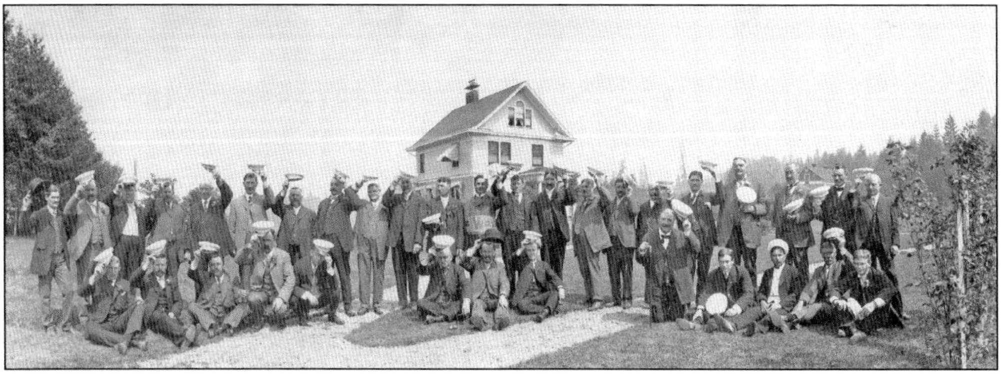

In 1904, brewery owner Leopold Schmidt and his wife, Johanna, built a grand new house on the bluff above the original Olympia Brewing Company. In this photograph, Leopold Schmidt (center, with bowler hat) entertains Olympia beer distributors on the lawn of the Schmidt House in 1907. For reasons lost to posterity, the family called their new home "Three Meter"—a nickname still used today. The Schmidt House is listed on both the National Register of Historic Places and the Tumwater Historical Register. (Courtesy of Olympia Tumwater Foundation.)

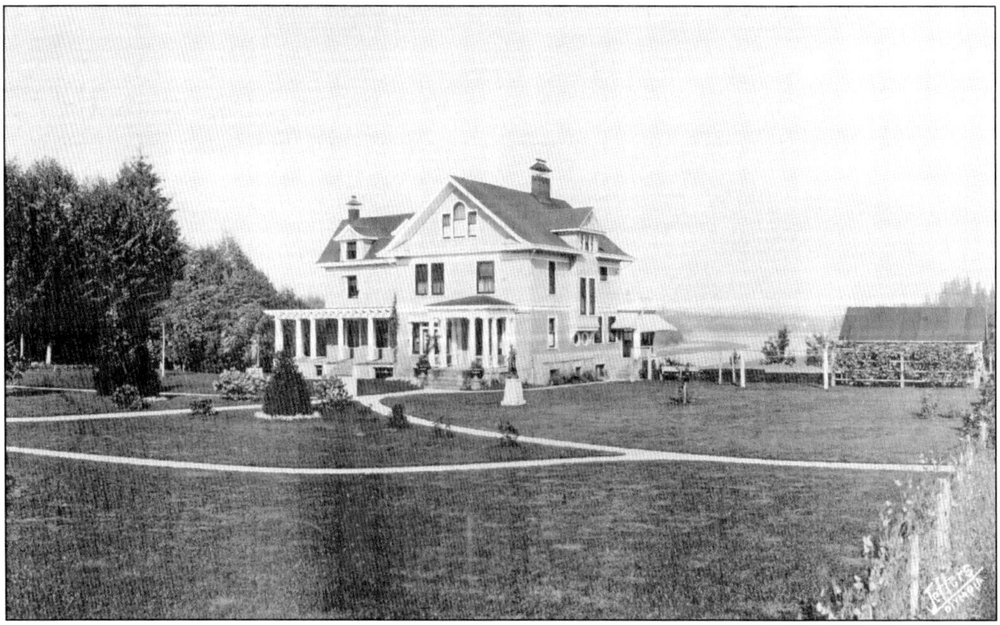

Around 1910, as his health began to decline, Schmidt added a conference-room wing onto the east side of the house so he could meet with his sons about brewery business without making the long walk down to the company office. After the deaths of Johanna (1911) and Leopold (1914), Three Meter passed to their eldest son, Peter G. Schmidt Sr., and his wife, Clara Muench Schmidt, who raised five children there. (Courtesy of Peter G. Schmidt Jr.)

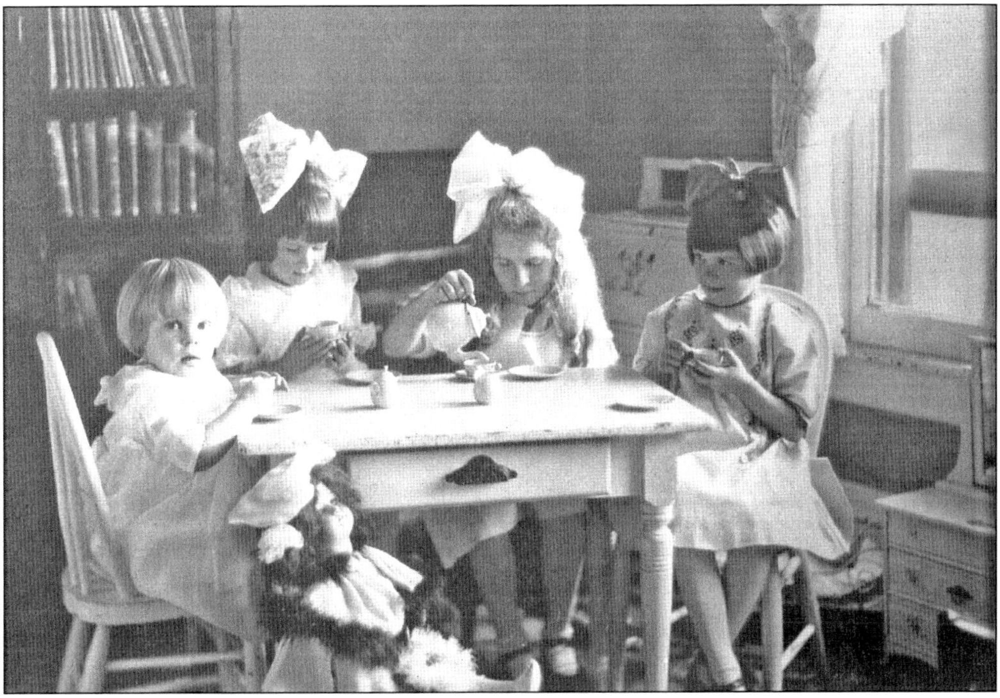

Peter G. and Clara Schmidt's four daughters enjoy a tea party inside the their house, around 1920. From left to right are Alice (nicknamed "Oodie"), Marie ("Sis"), Clara ("Nootchie"), and Margaret ("Gradie"). (Courtesy of Olympia Tumwater Foundation.)

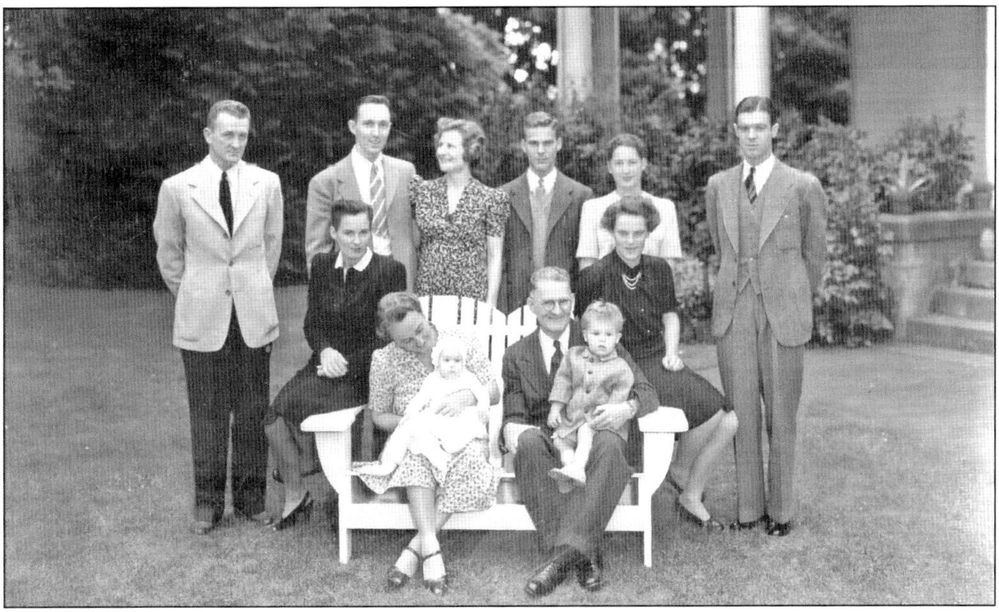

The Peter and Clara Schmidt family poses outside the Schmidt House in 1941. From left to right are (first row, seated) Marie Schmidt Campbell (Strang), Clara Schmidt holding Louise Huffine, Peter G. Schmidt Sr. holding Peter Barkley, and Alice Schmidt Barkley; (second row, standing) Rex Campbell, Sherman Huffine, Clara Schmidt Huffine, Peter Schmidt Jr., Margaret Schmidt, and Richard Barkley. (Courtesy of Olympia Tumwater Foundation.)

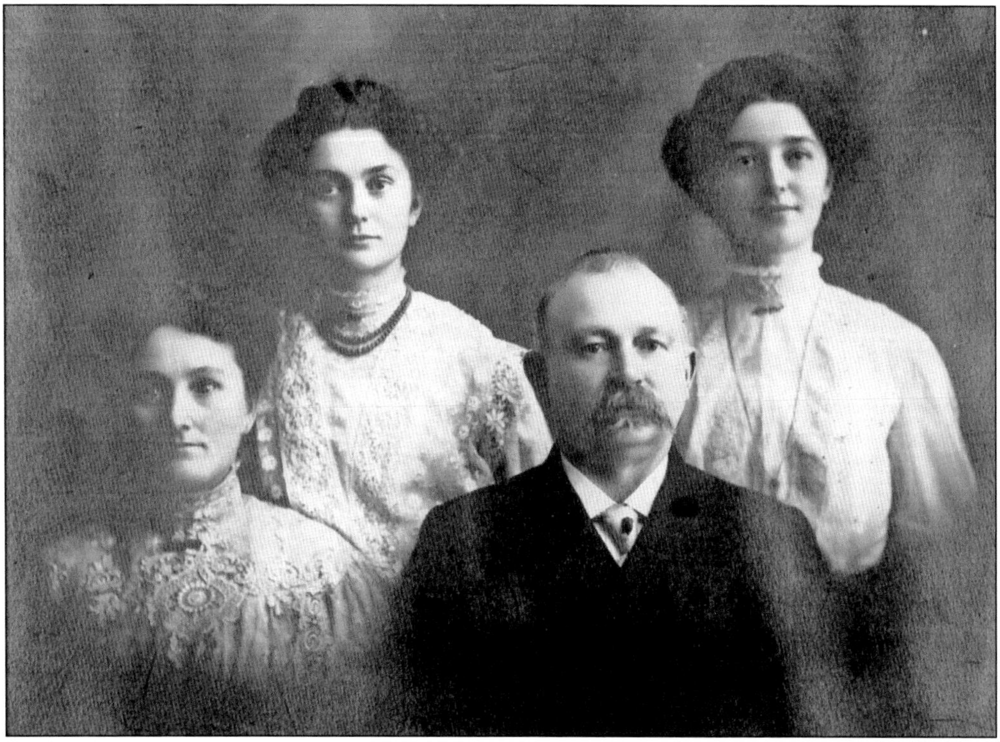

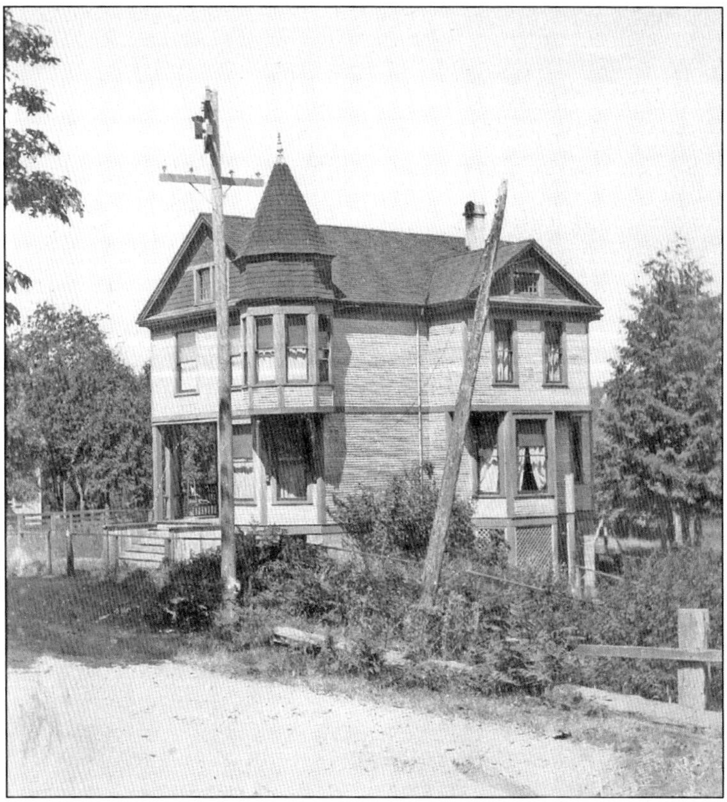

German immigrant William Naumann, pictured above with his wife, Louise, and daughters, Freya (rear left) and Martha, was a brewmaster at the Olympia Brewing Company when he built a new house on Reserve Street (Deschutes Way) in 1905. The Naumann house was considered quite modern for its time, boasting such conveniences as hot and cold running water, radiator heating, and electric lights in each room. (Above, courtesy of Charlene Freya Chambers; at left, courtesy of Henderson House Museum, No. 478.)

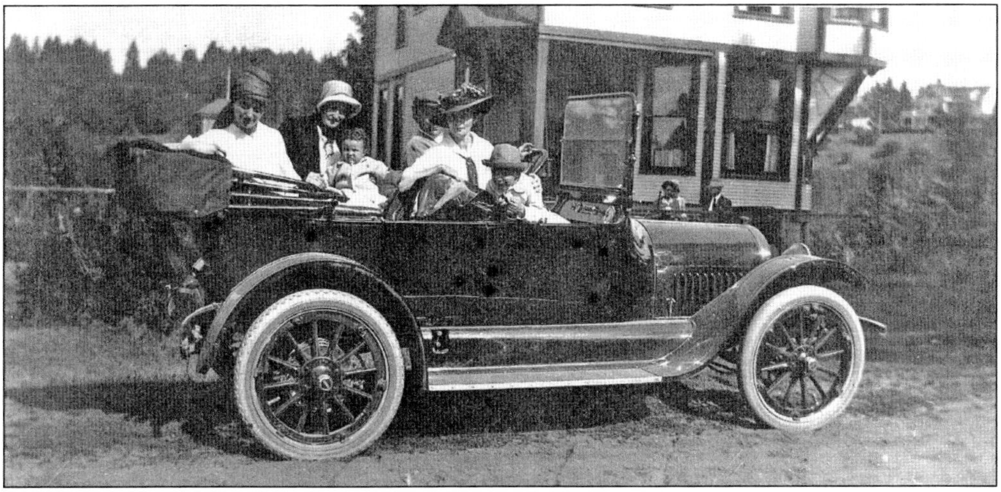

The Naumanns sold the house to John and Catherine Rohrbeck in 1909 but returned for a visit six years later, when this photograph was snapped. Louise Naumann (in white cloche hat) is flanked by grown daughters Martha and Freya, along with Freya's two children. Son-in-law William Meyer is at the wheel. The brick tower of the Old Brewhouse and the roof of the Schmidt House are both visible in the background. (Courtesy of Henderson House Museum, No. 475.)

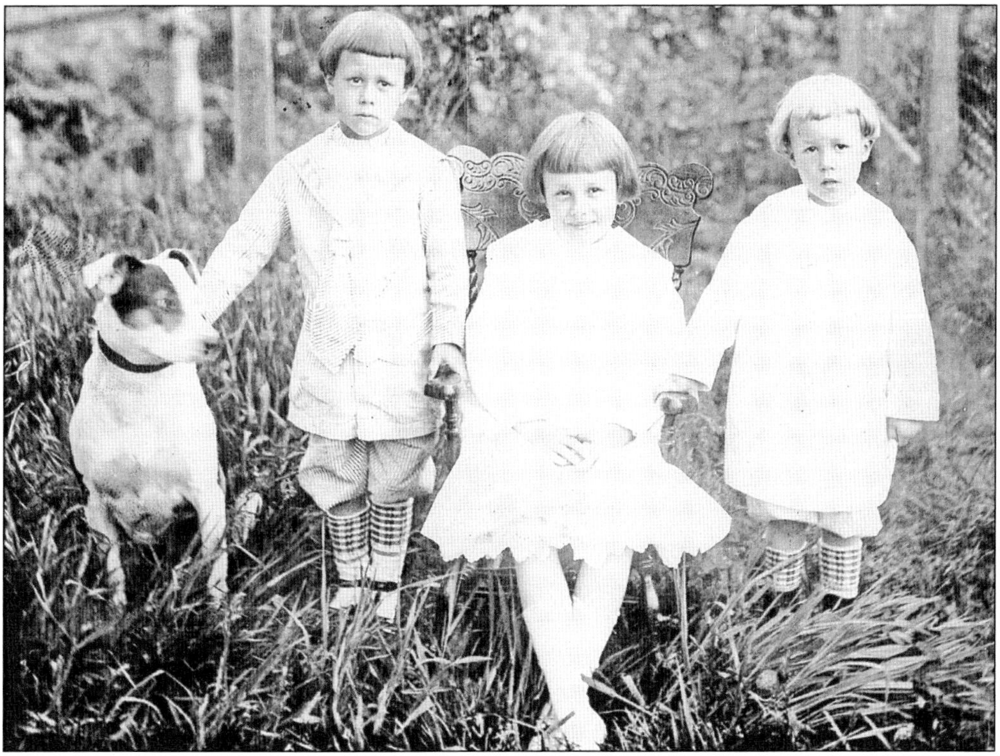

Alfred, Mildred, and Harold Rohrbeck pose with their dog, Paddy, on the grounds of the Henderson house in 1914. The children's father, John Rohrbeck, worked in the accounting office of the Olympia Brewing Company (see page 36). Like most of their neighbors, the family grew vegetables on their large lot and also kept a dairy cow. Mildred remembered carrying milk across the river to the brewery as a treat for the brewhouse cats. (Courtesy of the Mildred Rohrbeck Hotop family.)

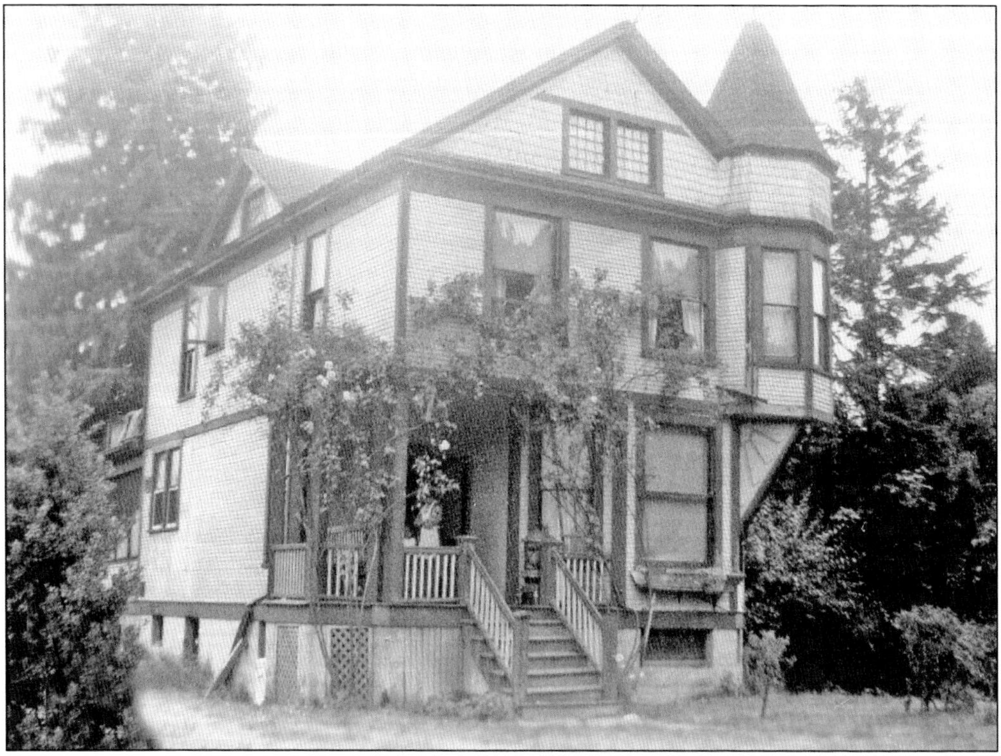

The Naumann house changed hands twice in the 1920s, then sat empty for a time during the Great Depression. In 1939, about the time this photograph was taken, it was purchased by the Frank and Agnes Henderson family, who remained in the house for nearly 40 years. (Courtesy of Washington State Archives.)

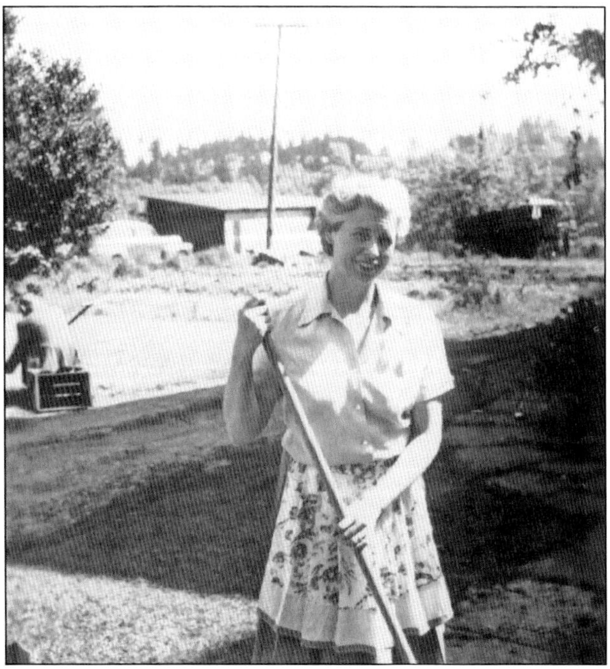

In 1977, the City of Tumwater purchased the house from Agnes Henderson (shown at left) with the aim of preserving one of the city's remaining historic homes and using it as a museum. Careful work was required to restore original details that had been lost and altered over the years. Known today as the Henderson House Museum, the house built by William and Louise Naumann looks much the same now as it did in 1905. It is listed on both the National and Washington State Registers of Historic Places and on the Tumwater Historical Register. (Courtesy of the Henderson family.)

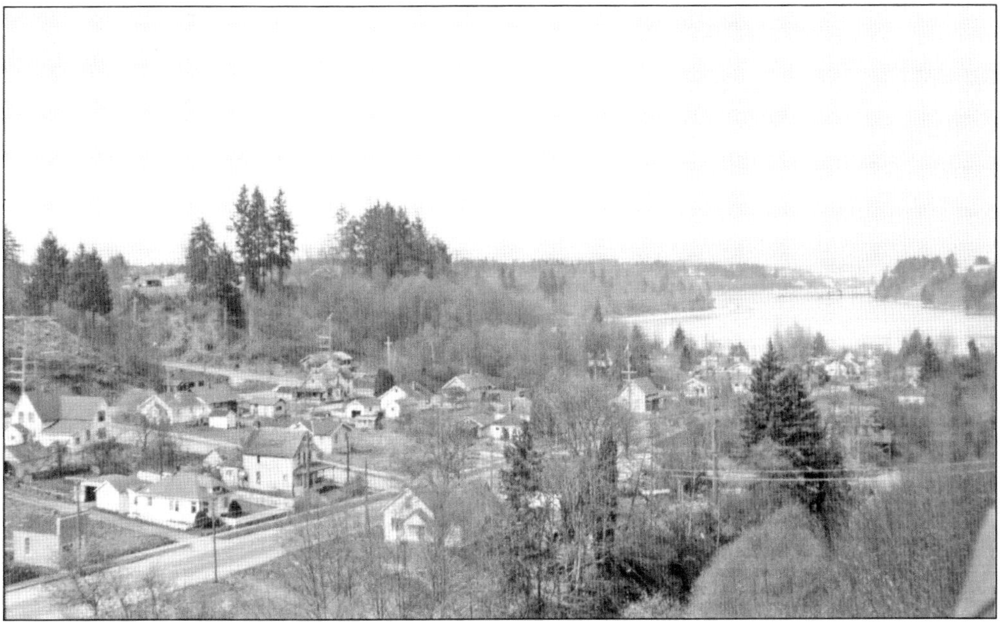

This view from 1954, looking north from above the Boston Street Bridge, shows Tumwater's central neighborhood stretching along Deschutes Way all the way down to the water. By this time, the mouth of the river has been dammed to create Capitol Lake. The Crosby and Naumann/Henderson houses stand at the farthest end of the street. (Courtesy of Henderson House Museum, No. 1438.)

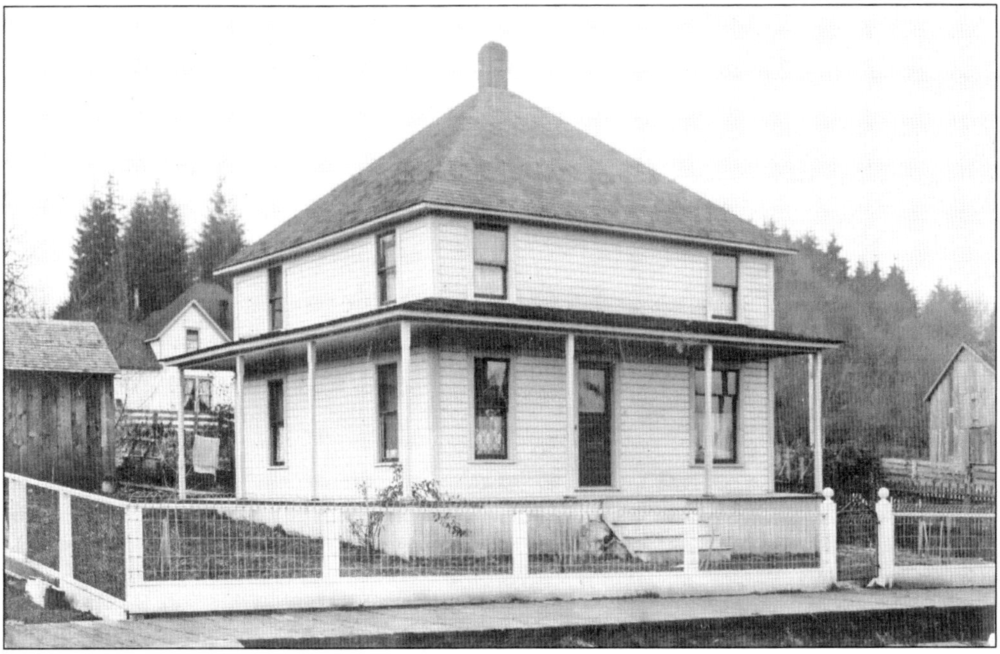

The Brown family residence was one of nearly 100 Tumwater houses that were either moved or demolished in 1955 to make way for Interstate 5. This house, located on Deschutes Way, was the boyhood home of Jake, Vince, and Jim Brown, who appear on page 83. (Courtesy of Jim Brown.)

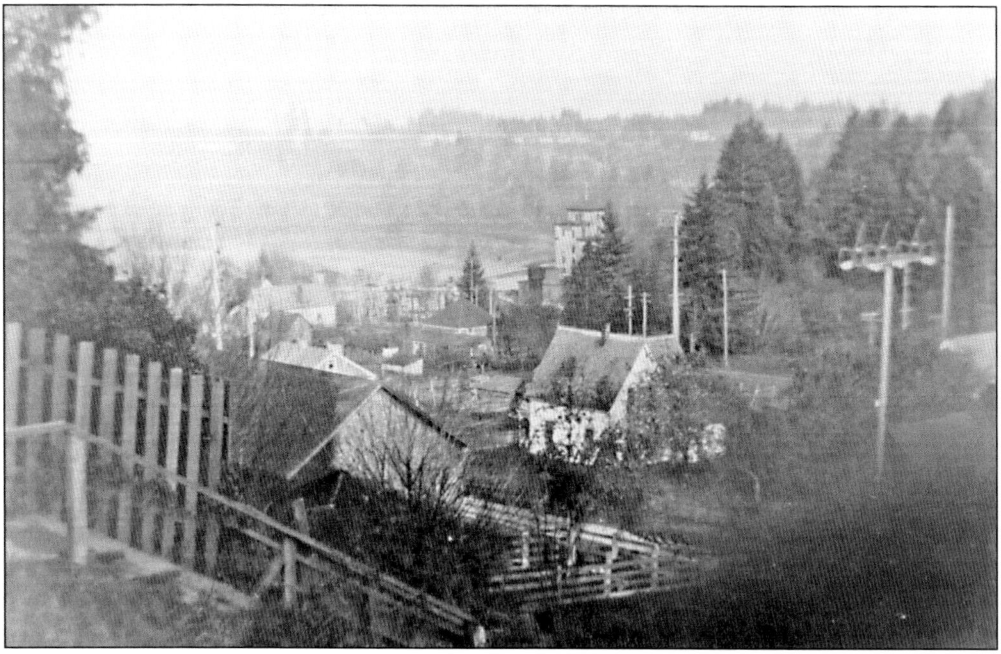

This 1930s photograph was taken from the steps on Tumwater Hill just above Second Avenue, looking east across the waterway toward the tower of the 1906 brick brewhouse and Capitol Boulevard on the ridge beyond. The pyramid roof of the Cannon/Franco House (see page 61) is visible down the hill in the center of the shot. (Courtesy of Henderson House Museum, No. 1484.)

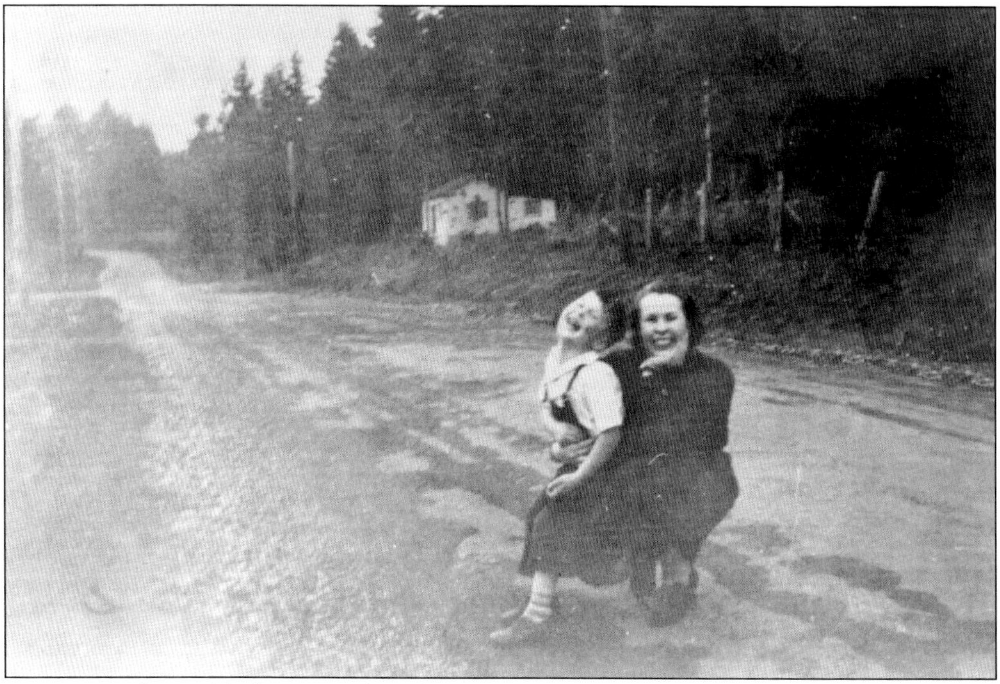

Houses were few and far between when this 1938 photograph was taken on North Sixth Avenue looking south from DeSoto Street toward Bates. The happy boy is Ronald Nielsen, enjoying a laugh with his sister Marie Nielsen Ayers. (Courtesy of Henderson House Museum, No. 527.)

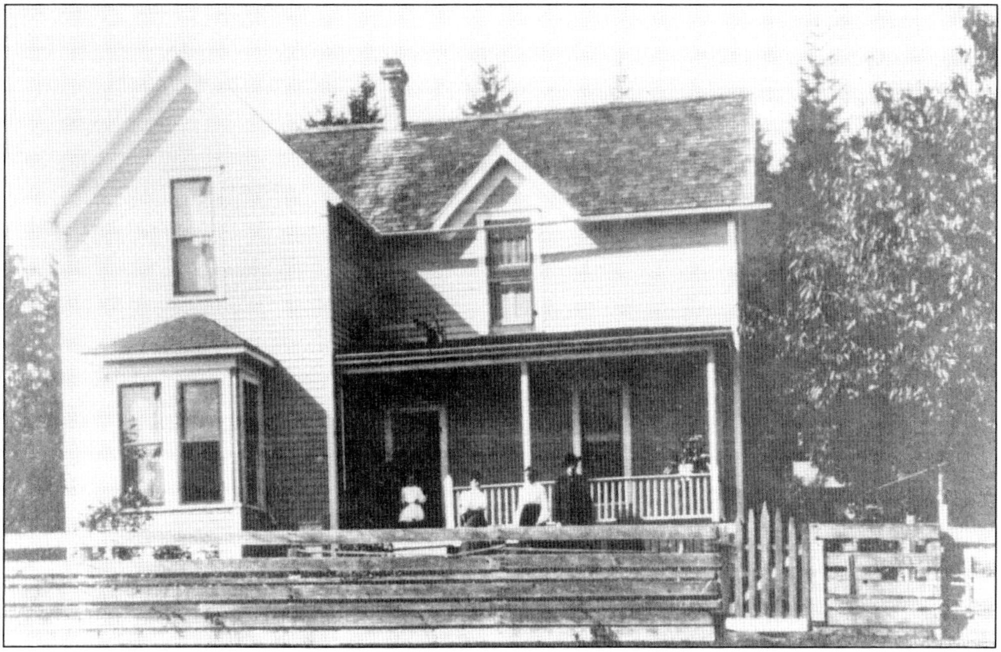

The Brower House was built in 1895 for Benjamin and Jennie Brower, who had arrived in Tumwater five years before. Benjamin Brower, a Civil War veteran on the Union side, worked in local sawmills and for the Olympia Light and Power Company. The house, still standing on Tumwater Hill, remained in the Brower family for three generations. It is listed on the Tumwater Historical Register. (Courtesy of Henderson House Museum, No. 439.)

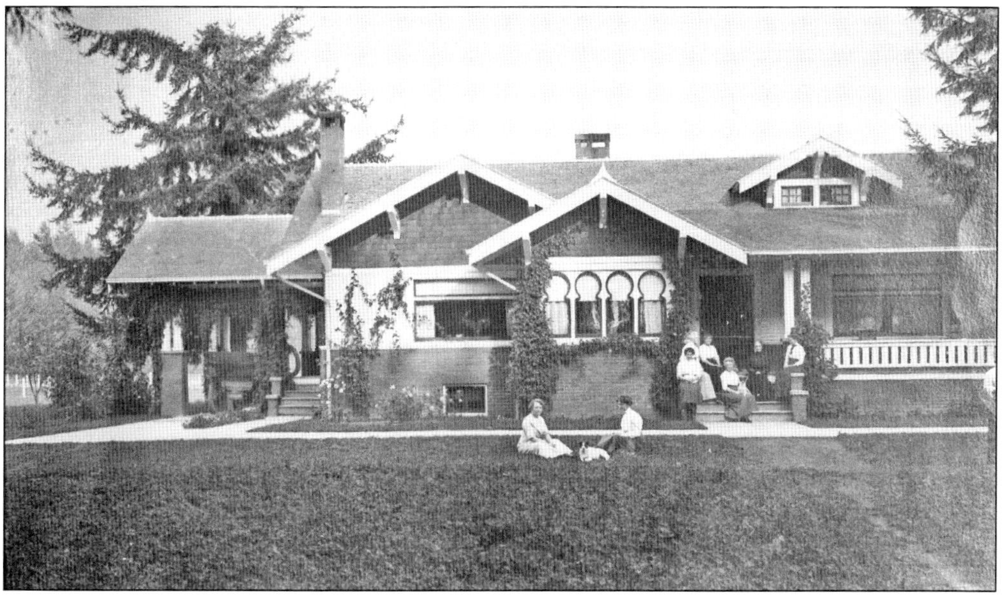

Real estate developer Fred Carlyon, brother of Olympia mayor and civic booster P. H. "Doc" Carlyon, built this large, striking craftsman-style home in 1908 on Capitol Boulevard. It was torn down in 1956 to make way for the Sunset Life Insurance building (later the office of the state auditor). In the 1920s, Fred Carlyon developed the Carlyon neighborhood behind his own handsome house. (Courtesy of Washington State Historical Society, C2010.0.3.)

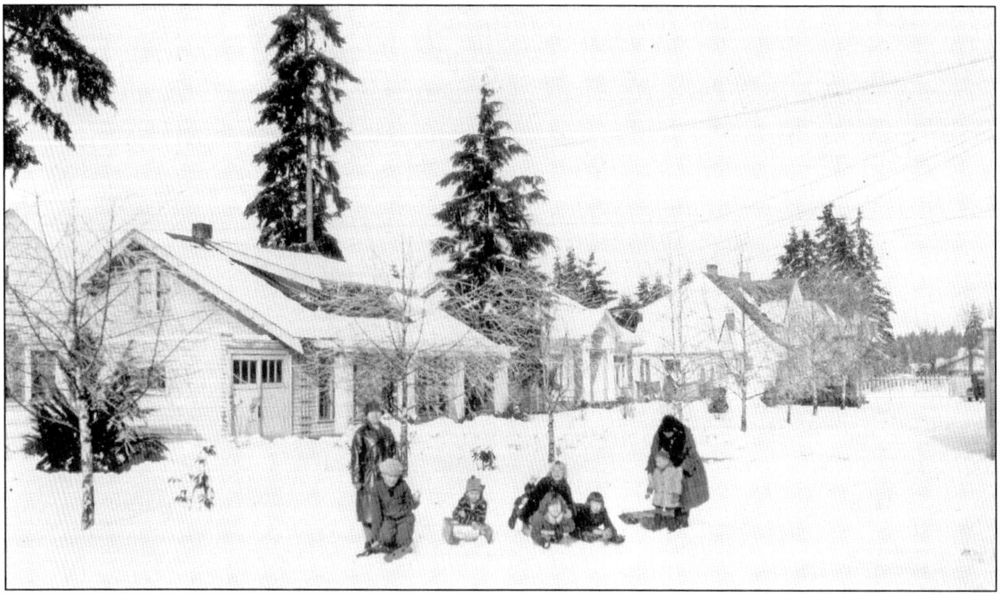

The Tumwater Lumber Mills Company (TLM), the last sawmill in town, produced a successful line of "kit" houses called Tumwater Ready-Cut Homes during the 1920s and 1930s. Each house came as a ready-to-assemble kit of precut lumber, windows, cabinets, floors, doors, and a roof. A long row of TLM homes in the 3200 block of Capitol Boulevard (above) served as a life-sized advertisement for the company. The block was nicknamed "Swede Row," a reference to the five Swedish-born Anderson brothers who owned the company and initially lived in the houses. Amy Anderson, their sister and company bookkeeper, owned the English Revival–style house (below) with the shutters and window box. (Both, courtesy of Kurt and Kit Anderson.)

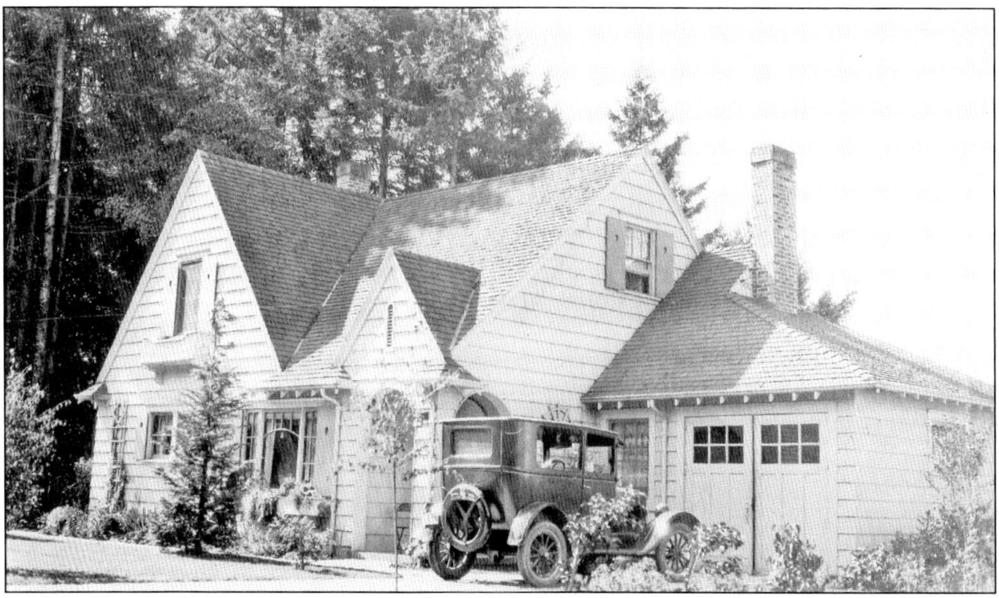

Four

Tumwater at Work

While the Olympia Brewing Company hired far more employees than any other local business, not everyone in Old Tumwater worked there. From the days of the pioneer sawmills until the Tumwater Lumber Mills Company left town in the 1930s, a significant number of residents were employed in the timber trade. Farming, too, was a way of life for many Tumwater families. Early settlers typically built farms on their pioneer land claims—especially on the open prairie south and east of the river—and working farms could be found around town as late as the 1960s.

In addition to farming and industry, Tumwater offered the usual shops and services of an American small town: grocery stores, drugstores, a butcher shop, barber, hotel, and saloon. The 1911–1912 Polk City Directory listed 29 different local occupations and businesses, from beekeeper and dairy farmer to insurance agent and judge. In a significant sign of the changing times, listings appeared that year for both an old-fashioned blacksmith shop—gone before the directory actually went into print—and newfangled auto repair.

Perhaps because of Tumwater's proximity to the larger capital city of Olympia, some occupations and industries never seemed to take hold. The town at the falls had no bank, no newspaper, and no theater or movie house (although later, in 1949, Tumwater would claim the first drive-in theater in Thurston County). Especially after 1892, when electric streetcar service began along Capitol Boulevard, residents increasingly looked to Olympia for shopping and entertainment. But it was Tumwater's electrical power plant, staffed in shifts around the clock, that lit up Olympia's streets at night and made the trolley cars run.

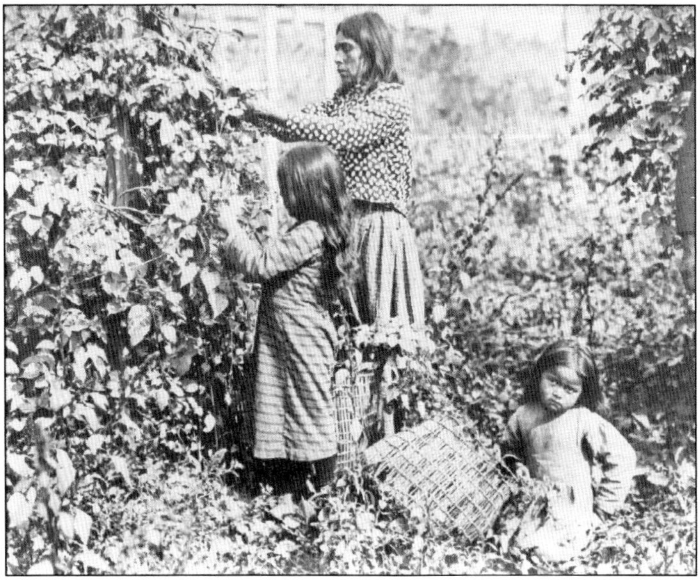

Unable to continue their traditional way of living, American Indians looked for work in the new American economy. One place they found it was in low-paying, transient jobs at harvest time. These American Indian girls are picking hops with their elders. (Courtesy of Squaxin Island Tribe Museum, Library, and Research Center.)

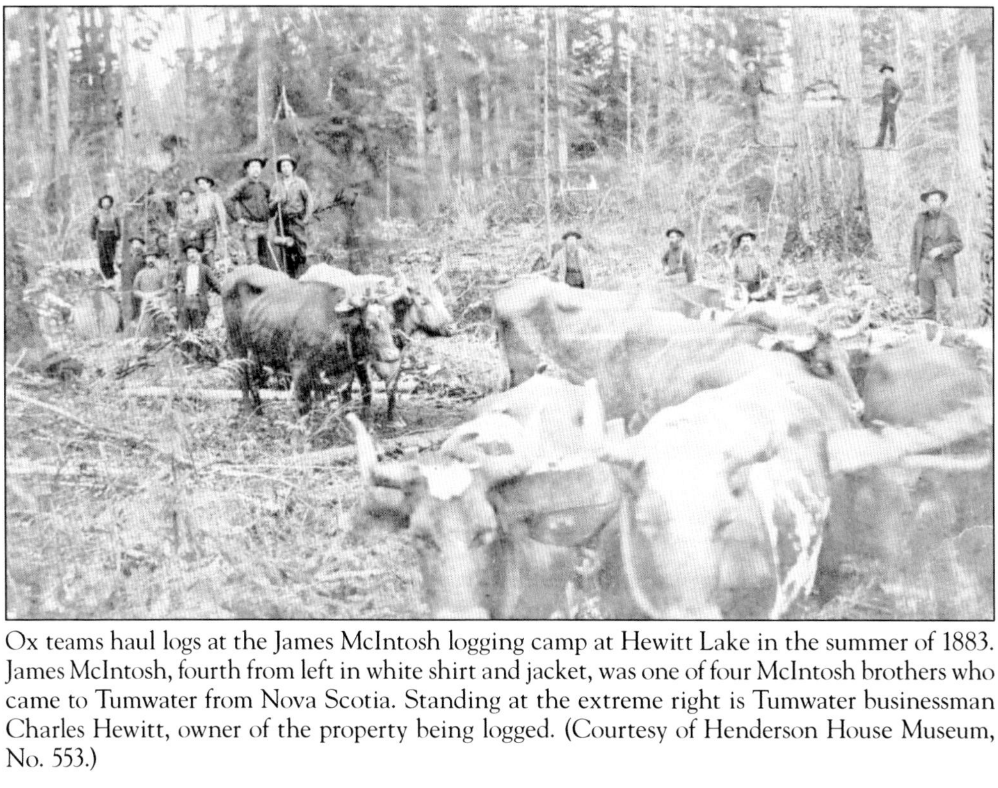

Ox teams haul logs at the James McIntosh logging camp at Hewitt Lake in the summer of 1883. James McIntosh, fourth from left in white shirt and jacket, was one of four McIntosh brothers who came to Tumwater from Nova Scotia. Standing at the extreme right is Tumwater businessman Charles Hewitt, owner of the property being logged. (Courtesy of Henderson House Museum, No. 553.)

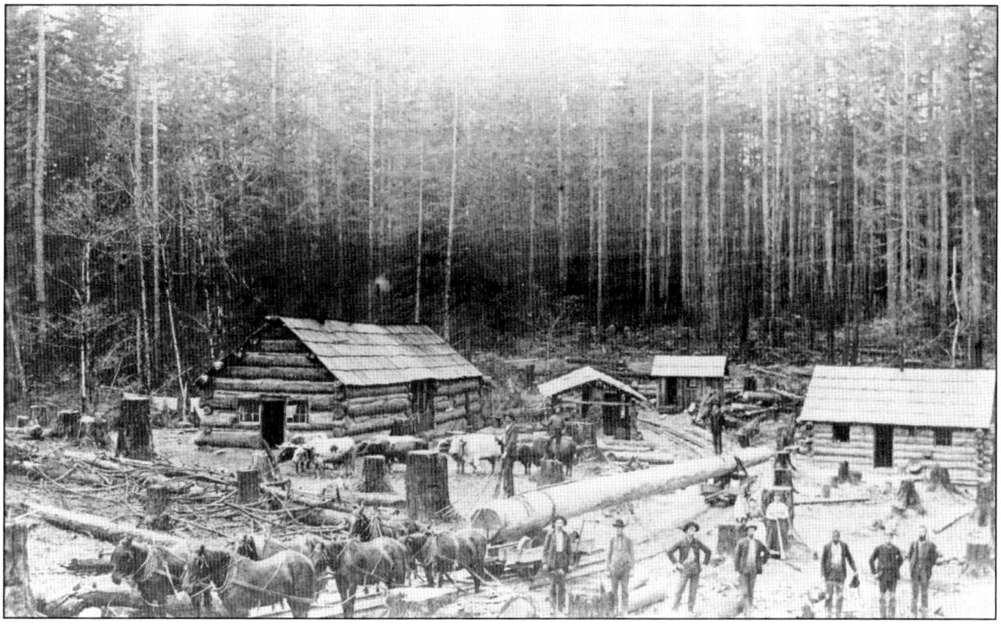

Both oxen and horse teams are in use at this Black Lake logging camp around 1890. Note the size of the log being hauled and the size of the stumps left behind. (Courtesy Henderson House Museum, No. 759.)

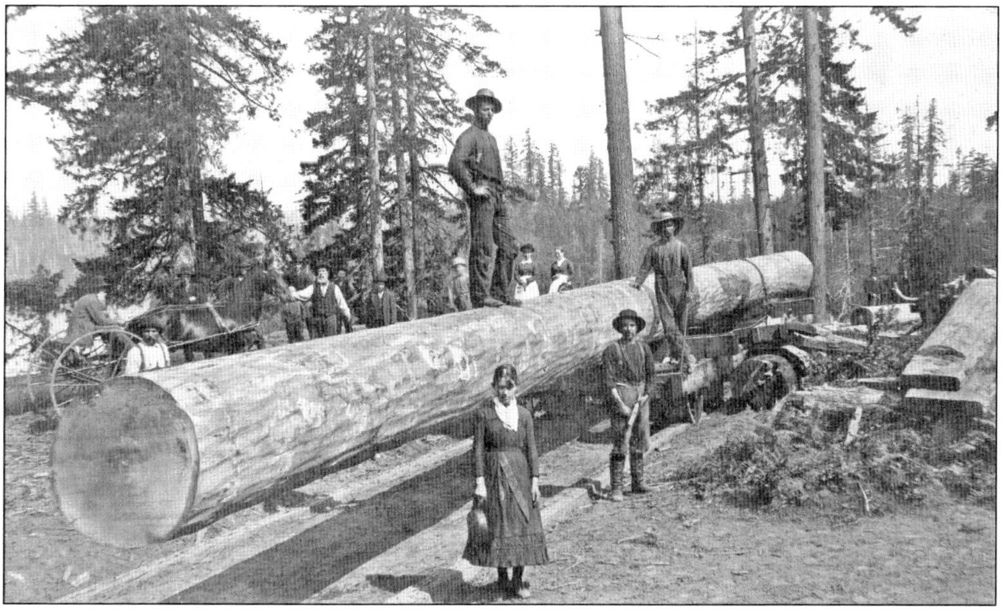

Loggers clear the forest east of the river in 1884 near the present-day intersection of Carlyon Avenue and Capitol Boulevard. Logs were hauled on small railcars to the brink of the bluff and dumped down the hill to the Deschutes waterway, then floated in rafts to the mills. Eight thousand board feet of lumber were eventually sawed from this 100-foot log. (Courtesy of Henderson House Museum, No. 566.)

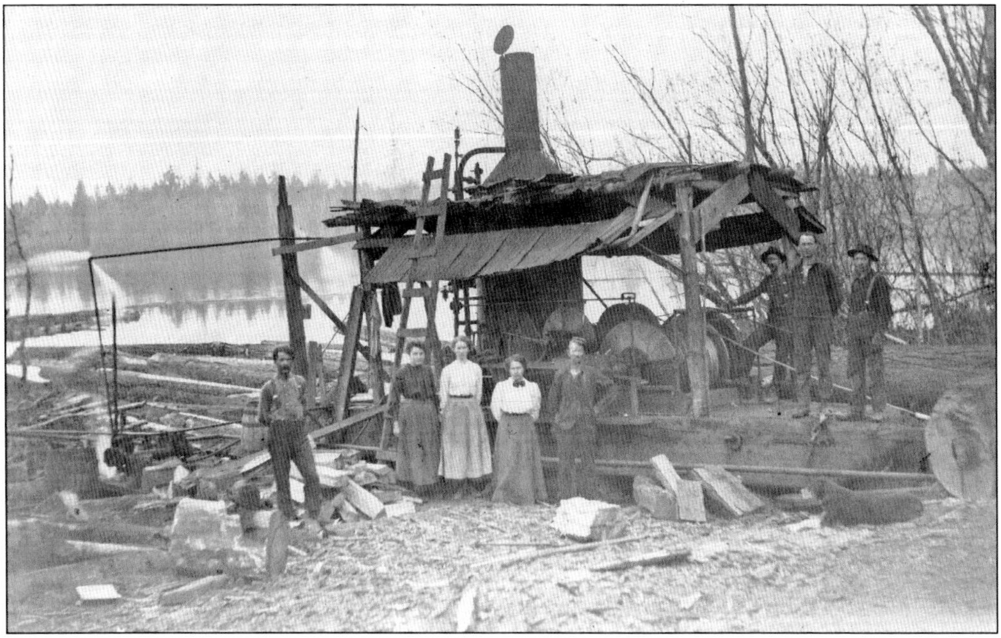

Crisply dressed women pose with somewhat grubbier loggers near a donkey engine at Black Lake. The steam-powered donkey provided the brawn to haul logs from the woods with cables, eliminating the need for ox teams. (Courtesy of Henderson House Museum, No. 890.)

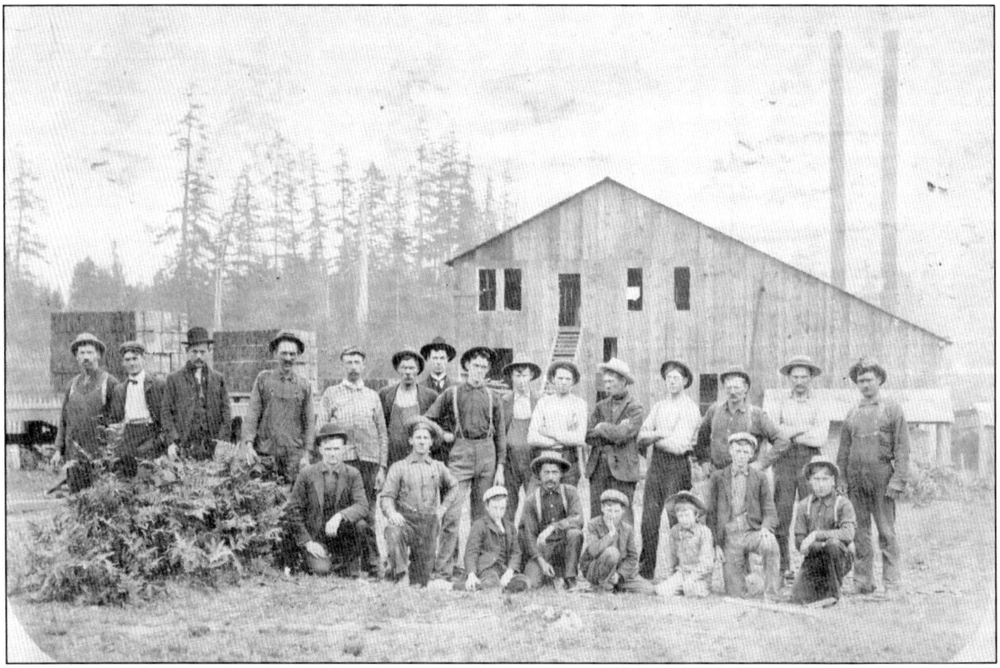

The Lea Lumber and Shingle Mill was constructed at the Upper Falls in 1904, replacing the original pioneer sawmill that burned in 1891. The earlier mill had been powered by the falls, but the new one ran on electricity. The building behind the crew is the kiln; the mill is out of view to the left. In 1919, the Lea operation was purchased by the Anderson brothers, who transformed it into the Tumwater Lumber Mills Company. (Courtesy of Henderson House Museum, No. 049.)

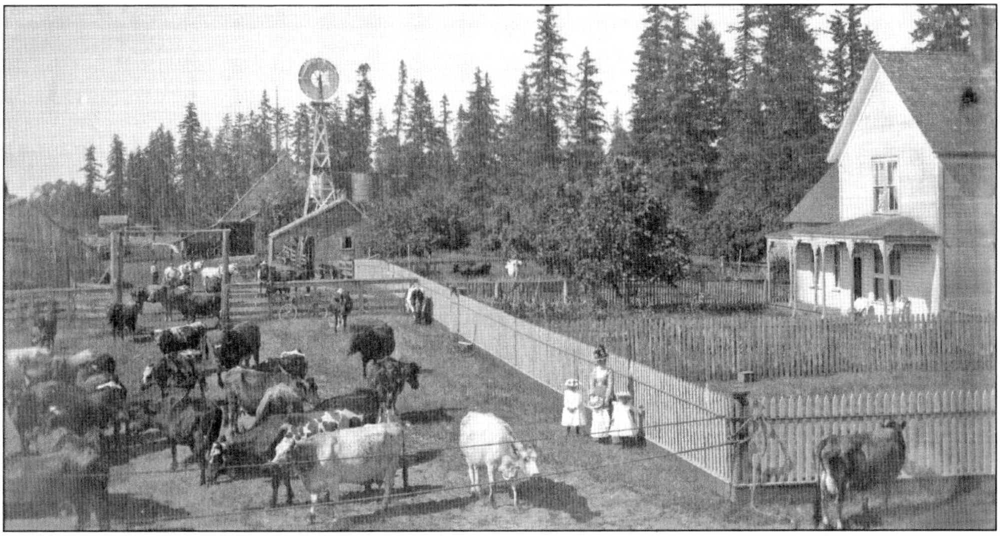

Swiss immigrants Joseph and Magdalena Wickie rented and worked the Arthur Jones farm south of town (near the present-day Olympia Airport) when this picture was taken around 1901. Magdalena stands at right with daughters Marie, Lena, and Jennie, while Joseph sits on the fence rail in the background. By arrangement with the Olympia Brewing Company, Joseph Wickie collected the spent mash from the brewery and sold it to local dairy farmers as feed. Eventually the Wickies owned the Pioneer Dairy on the Yelm Highway, where the neighborhood known as The Farm was built in the 1990s. (Courtesy of Henderson House Museum, No. 492.)

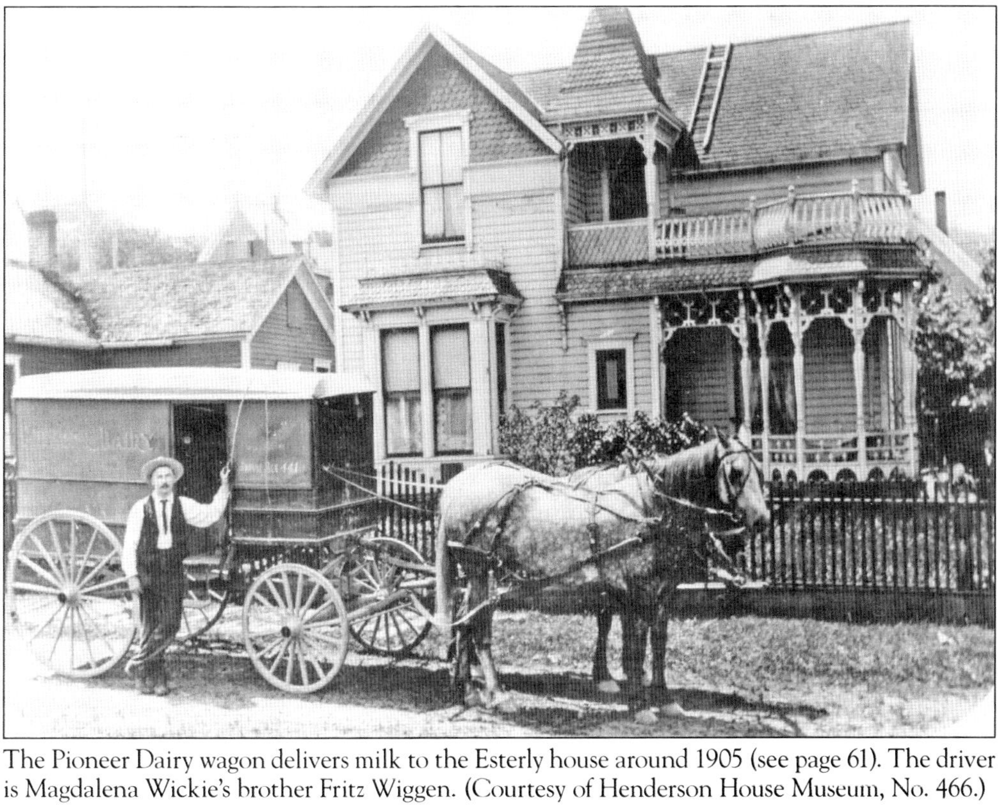

The Pioneer Dairy wagon delivers milk to the Esterly house around 1905 (see page 61). The driver is Magdalena Wickie's brother Fritz Wiggen. (Courtesy of Henderson House Museum, No. 466.)

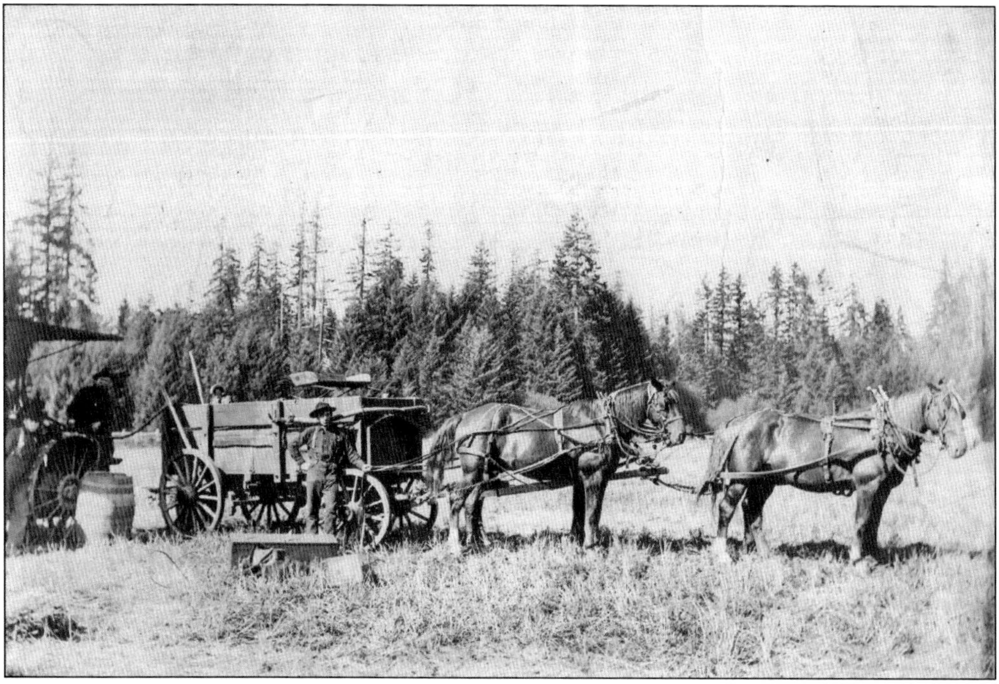

A two-horse team stands hitched to a springboard wagon at the Drewry Ranch in 1906. The Drewry property was located south of town, near Bush Prairie, where the equestrian center called Trails End later stood. (Courtesy of Henderson House Museum, No. 348.)

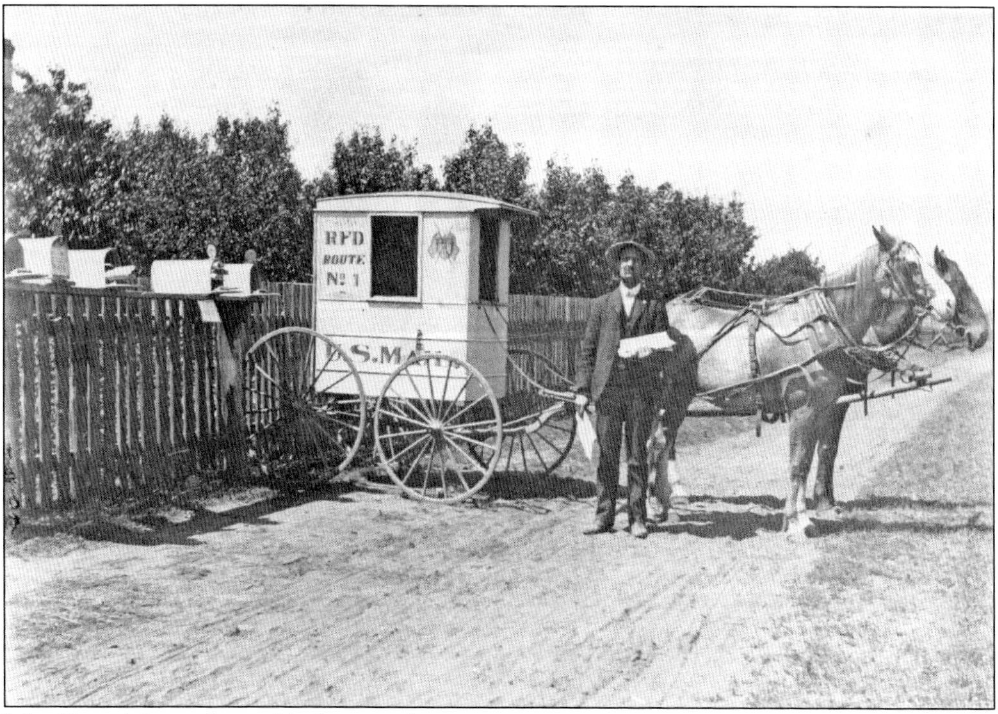

John Hopp delivers the mail by horse and wagon on RFD Route 1, south of Tumwater. Hopp started the job in 1902 and held it for 40 years. (Courtesy of Henderson House Museum, No. 755.)

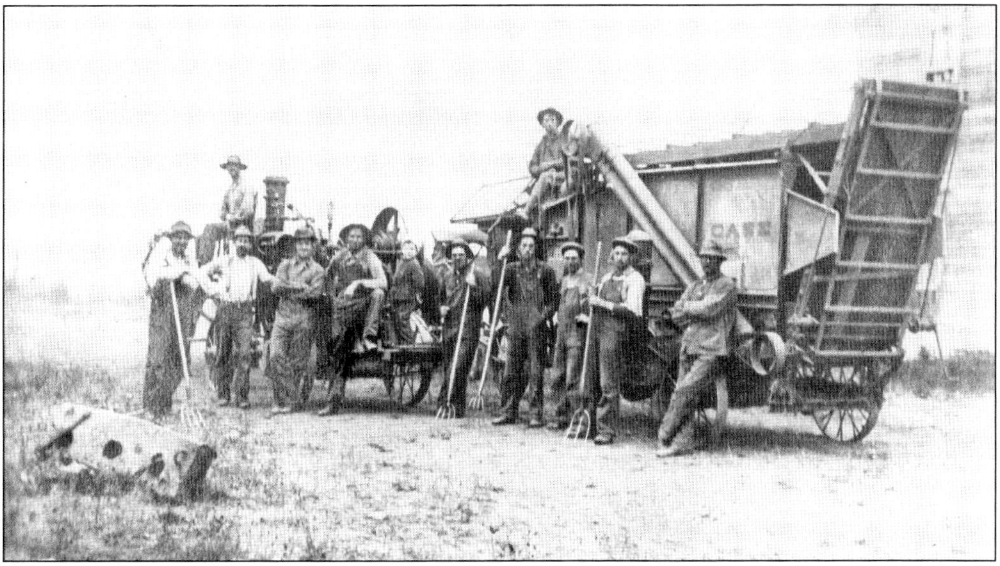

A crew prepares for threshing on Fred Lewis's farm in 1916. Ten years after the picture on the opposite page was taken, farm machinery had advanced from horses to gasoline engines. The Lewis farm was located off Israel Road, where the Sunset Drive-In Theater would go up in 1949, followed in 1988 by Tumwater City Hall. (Courtesy of Henderson House Museum, No. 351.)

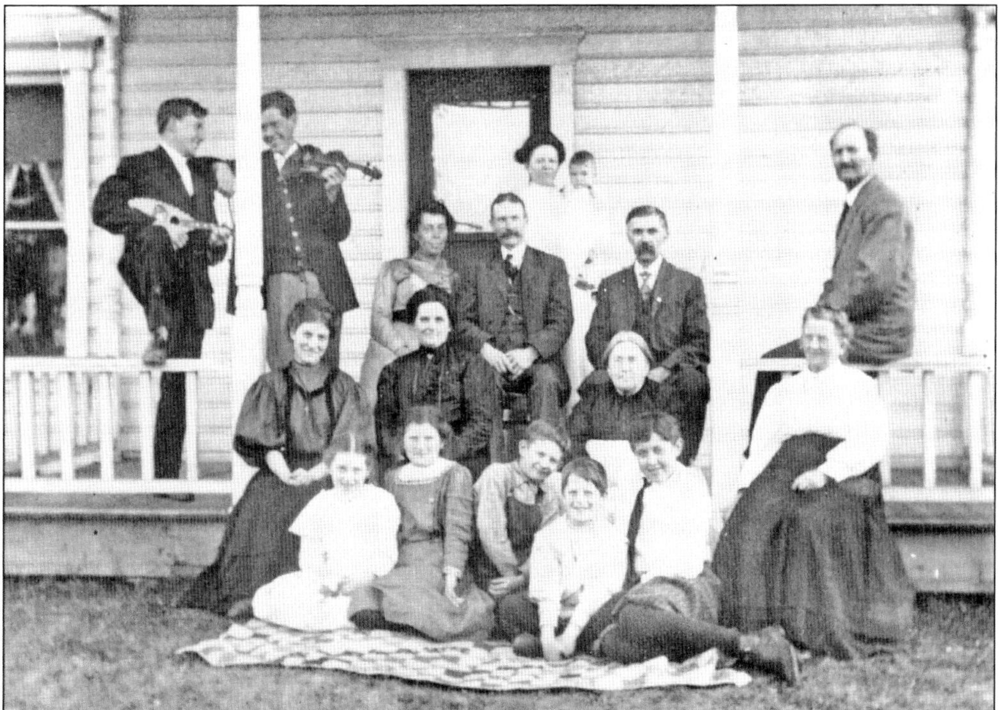

The families of rural mail carrier John Hopp and farmer Fred Lewis gather on the porch of what is probably the Lewis farmhouse. Lewis is the man seated second from right; his wife and child stand behind him. Hopp sits at the right, on the railing. The two musicians on the left add a charming touch to the scene. (Courtesy of Henderson House Museum, No. 733.)

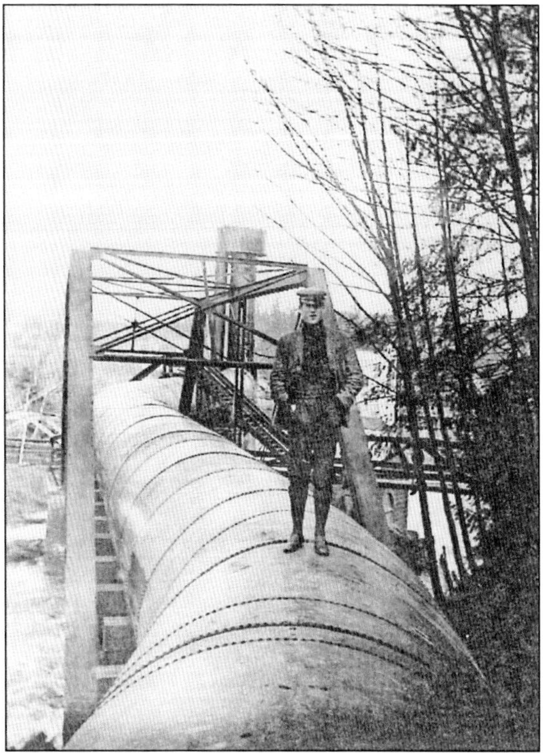

Harry L. Cusack, son of Tumwater mayor Harry B. Cusack, balances on the penstock leading to the Olympia Light and Power Company plant at the Lower Falls. The penstock was apparently a favorite pedestrian route up and down the canyon. Tumwater resident Ed McDonald remembered his father walking on top of the huge pipe to his midnight shift at the powerhouse. (Courtesy of Olympia Tumwater Foundation.)

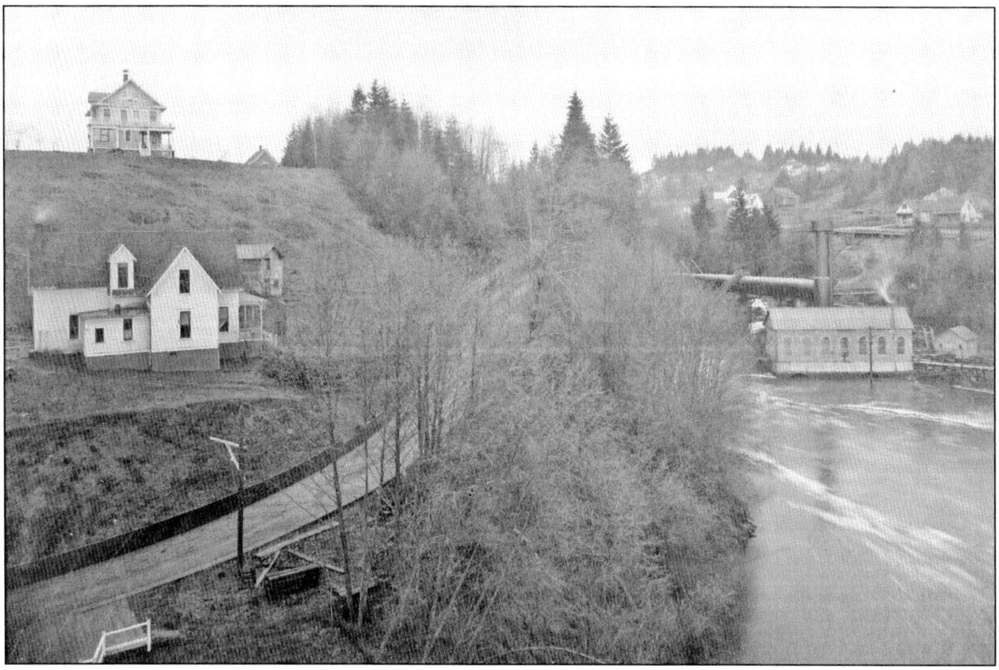

This unusual view, most likely taken from the tower of the 1906 brewhouse, shows where the penstock from the Upper Falls crossed the river to Powerhouse No. 2. The 1904 Schmidt House stands on top of the bluff; the special brewery spur of the local streetcar line runs downhill toward the left. (Courtesy of Olympia Tumwater Foundation.)

Burntrager's grocery store stood on Reserve Street (Deschutes Way) near the west end of the Boston Street Bridge. Planked sidewalks, well above the level of the unpaved street, gave the town's business district an up-and-coming air in the 1890s. (Courtesy of Henderson House Museum, No. 021.)

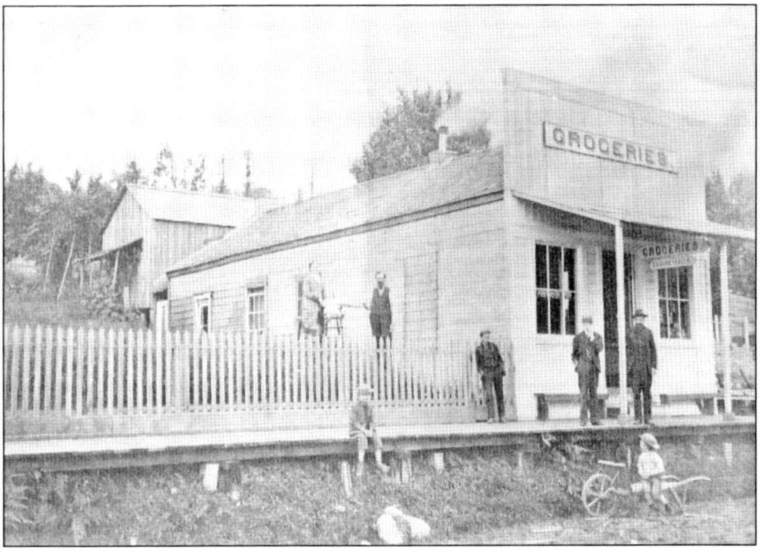

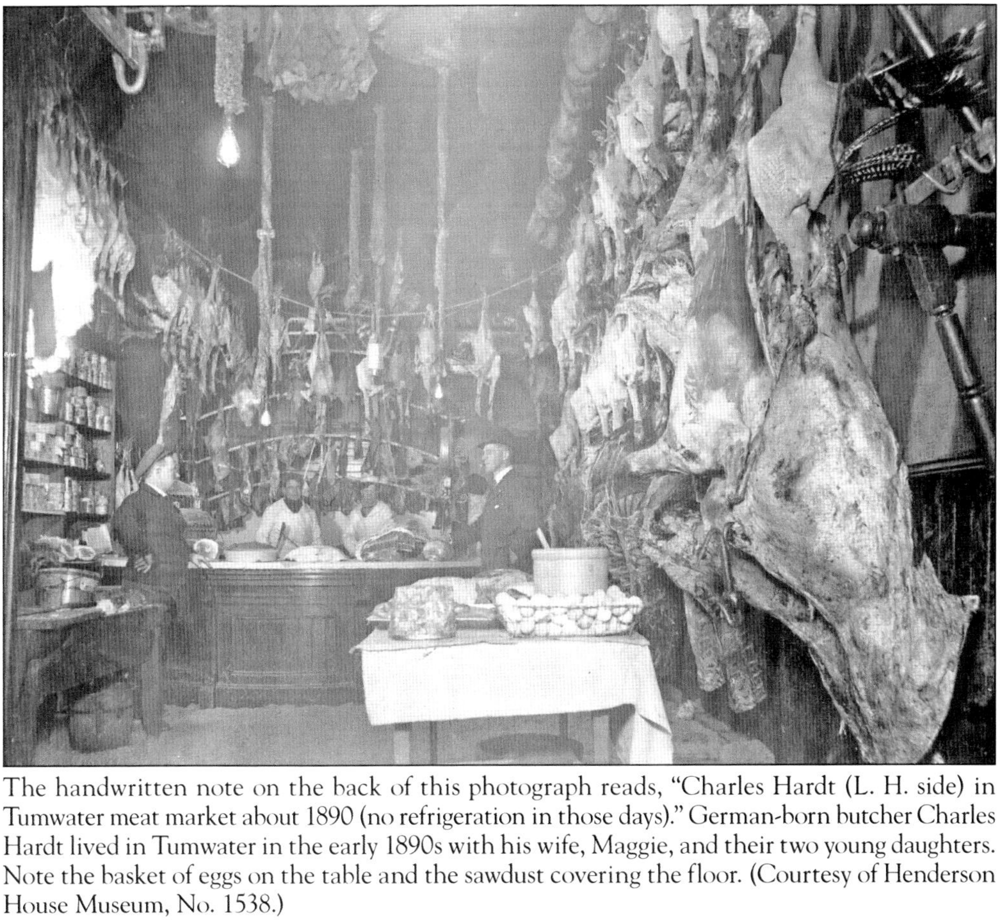

The handwritten note on the back of this photograph reads, "Charles Hardt (L. H. side) in Tumwater meat market about 1890 (no refrigeration in those days)." German-born butcher Charles Hardt lived in Tumwater in the early 1890s with his wife, Maggie, and their two young daughters. Note the basket of eggs on the table and the sawdust covering the floor. (Courtesy of Henderson House Museum, No. 1538.)

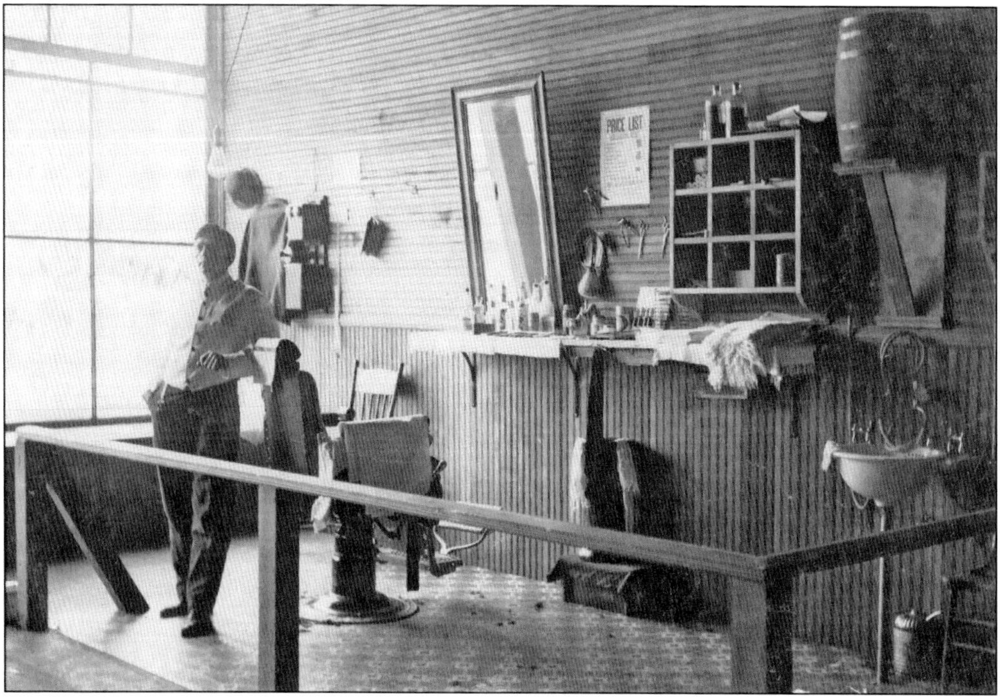

Ranson Albert Padget leans against the chair in his barbershop at the east end of the Boston Street Bridge, next door to the trolley station, around 1912. (Courtesy of Henderson House Museum, No. 959.)

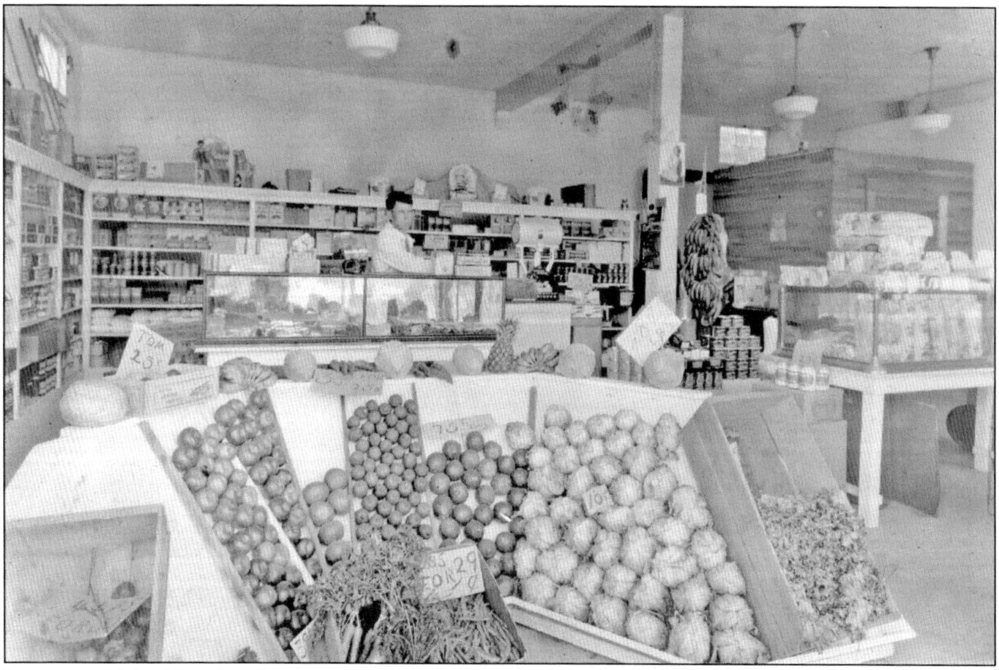

Lettuce sold for 10¢ a head when Frank Phillips opened his Tumwater grocery store in 1929. Phillips later rented freezer lockers where local residents stored their self-raised poultry and meat. He was also mayor of Tumwater from 1958 to 1962. (Courtesy of Henderson House Museum, No. 058.)

Charles Hewitt arrives at his drugstore with a wheelbarrow full of mail, around 1919. Mail came from Olympia by streetcar, and Hewitt wheeled his cart across the Boston Street Bridge every day to collect the sacks from the trolley station on the east bank. The town post office remained inside the Hewitt Drugstore from 1900 to 1942, with Hewitt's wife, Eva, taking over from her husband as postmistress in 1915. (Courtesy of Henderson House Museum, No. 385.)

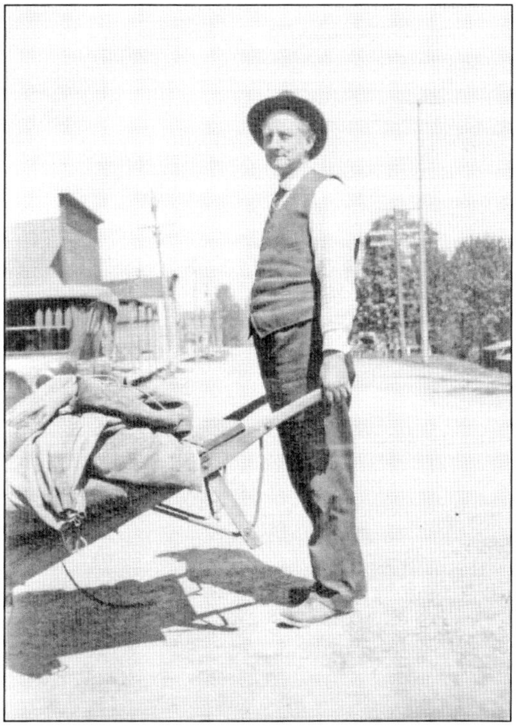

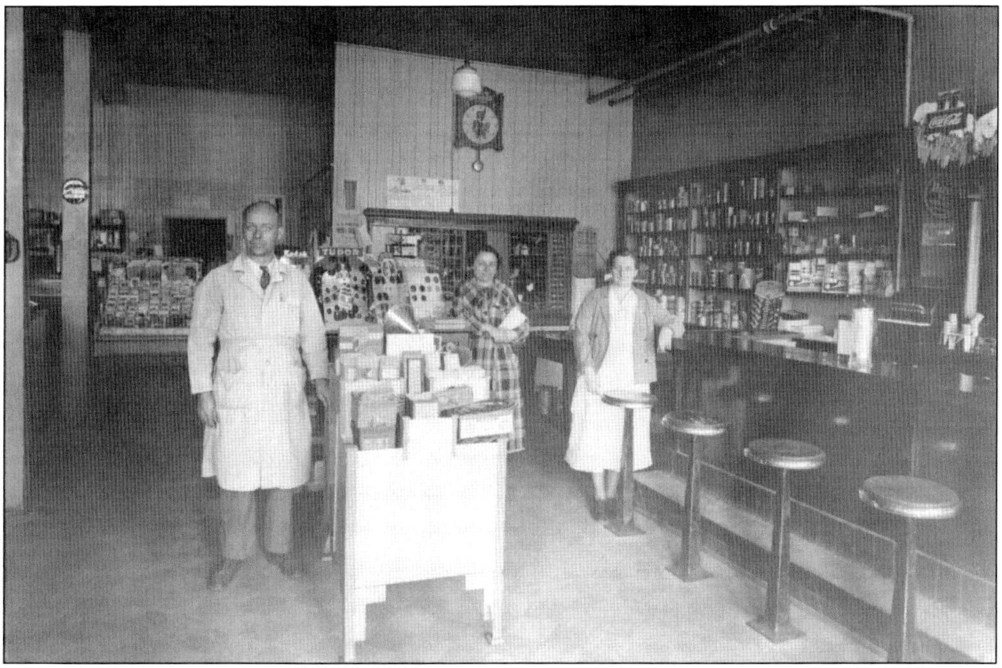

The Hewitts' daughter Laura Hewitt Henry ran the family business with her mother after Charles Hewitt's death in 1927. She is pictured here (right) inside the drugstore with her husband, Phil Henry, and customer Blanche Beigh. The post office window where postmistress Eva Hewitt reigned for 27 years can be seen at the rear of the store. (Courtesy of Henderson House Museum, No. 1016.)

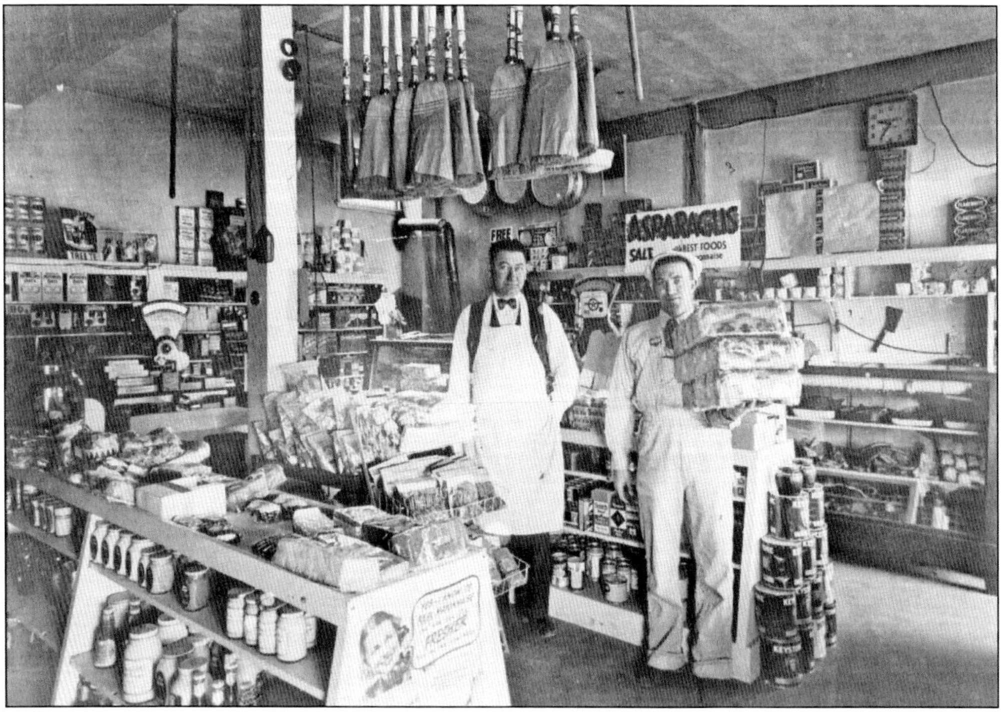

Brothers Norm and Joe O'Hare owned a grocery store on Deschutes Way at Division Street during the 1930s. Joe later opened his own store inside the roller-skating rink on Capitol Boulevard (see page 103). Here Norm O'Hare (left) stands inside the original store with an unidentified bakery truck driver. (Courtesy of Henderson House Museum, No. 953.)

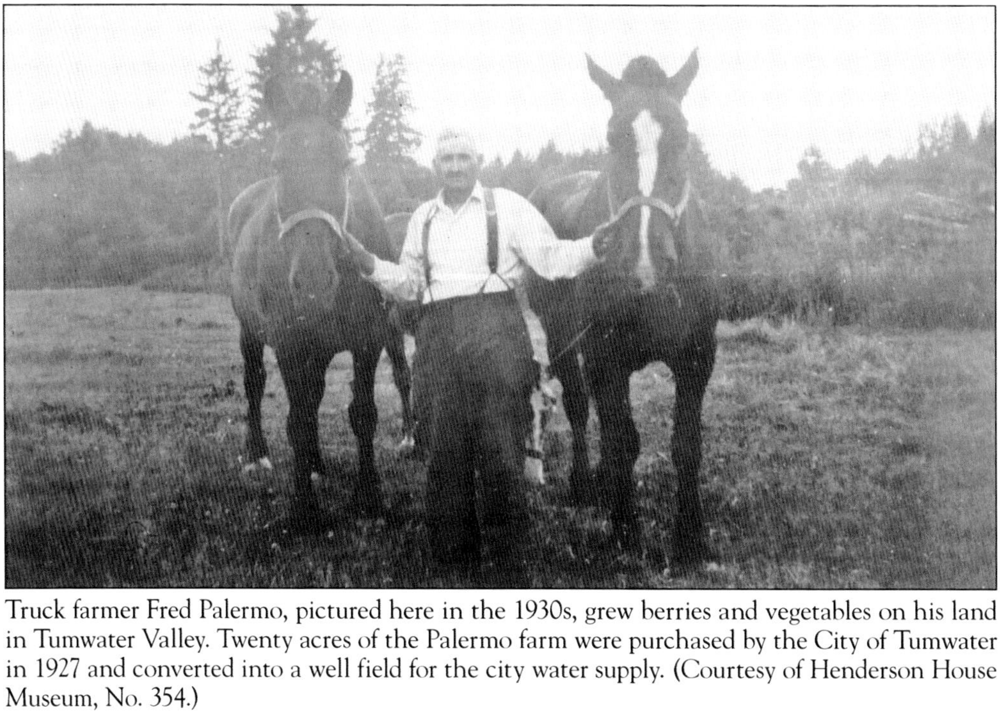

Truck farmer Fred Palermo, pictured here in the 1930s, grew berries and vegetables on his land in Tumwater Valley. Twenty acres of the Palermo farm were purchased by the City of Tumwater in 1927 and converted into a well field for the city water supply. (Courtesy of Henderson House Museum, No. 354.)

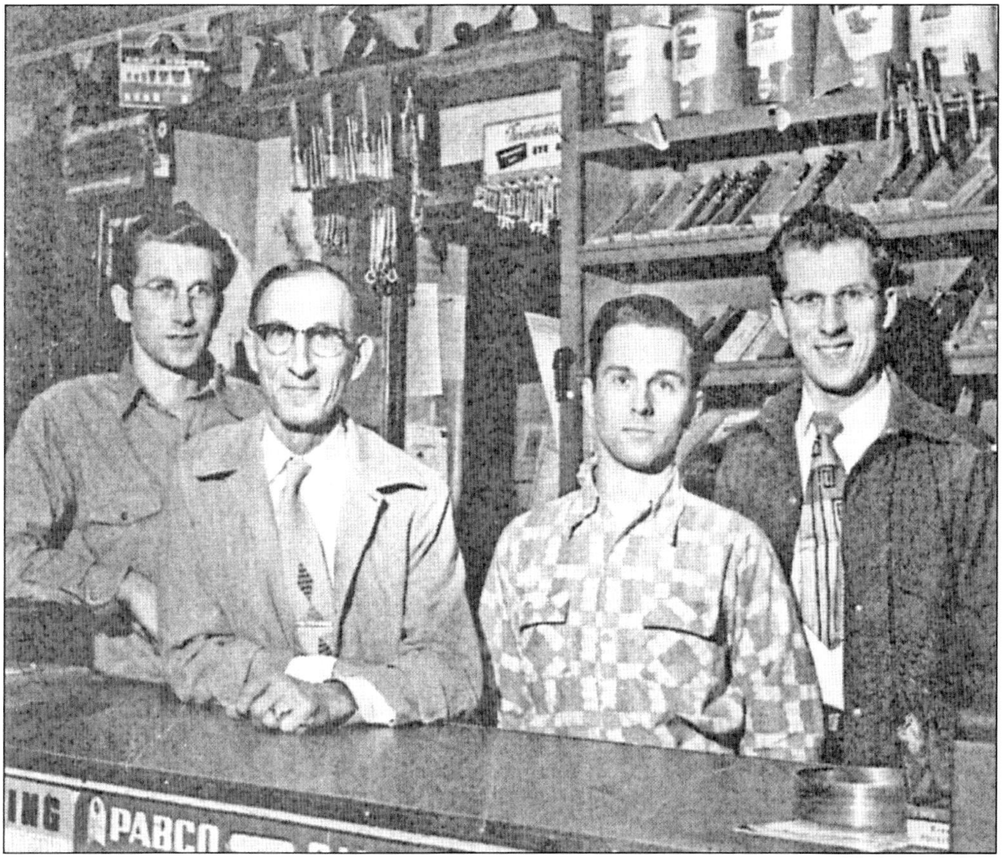

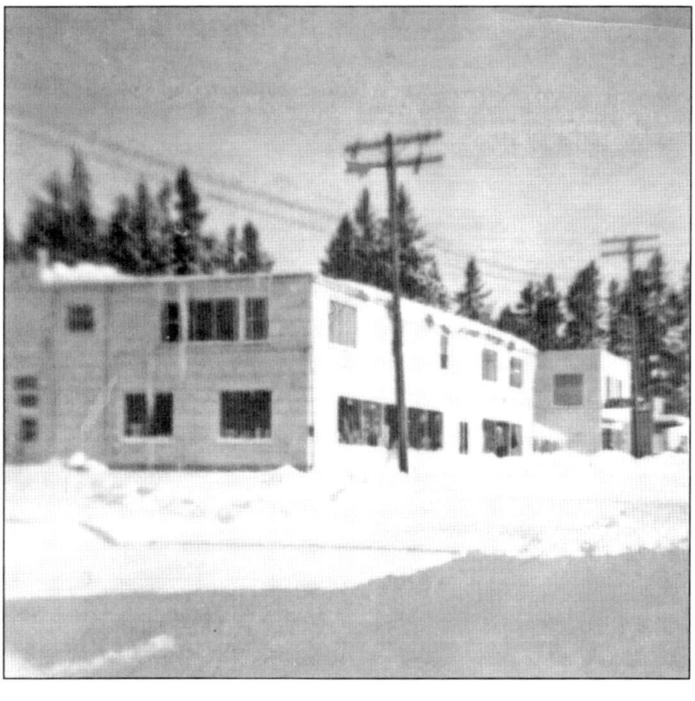

Emmett Brown (above, second from left) poses with sons, from left to right, Jake, Vince, and Jim at the front counter of the family's construction and hardware business around 1955. City Lumber and Builders (at right) stood on Custer Way, between Cleveland Avenue and Capitol Boulevard, and operated under the slogan "Brown's Boards Build Better Buildings." The Browns built dozens of local houses and businesses, including the Falls Terrace Restaurant overlooking the Upper Falls. (Both, courtesy of Jim Brown.)

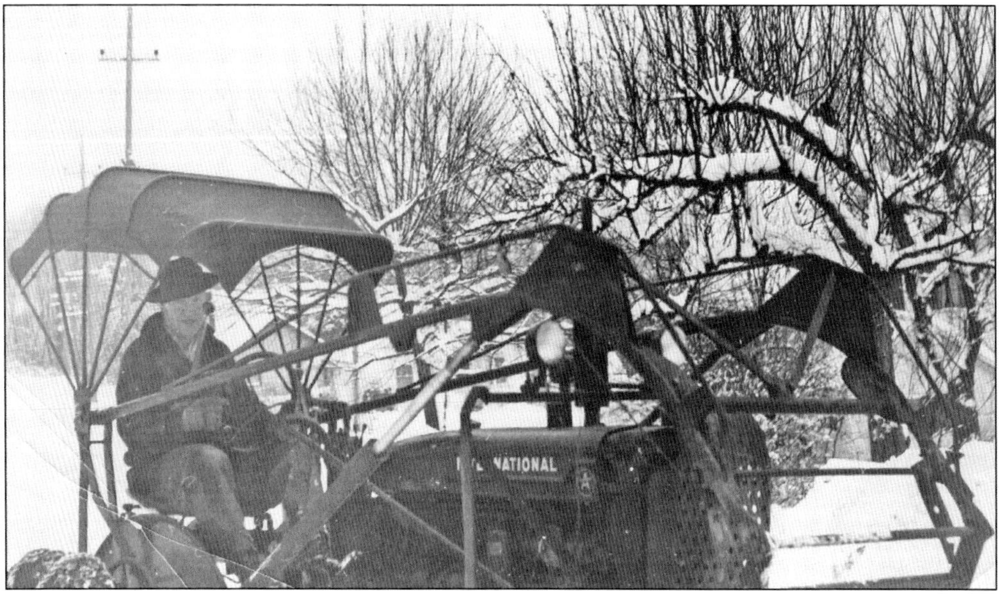

City street superintendant Charlie Meyers clears the road during a rare winter snowstorm. Most streets in town remained unpaved until the late 1950s. (Courtesy of Henderson House Museum, No. 1178.)

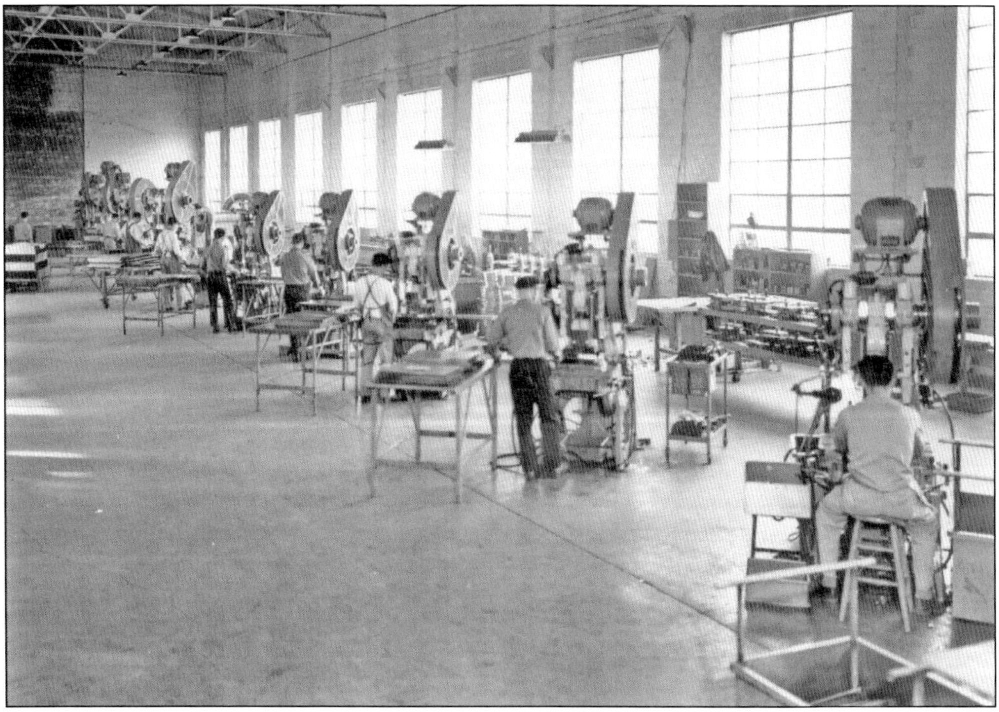

In the 1940s, new industry moved into the original Olympia Brewing complex at the foot of the Lower Falls. Jensvold Manufacturing produced airplane parts on the site as a subcontractor for the Boeing Company during World War II. After the war, employees of General Metalcraft (shown here) turned out steel kitchen cabinets in the shadow of Leopold Schmidt's 1906 brick brewhouse. (Courtesy of Henderson House Museum.)

Five

Community Life

In the days before streetcars and telephones, local life revolved around harvest time in the summer and socializing in winter. American Indians gathered food in the warm, dry months and returned to their winter villages for the ceremonial season—a time of ritual stories and dances, gaming, and feasting with guests. Pioneer settlers, too, worked on their farms in summer and turned to indoor pursuits in the winter: lessons in the classroom, dances above the Lee and Biles store, lively meetings of the Tumwater Literary Association or the local lodge of the Good Templars, who fought against drink and saloons.

By the early 1870s, Tumwater was an incorporated town with a school, a church, and two public halls. When it came to civic issues, citizens cared about street improvements, acquiring a rail line, and attracting new business and industry. They did not, it seems, care quite as much about voting rights for women. "Tumwater, Wash[ington] Ter[ritory]," famous suffragist Susan B. Anthony scribbled in her diary after a stop on her lecture tour in 1871. "Very small audience."

By the early 20th century, the Olympia Brewing Company stood at the heart of town life. When workers formed a social club in 1908, the Schmidt family built a clubhouse for them on the hilltop east of the brewery. Although Prohibition brought an official end to the Tumwater Club, the hall remained an essential part of Tumwater life for decades—serving, at various times, as the local Red Cross headquarters, a roller-skating rink, and a bowling alley.

For children raised in Tumwater in the 1930s and 1940s, nothing beat the Deschutes River as a place to hang out and play. "We practically lived at that river," remembered Margaret Henderson Lee, who grew up in the Naumann/Henderson House. "It was so much fun."

"There was such a feeling of closeness before the freeway," former Tumwater resident Maureen Hannah recalled. "We'd walk from Tumwater Hill, across the Boston Street Bridge, and then head down Capitol Way to Olympia—we walked and walked. The freeway changed that. We went from being a tiny community to being part of the real world."

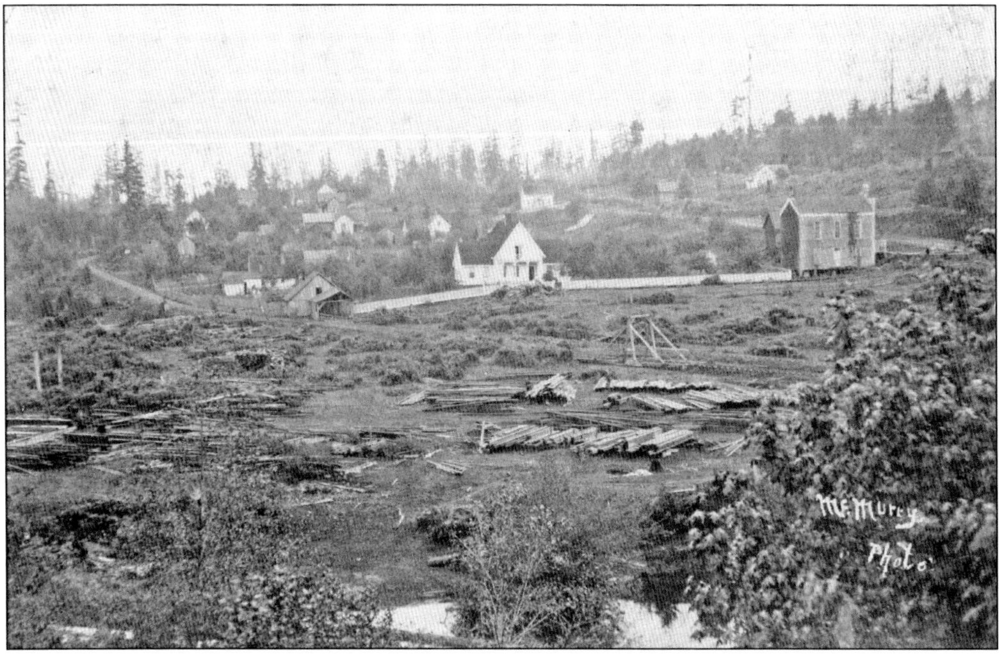

The Tumwater Literary Association dedicated its new meeting hall (right) with a fund-raising ball in April 1873. The structure cost $1,143.44 to build; the dance netted $25. The association sponsored a lending library and a debating club and briefly housed the town school. Its two-story hall stood on Reserve Street (Deschutes Way) at what is now C Street. Mill owner Ira Ward's second house stands at the center of the scene. (Courtesy of Henderson House Museum, No. 633.)

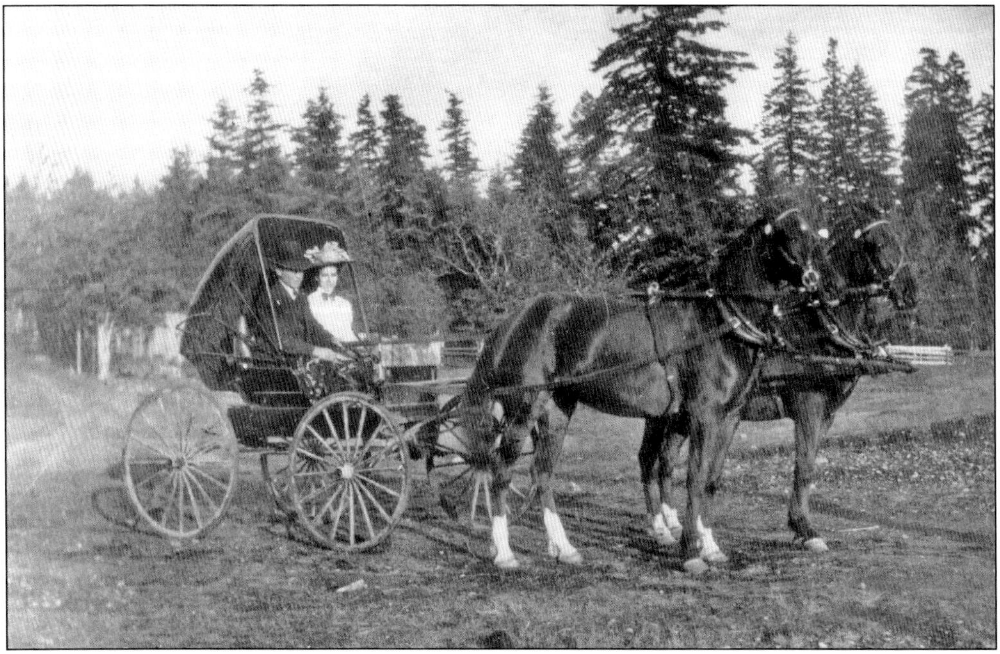

A four-wheel, two-horse phaeton was still a fashionable ride in 1909 when Gus and Pearl (Spirlock) Nelson set out on their wedding trip. The couple's descendants continue to farm near Tumwater on land purchased by the Spirlock family in 1861. (Courtesy of Henderson House Museum, No. 758.)

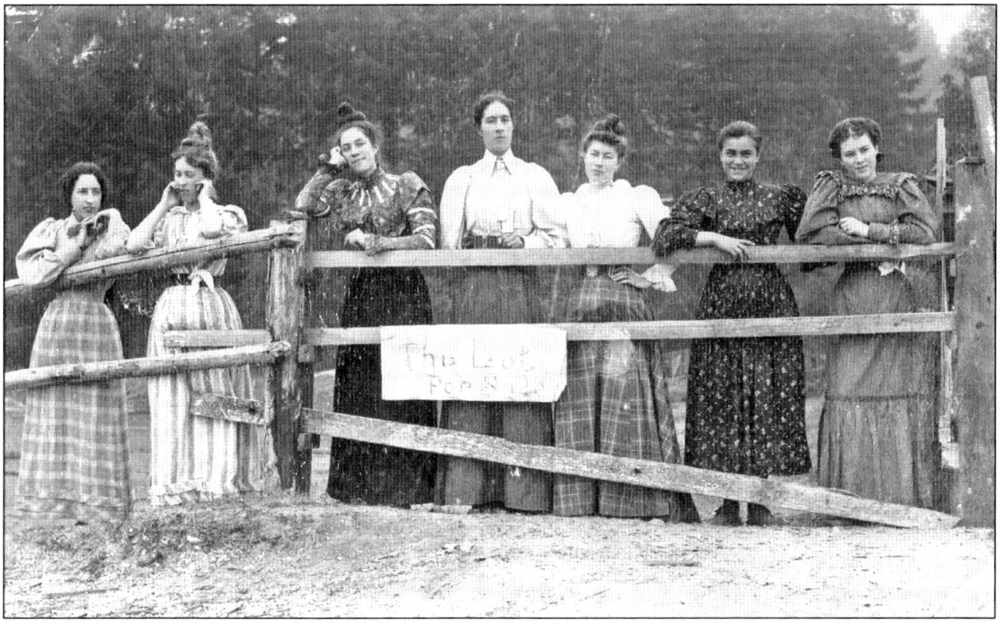

Young women share a sly joke with the photographer (the sign reads, "This Lot for Sale") along a rural rail fence. Given the fashions and hair styles, the picture was probably taken in the late 1890s. (Courtesy of Henderson House Museum, No. 1035.)

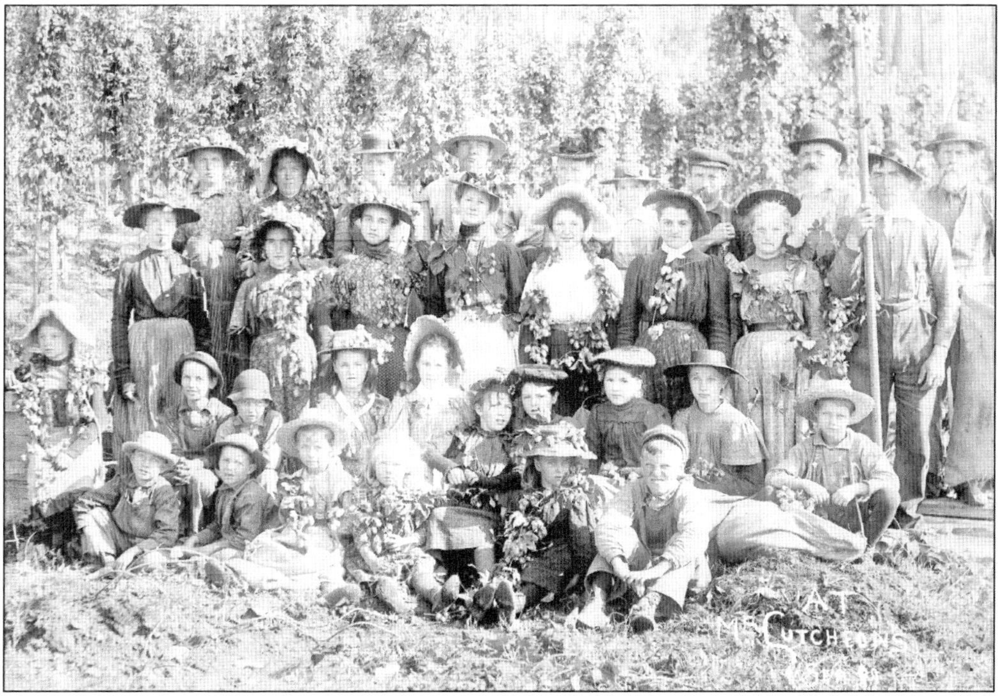

Black Lake residents drape themselves in hop vines for the local Hops Festival around 1899. There would not be many more such local festivals. Aphids known as "hop lice" decimated Western Washington hop fields during the 1890s. (Courtesy of Henderson House Museum, No. 357.)

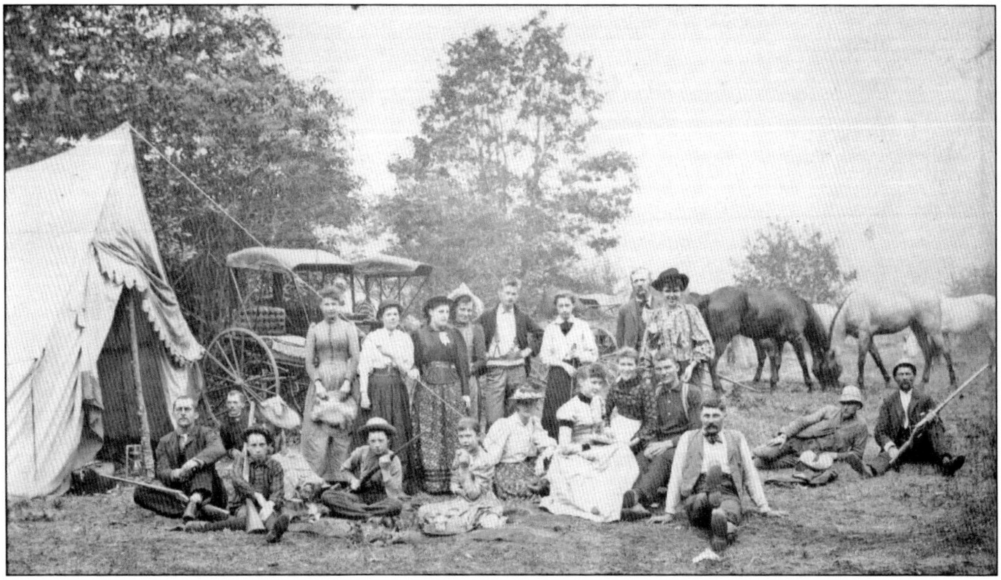

Tumwater friends enjoy a camping excursion to nearby Black Lake in the summer of 1891. Note the heavy canvas tent, the horse-and-buggy transportation, and the proliferation of shotguns. From left to right are (first row) Frank Kotick, Harry Biles, Kate Ward, unidentified, ? Donns, Linnie Barnes, Ada Sprague Mowell, two unidentified people, and George Gelbach; (second row) John Mowell (seated), unidentified, Etta Sprague Gelbach, Sadie Harris, Fannie Biles, Rod Sprague, unidentified, Clark Biles, and Minnie Sargent. The two men seated, to the far right, are unidentified. (Courtesy of Henderson House Museum, No. 691.)

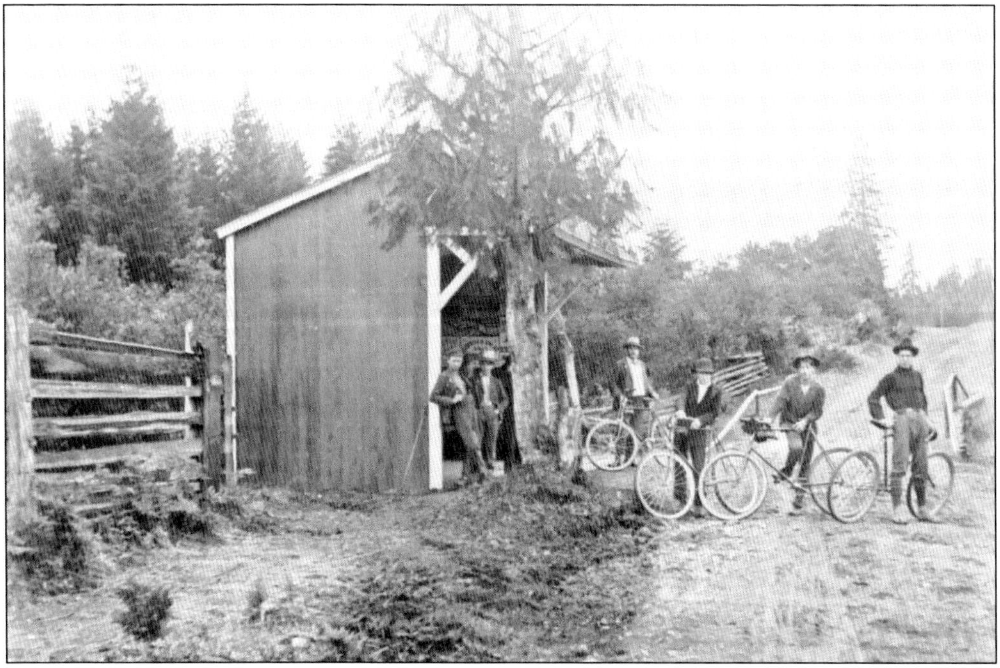

Bicycles brought unprecedented freedom to ordinary citizens, allowing them to travel moderate distances without the trouble and expense of a horse. Here six members of a local bicycle club enjoy a ride in the country. (Courtesy of Henderson House Museum, No. 711.)

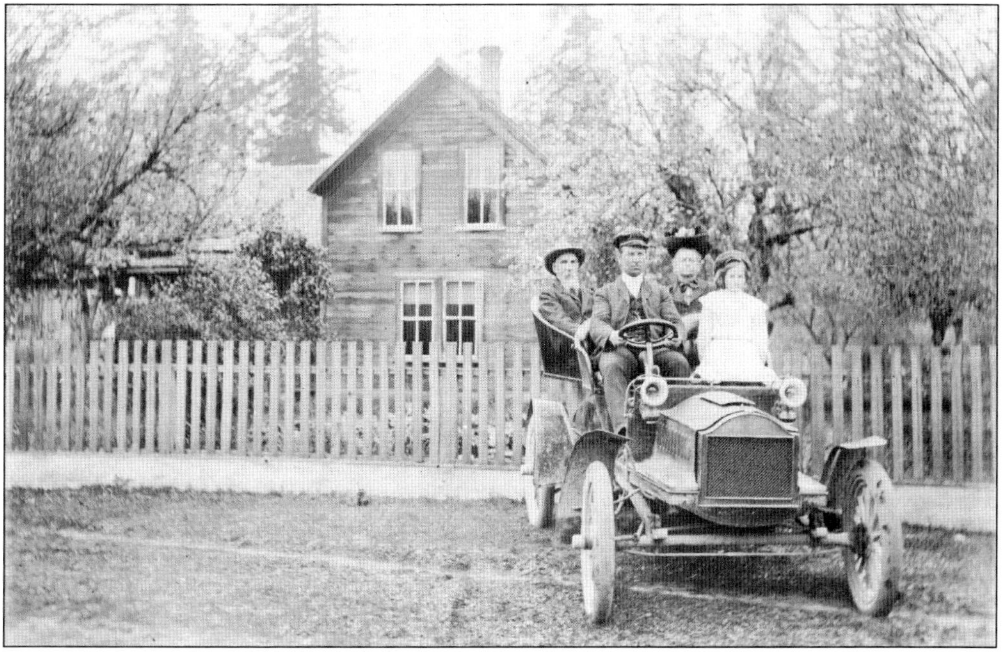

Businessman Wilbur Ashley, who once ran a bicycle shop in town (see page 23), later sold motorcycles and cars in Olympia. He is pictured here behind the wheel of a 10-horsepower Oldsmobile, which he insisted was the first car in the Olympia-Tumwater area. His claim was hotly challenged, however, by two other Olympia driving enthusiasts who acquired their cars during the same week of 1904. In this photograph, taken on Littlerock Road, Ashley is joined by young Laura Hewitt (Henry) in the passenger seat and Ashley's parents, George and Mary, in the back. (Courtesy of Henderson House Museum, No. 1106.)

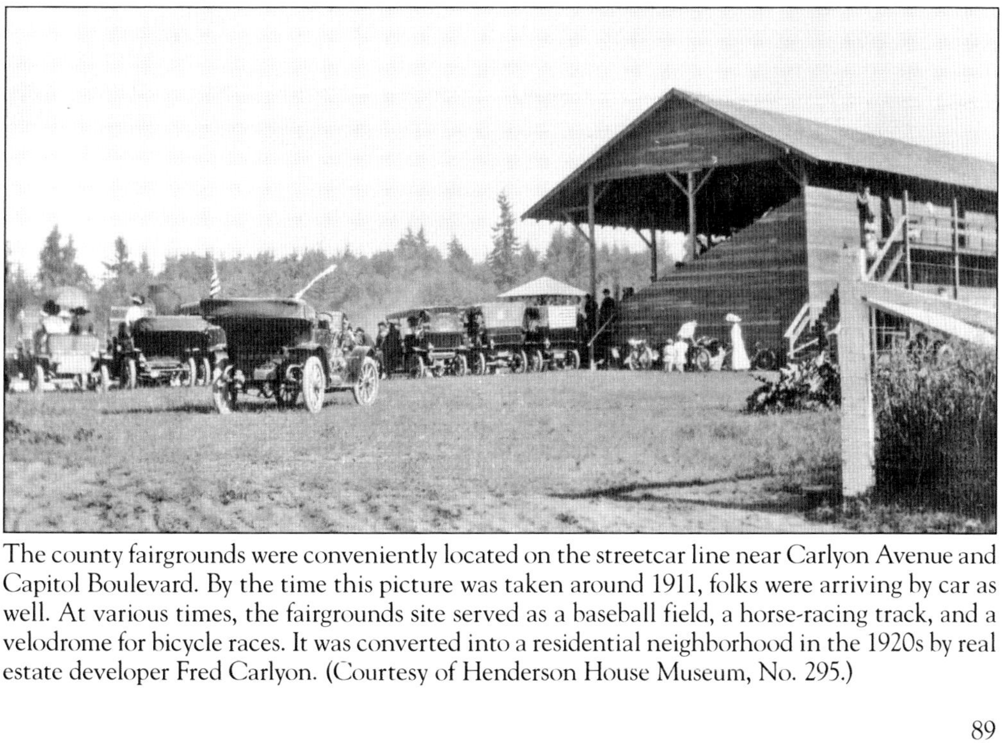

The county fairgrounds were conveniently located on the streetcar line near Carlyon Avenue and Capitol Boulevard. By the time this picture was taken around 1911, folks were arriving by car as well. At various times, the fairgrounds site served as a baseball field, a horse-racing track, and a velodrome for bicycle races. It was converted into a residential neighborhood in the 1920s by real estate developer Fred Carlyon. (Courtesy of Henderson House Museum, No. 295.)

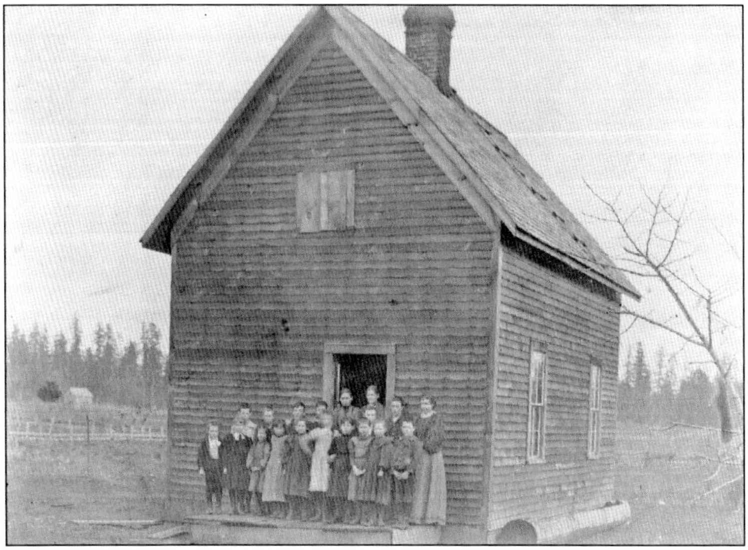

Local children were initially educated in small schoolhouses scattered throughout the area. This photograph is identified as the first schoolhouse of the Brighton Park School District, which was established south of Tumwater in 1897. (Courtesy of Henderson House Museum, No. 284.)

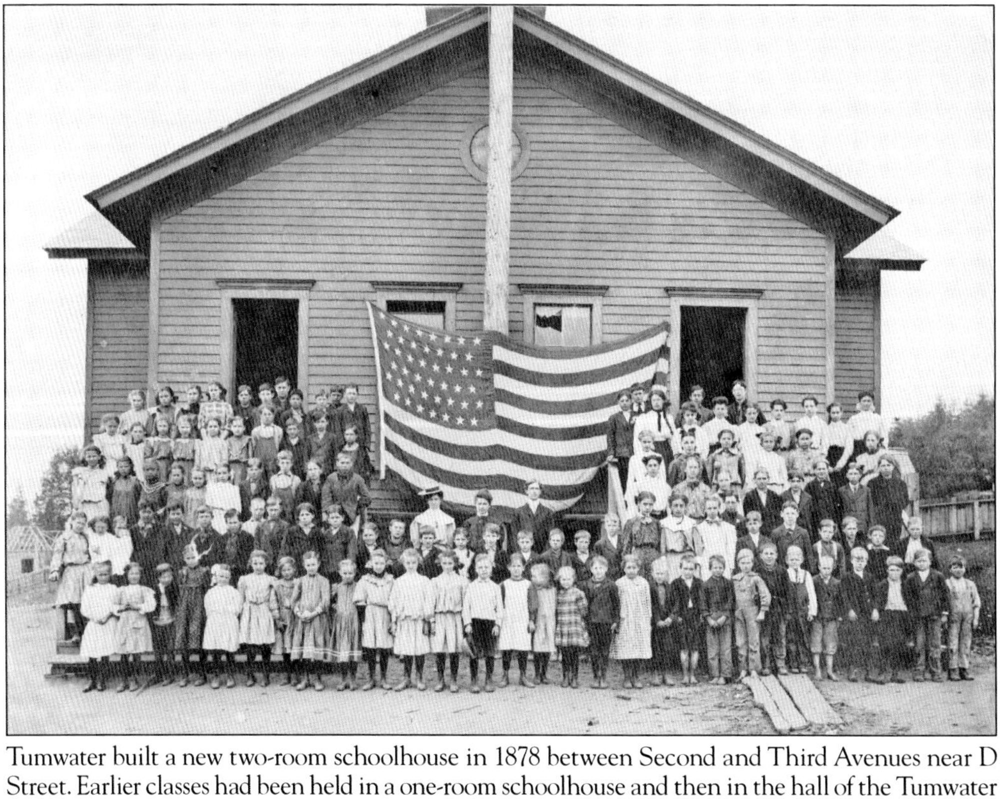

Tumwater built a new two-room schoolhouse in 1878 between Second and Third Avenues near D Street. Earlier classes had been held in a one-room schoolhouse and then in the hall of the Tumwater Literary Society. (See page 86.) More than 110 students, grades first through eighth, can be counted in this photograph from the 1890s. (Courtesy of Henderson House Museum, No. 185.)

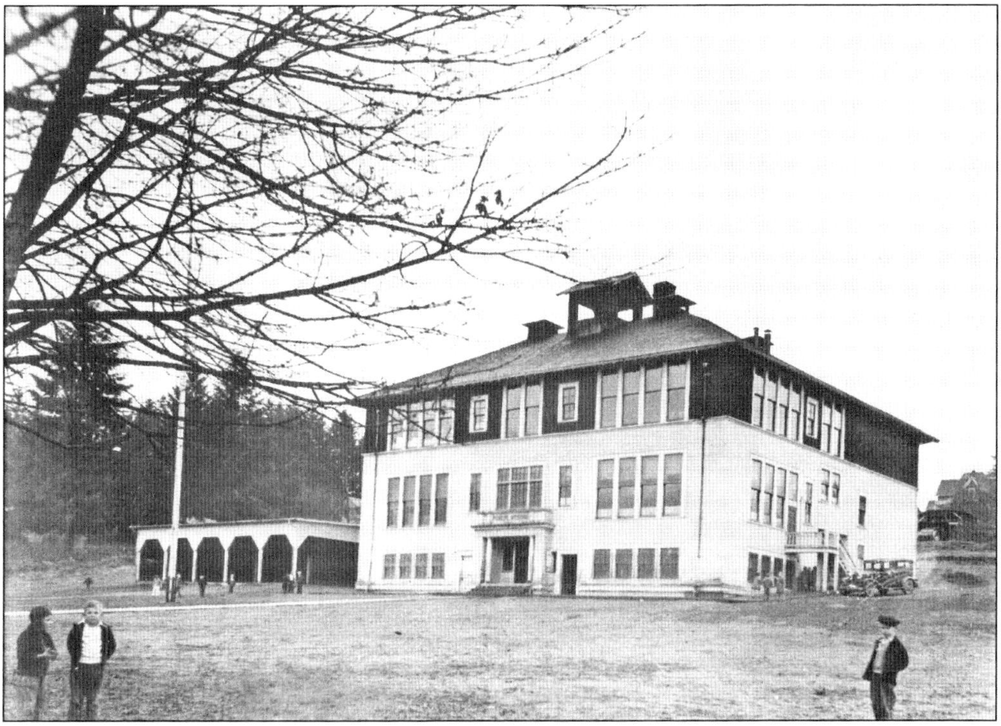

In 1908, the Tumwater School District opened a handsome two-story building, with a basement, at Second and C Streets to replace the two-room school. This school served Tumwater's students for three decades, until it was replaced by a new brick building on Linwood Avenue in 1937. (Courtesy of Tumwater School District.)

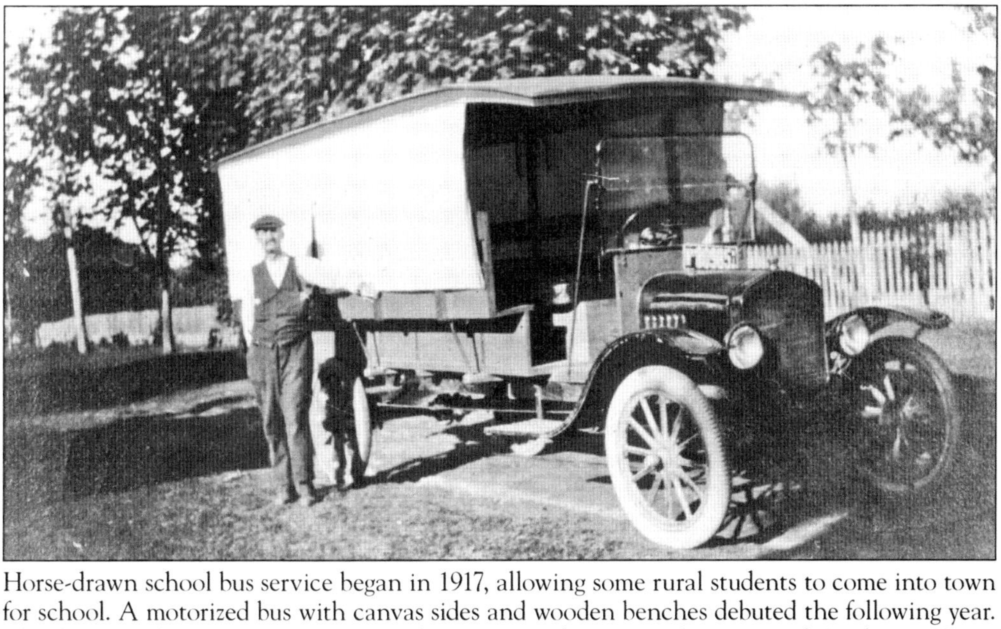

Horse-drawn school bus service began in 1917, allowing some rural students to come into town for school. A motorized bus with canvas sides and wooden benches debuted the following year. The driver in this picture is John Hopp, longtime rural postman. (Courtesy of Henderson House Museum, No. 292.)

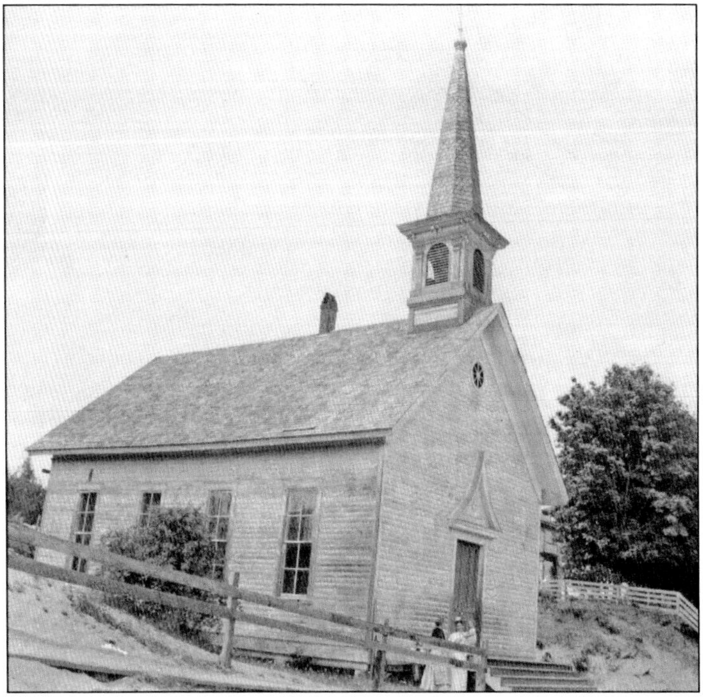

The first church in Tumwater was built as a community church but soon became associated with the Methodist denomination. A landmark on Second Avenue since 1872, the church has also housed Unitarian and Society of Friends congregations. (Courtesy of Henderson House Museum, No. 671.)

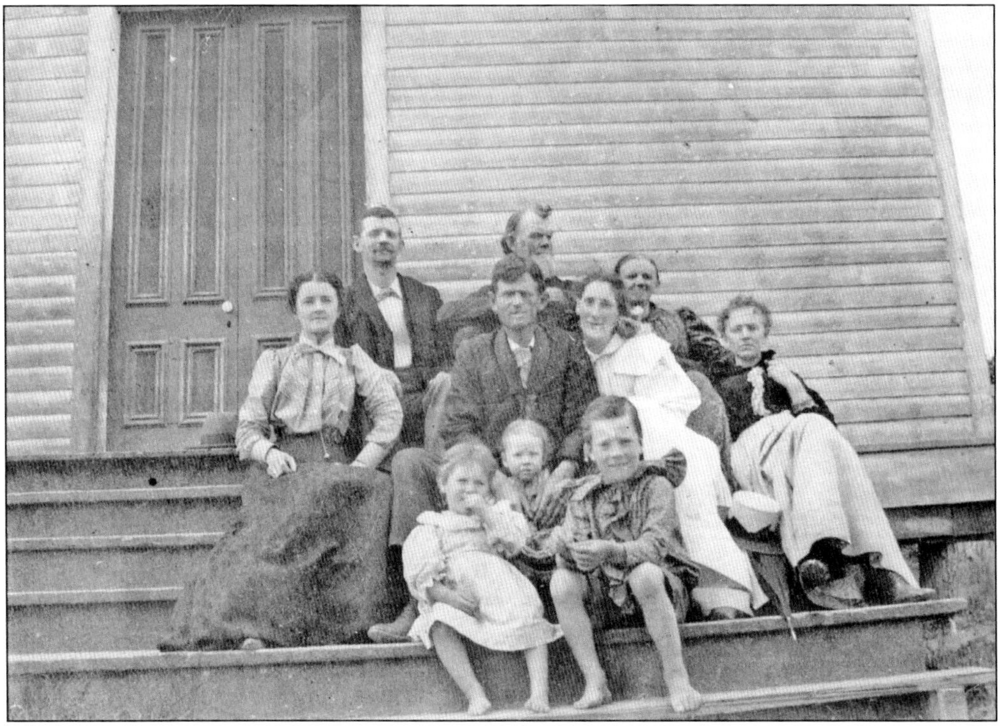

The Reverend Ebenezer Hopkins's family sits for a group portrait on the steps of the pioneer church. Hopkins (rear row, with beard) served as the town's Methodist preacher three times between 1885 and 1904. He retired in Tumwater and stayed for the rest of his life. (Courtesy of Henderson House Museum, No. 673.)

The Reverend Ebenezer Hopkins officiates at the wedding of Bill Lozier and Mary Bechtel, with Robert Hannah (mayor of Tumwater 1929–1930) and Florence Bechtel attending the bridal couple. (Courtesy of Henderson House Museum, No. 676.)

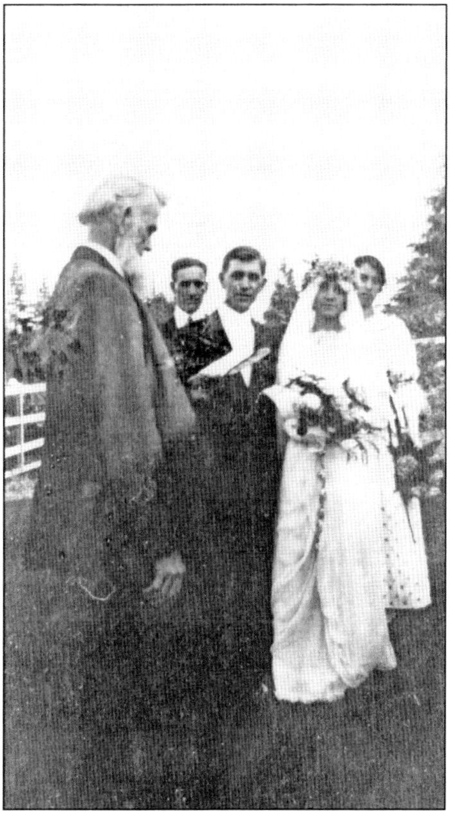

Early Tumwater Baptists met in the homes of members and held full-immersion baptisms in the Deschutes River. In 1907, they established a formal congregation and 10 years later built the Tumwater First Baptist Church at the north end of Second Avenue. Pictured outside the church (below) are Rev. Wayland A. Nickerson and Deacon H. B. Lozier. (Courtesy of Henderson House Museum, No. 686.)

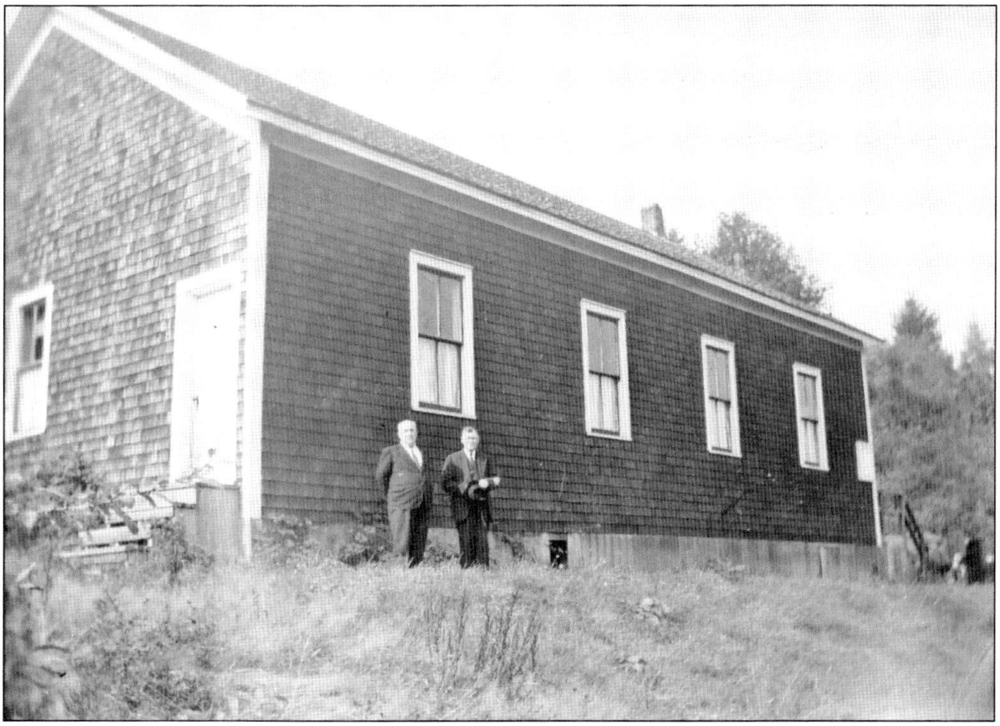

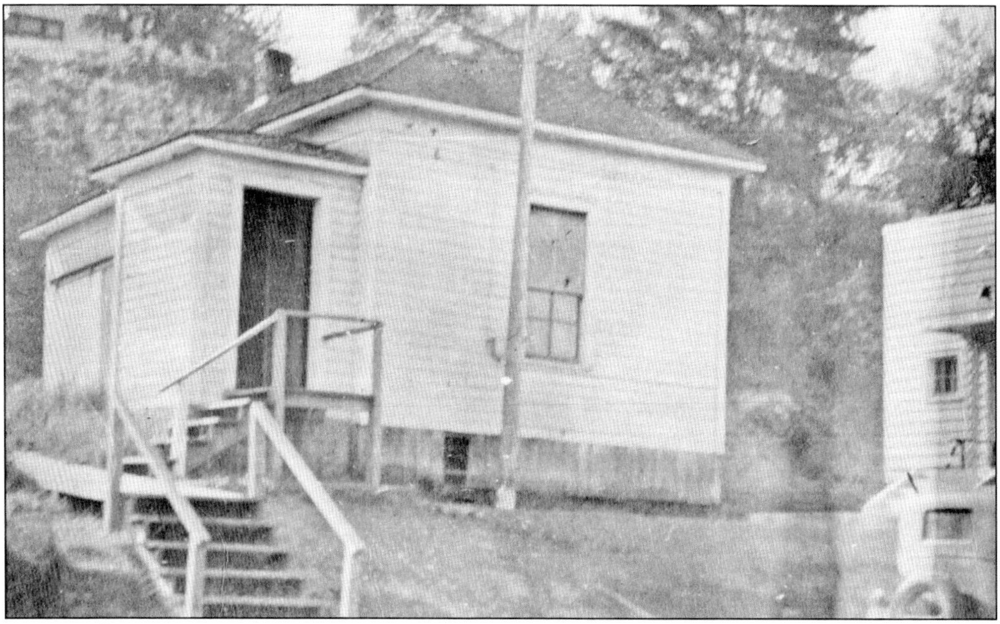

This small wooden structure on Second Avenue was the Tumwater City Hall until it was replaced by a larger building (just visible on the right) in 1939. (Courtesy of Henderson House Museum, No. 315.)

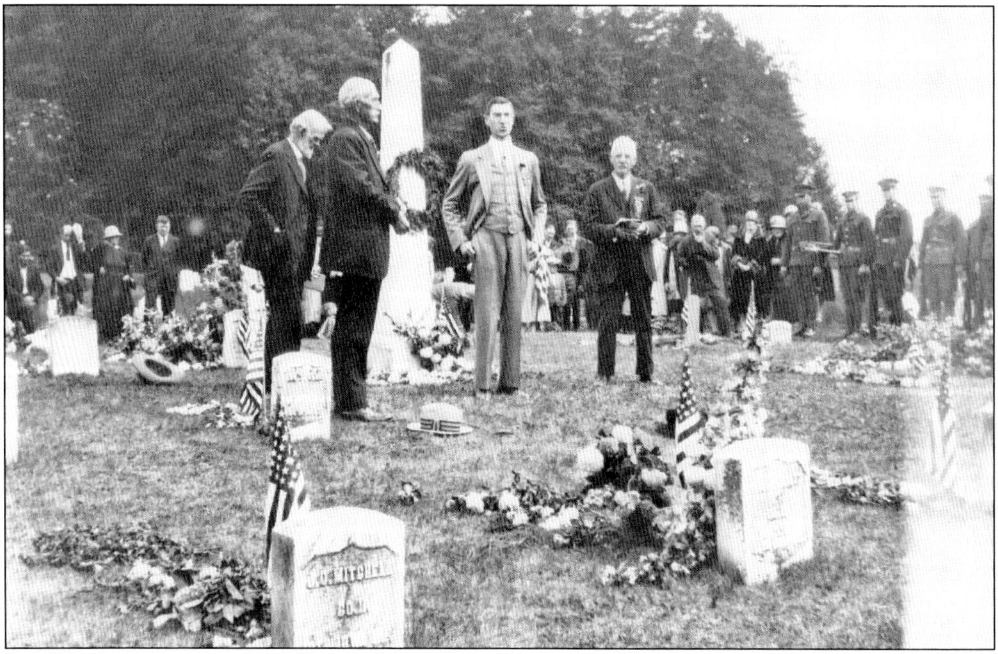

Citizens hold a commemorative ceremony in the veterans section of Masonic Memorial Park around 1925. (The Reverend Ebenezer Hopkins can be seen on the far left, standing.) Tumwater pioneer Smith Hays donated land for the cemetery to Olympia Lodge No. 1 of the Masons in 1858, although private burials had taken place there as early as 1852. South of town, pioneer Jesse Ferguson gave land for the Union Cemetery on Littlerock Road in 1867. (Courtesy of Henderson House Museum, No. 994.)

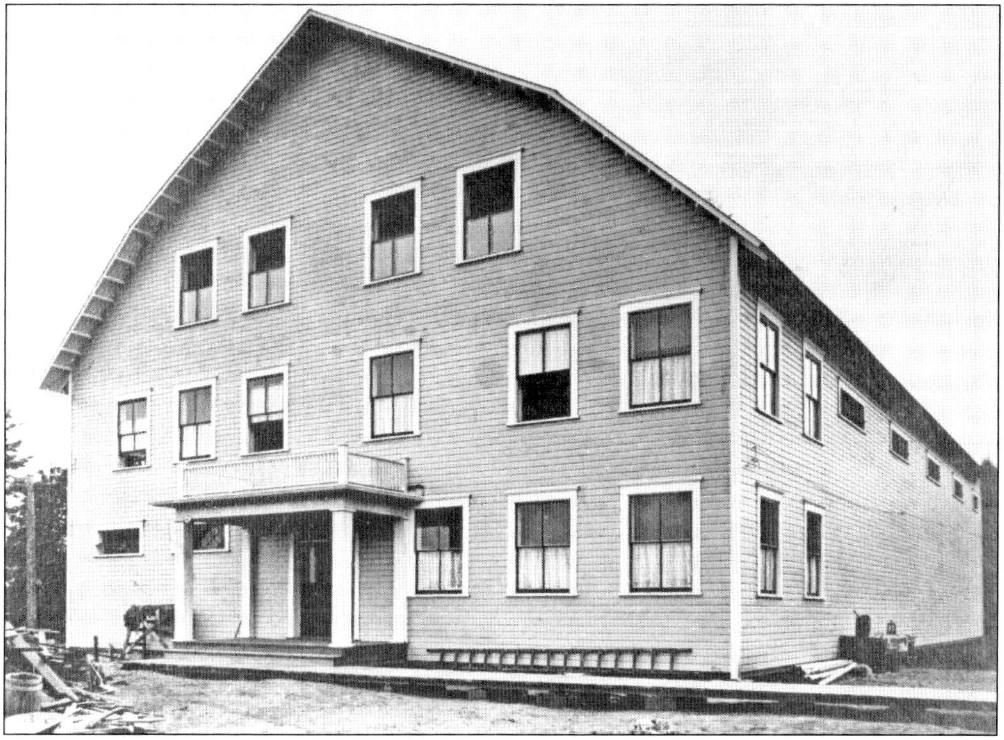

The barn-roofed Tumwater Club (above), located in what is now the 3300 block of Capitol Boulevard, was built in 1908 as an off-hours gathering place for Olympia Brewing Company employees. Its polished maple dance floor (below) hosted the legislative ball of 1908, Red Cross dances for Camp Lewis soldiers during World War I, and the inaugural ball of Gov. Louis Hart in 1921. (Both, courtesy of Henderson House Museum. Above, No. 1055; below, No. 1174.)

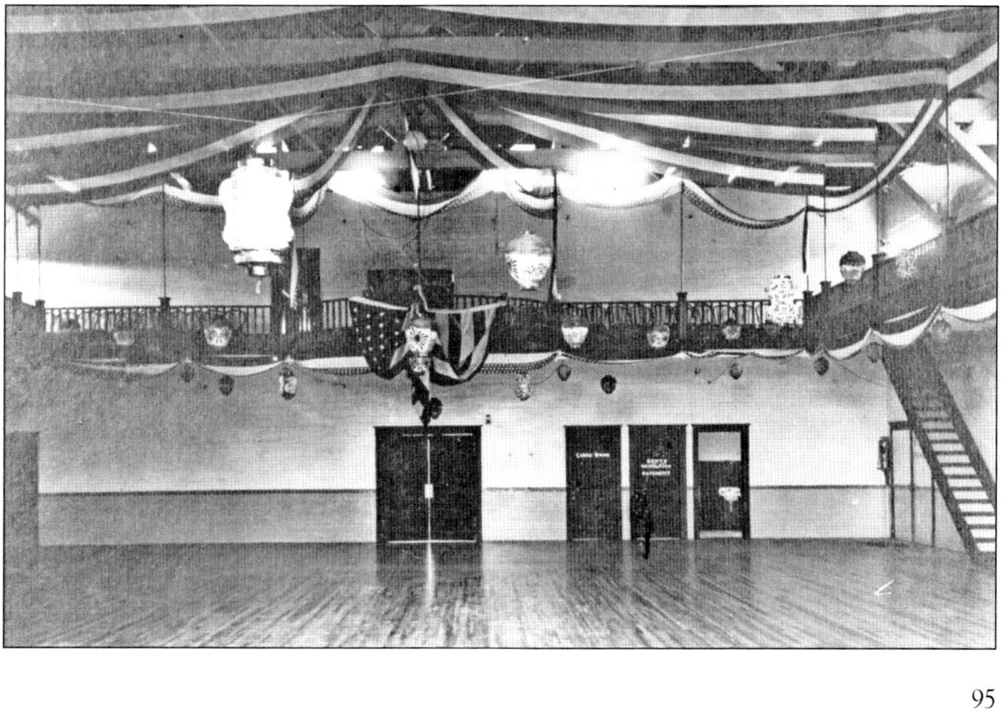

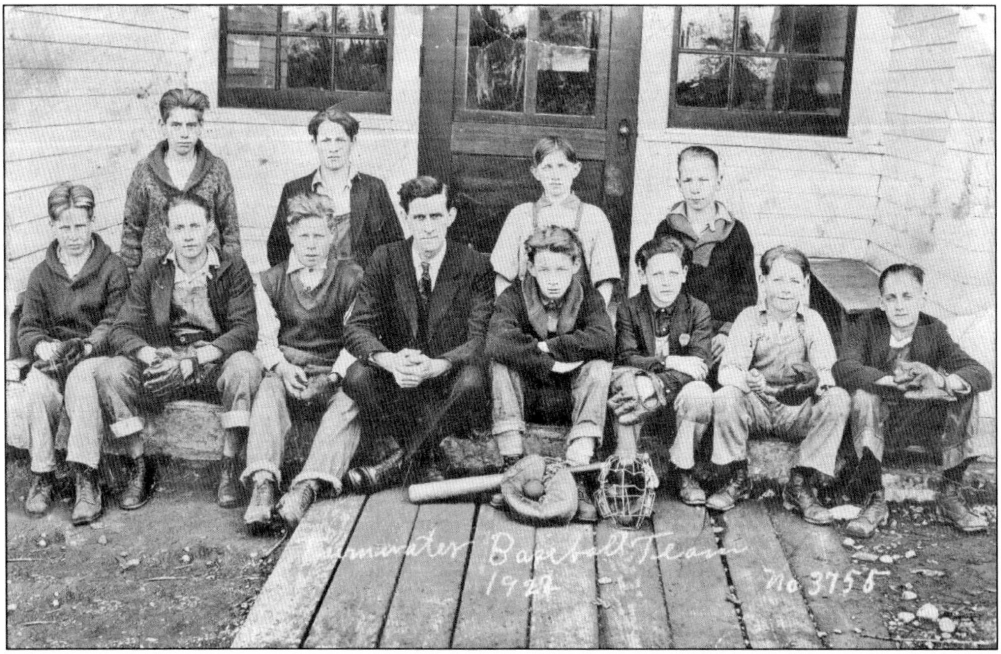

The 1922 Tumwater School baseball team poses for a portrait with principal W. E. McGuire. Shown here are the following: (first row, seated) Everett Dickison, Sam Shaw, Avery Dickison, W. E. McGuire, Edward Burley Godat, Clarence Dunn, Freddie Dunn, and Robert Hause; (second row, kneeling) Tom Lozier, Marvin Musgrove, Harold Brower, and Francis Peasley. McGuire was principal of the Tumwater School from 1915 to 1934. Tom Lozier, mayor of Tumwater in the late 1960s, remembered him as "a fine fellow." (Courtesy of Henderson House Museum, No. 716.)

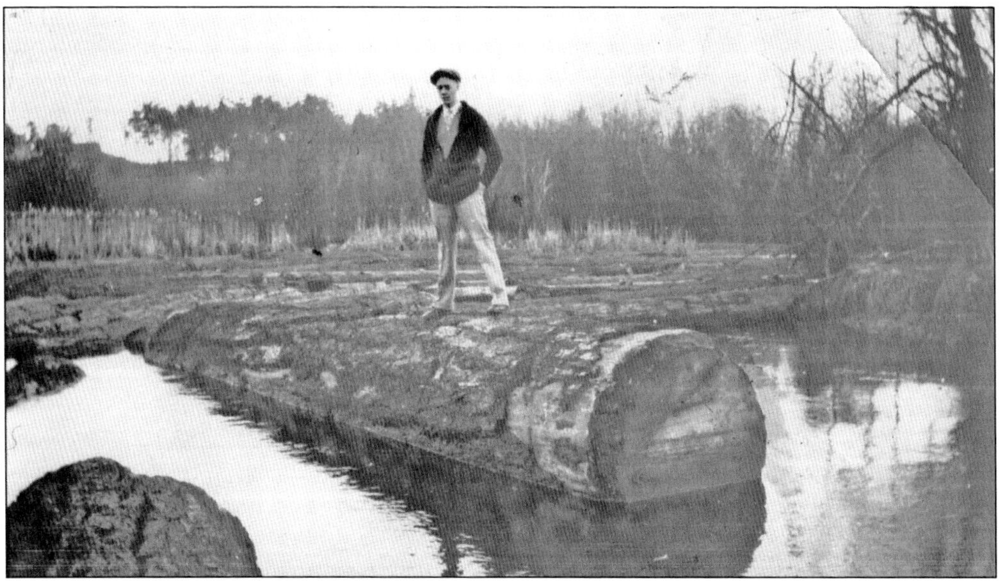

The note on this photograph reads, "Ralph on logs in the Deschutes River." Dress has become more casual in the 1930s, but "Ralph" still wears a necktie while larking about on the logs. (Courtesy of Henderson House Museum, No. 520.)

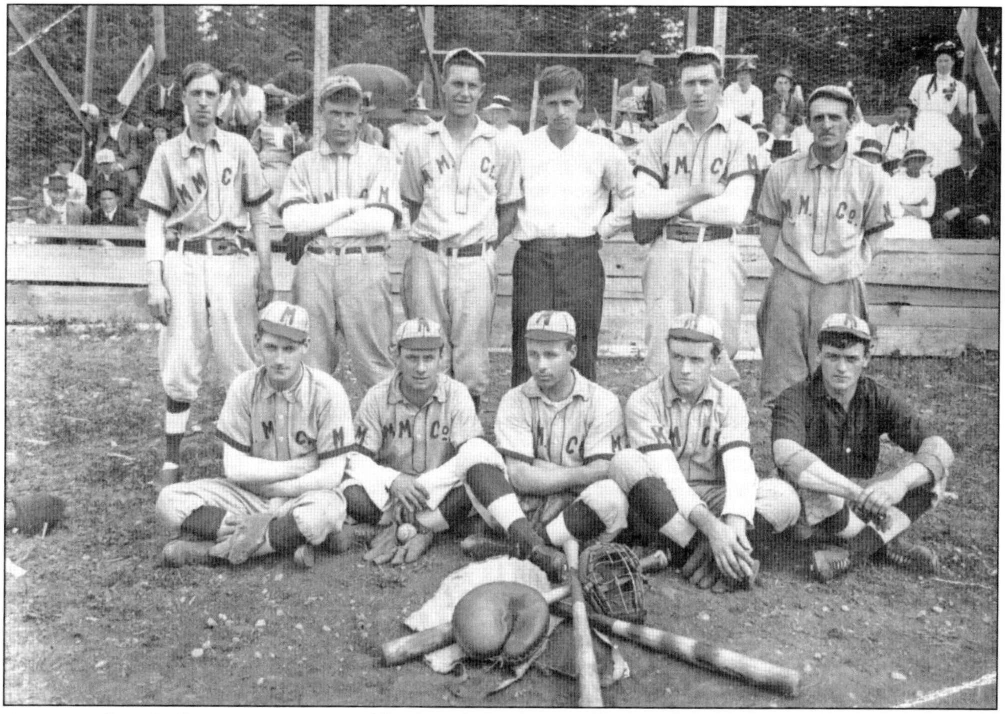

Amateur baseball teams sponsored by local lumber mills traveled from town to town to play against rival teams in the "Sawdust League." Pictured here is the Black Lake team of 1913–1914, sponsored by the Modern Mill Company. (Courtesy of Henderson House Museum, No. 996.)

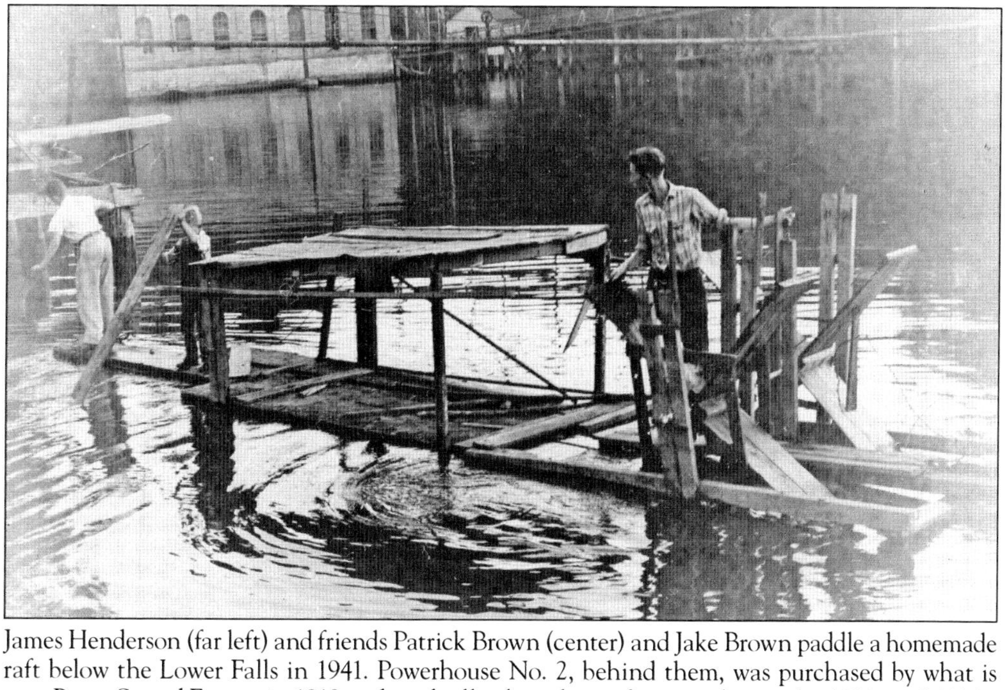

James Henderson (far left) and friends Patrick Brown (center) and Jake Brown paddle a homemade raft below the Lower Falls in 1941. Powerhouse No. 2, behind them, was purchased by what is now Puget Sound Energy in 1919 and gradually phased out of service during the 1920s and 1930s. (Courtesy of the Henderson family.)

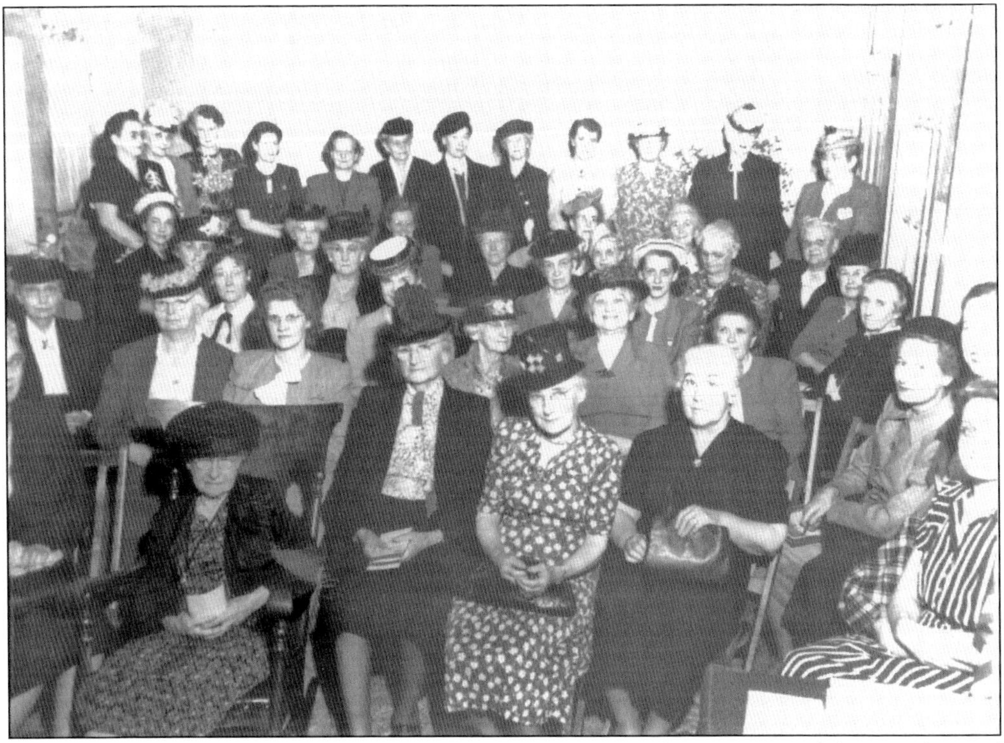

In 1947, the pioneer Crosby House was acquired by Olympia Chapter No. 4 of the Daughters of the Pioneers—pictured here—who repaired and furnished the historic home and opened it to the public. Donors to the project included the Schmidt family and Hollywood entertainer Bing Crosby, the famous grandson of Nathaniel and Cordelia Jane Crosby. The house was deeded to the City of Tumwater in 1981. (Courtesy of Daughters of the Pioneers, Olympia Chapter No. 4.)

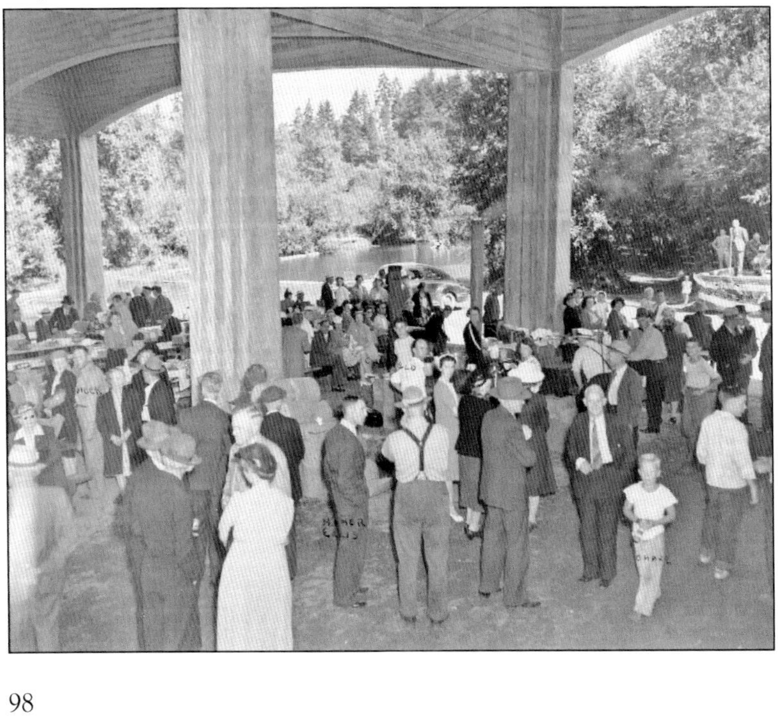

Citizens gather on the riverbank under the Capitol Boulevard Bridge for a picnic in 1945 celebrating the 100th anniversary of the founding of Tumwater. (Courtesy of Henderson House Museum, No. 312.)

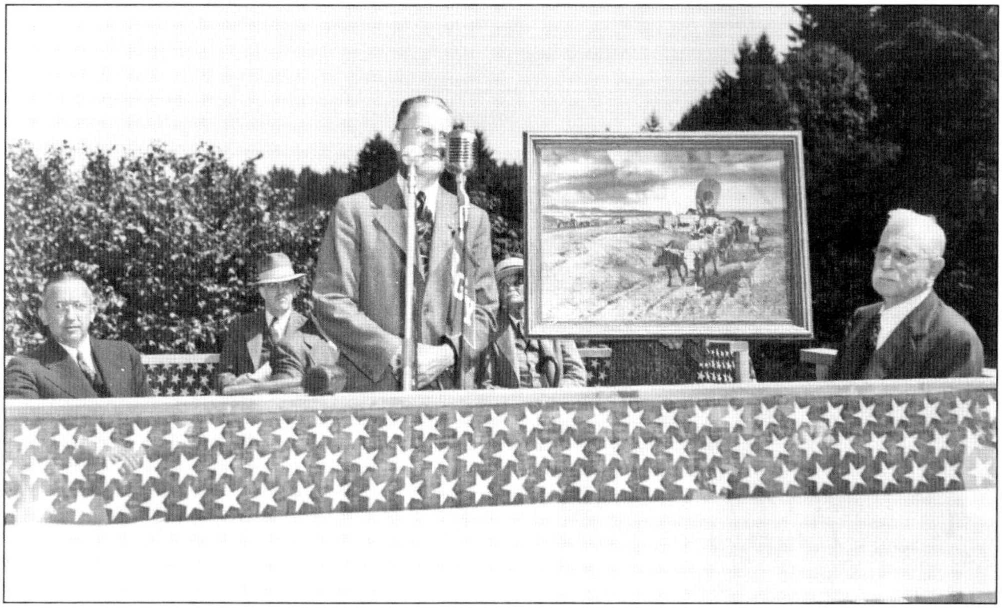

Brewery president Peter G. Schmidt Sr. presents a framed print of covered wagons crossing the plains to the City of Tumwater as part of the 1945 celebration of the town's centennial. (Courtesy of Henderson House Museum, No. 297.)

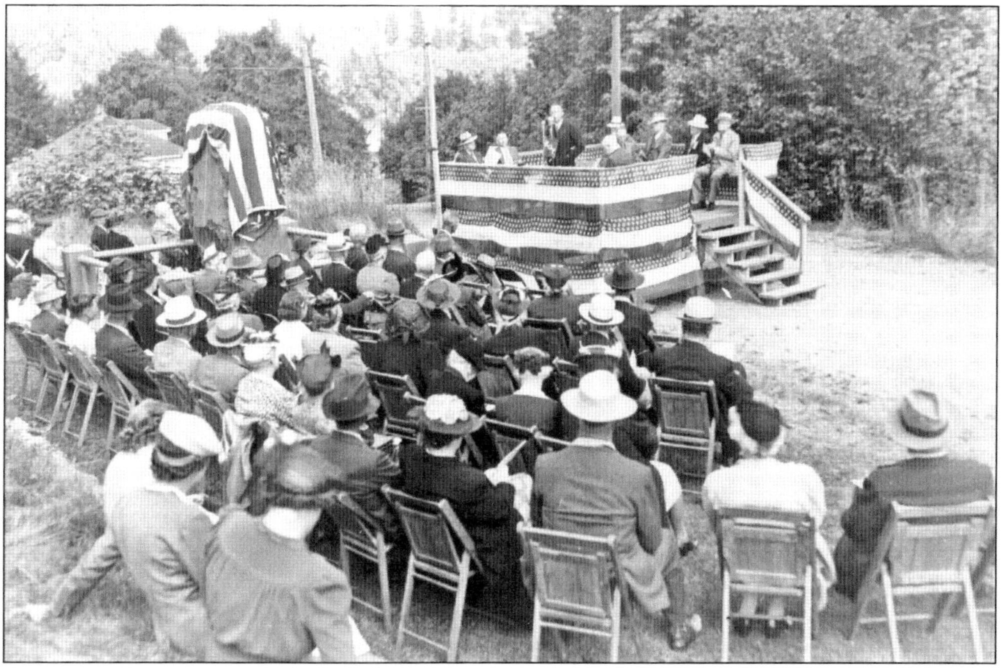

Mayor Ray Johnson addresses the crowd at the 1945 centennial celebration. Part of the ceremony included the rededication of a monument to Tumwater's founding pioneers, originally given in honor of brewery owner Leopold Schmidt by his children in 1916. The monument—under the bunting, at left—was located at the intersection of Deschutes Way and Simmons Road. It was later moved to its present location in Tumwater Falls Park. (Courtesy of Henderson House Museum, No. 296.)

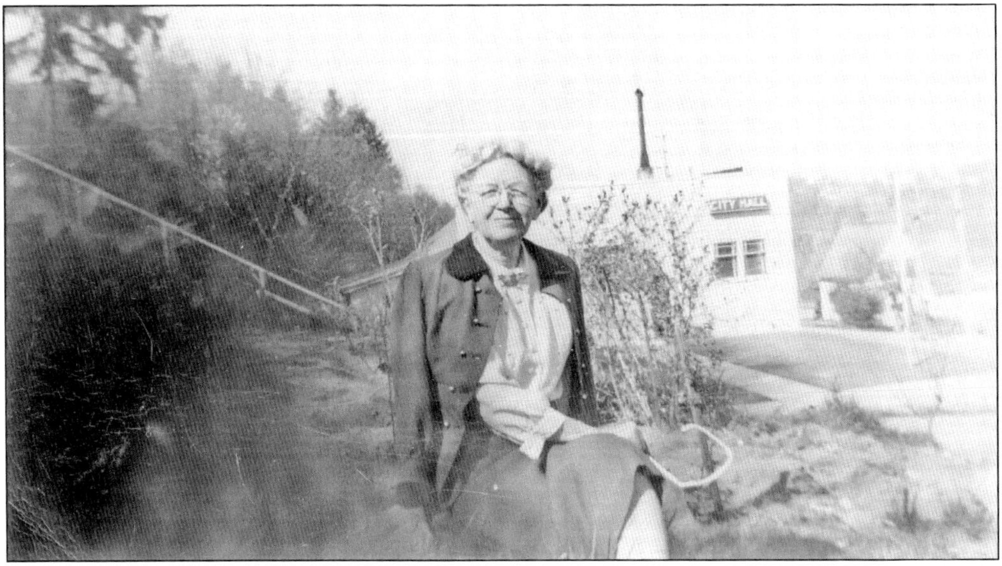

Amie Shattuck Cook, widow of Tumwater mayor and grocery store owner F. D. Cook, smiles for the camera near the old Tumwater City Hall (later Old Town Center) in 1951. Amie is seen as a little girl in the photograph of the Eastman/Shattuck families on page 57. (Courtesy of Gary Hopkins.)

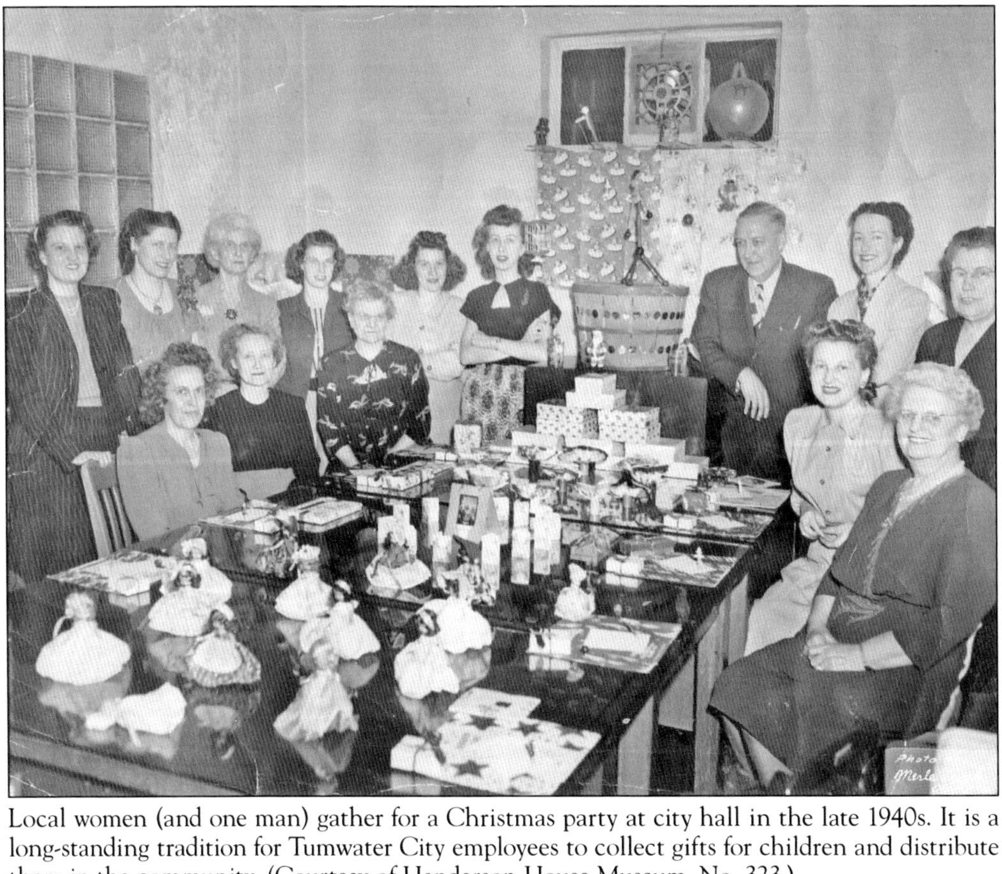

Local women (and one man) gather for a Christmas party at city hall in the late 1940s. It is a long-standing tradition for Tumwater City employees to collect gifts for children and distribute them in the community. (Courtesy of Henderson House Museum, No. 323.)

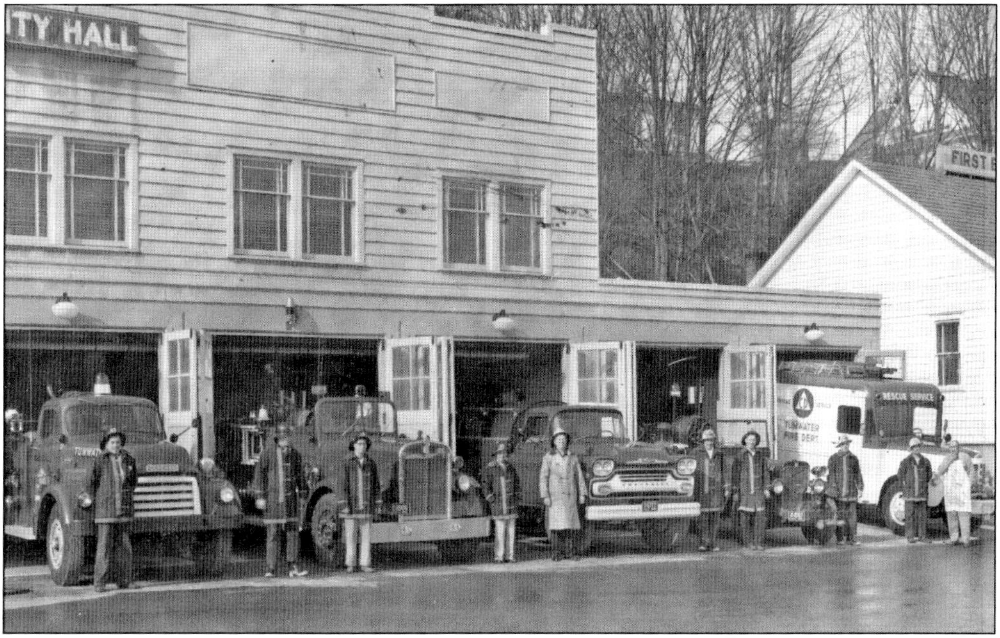

The Tumwater volunteer fire department—consisting mostly of Olympia Brewing Company employees—was created in 1934. Starting in 1944, volunteers were paid 75¢ per hour for practice drills and $1 per hour for fighting fires. Members of the department are shown here with their trucks at city hall in the mid-1950s. They are Joe Lennon, two unidentified, Don Corliss, Jimmy Lathrop, chief Al Reed, assistant chief Bud Ridgeway, Bill Webster, Warren Dibble, and Paul Childress. (Courtesy of Henderson House Museum, No. 1058.)

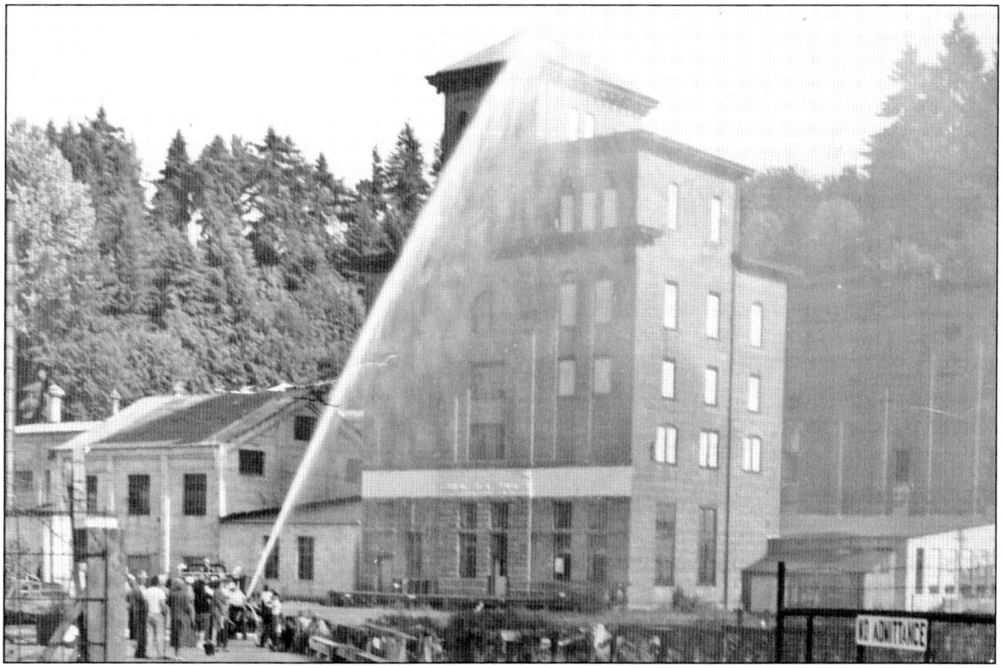

Firefighters test their pumps and hoses on the abandoned railway bridge near the old brick brewhouse around 1948. (Courtesy of Henderson House Museum, No. 1173.)

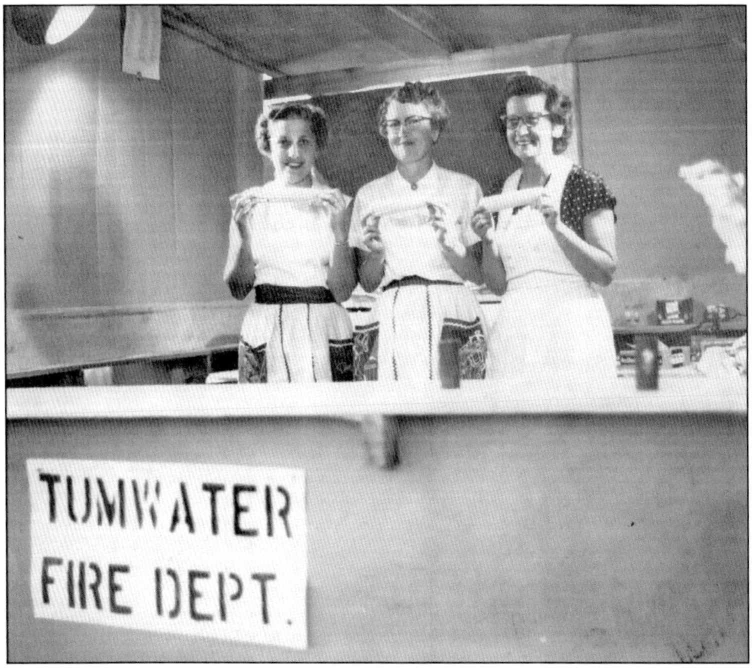

The Ladies Auxiliary of the Tumwater Fire Department held frequent events to raise money for the all-volunteer operation. In this c. 1955 picture, Beverly Webster, Hazel Devine, and Lilly Premo—all married to local firefighters—sell hot corn on the cob at the annual Thurston County Fire Show. (Courtesy of City of Tumwater Fire Department.)

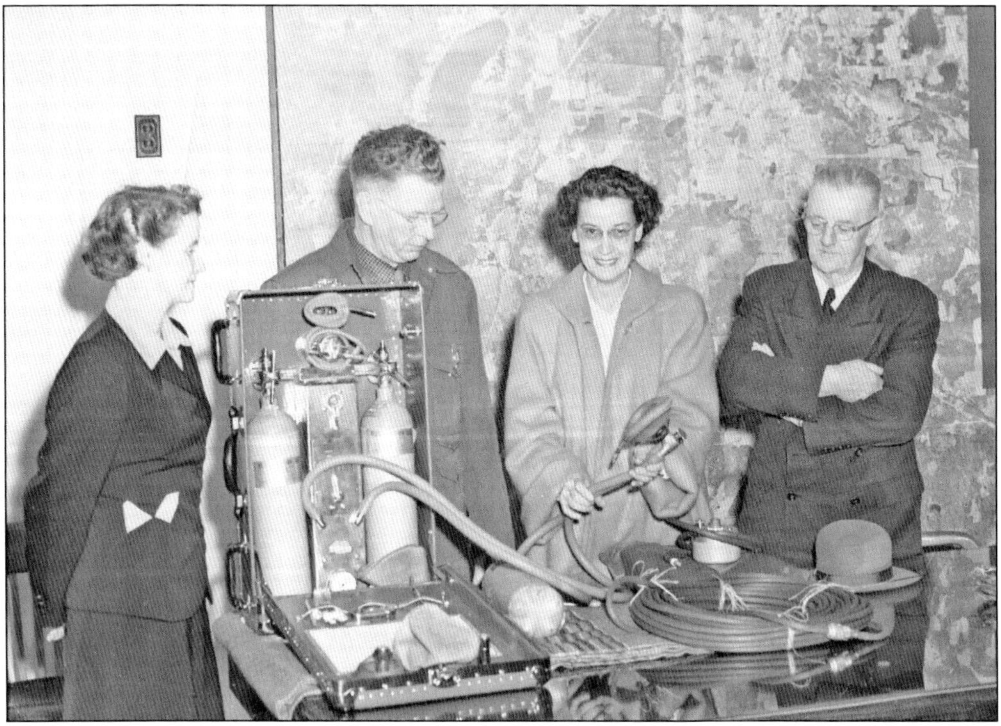

Auxiliary members proudly present new resuscitation equipment, purchased with Ladies Auxiliary funds, to the Tumwater Fire Department in 1952. From left to right are Mae Harnit, fire chief Al Reed, Lilly Premo, and state superintendant of fire training J. R. Cook. Reed, an engineer at the brewery, was Tumwater's unpaid fire chief from 1943 until his death in 1961. (Courtesy of City of Tumwater Fire Department.)

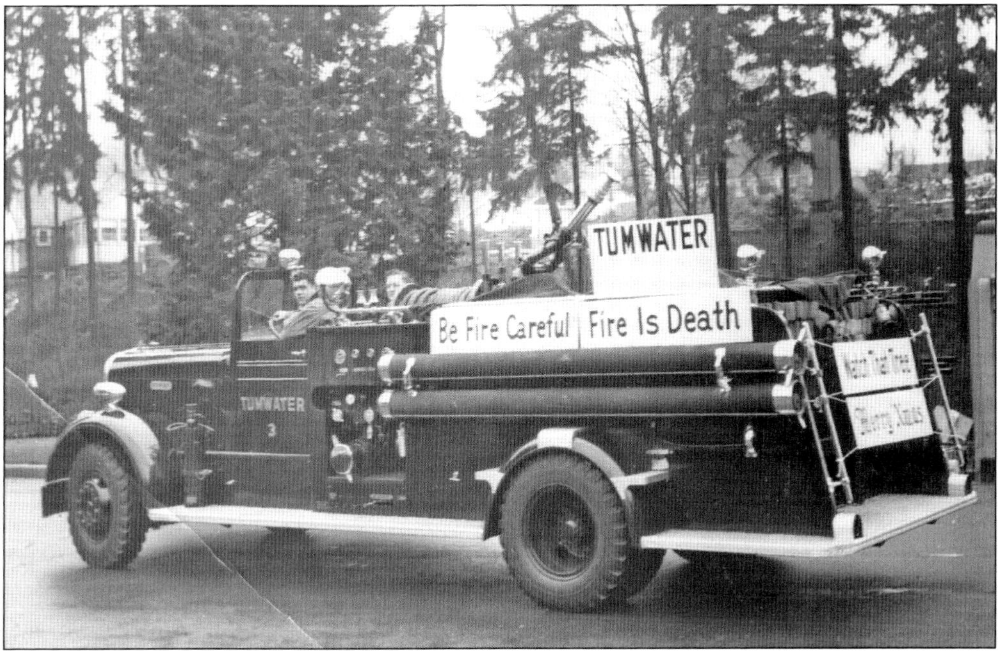

Volunteer firefighters mix safety warnings with season's greetings in this shot from the late 1950s. In later years, the "Santa Truck" was drafted to collect holiday donations for the Thurston County Food Bank, a tradition that continues in the 21st century. (Courtesy of Henderson House Museum, No. 1254.)

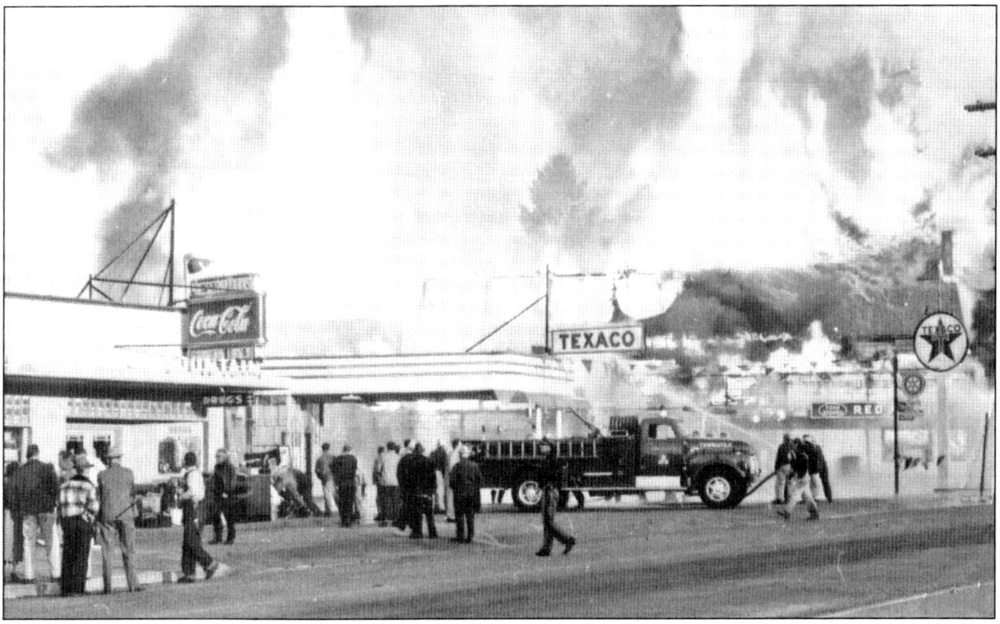

The former Tumwater Club went up in flames on December 20, 1955. The building had been used as a roller-skating rink throughout the 1930s and 1940s and was then converted into a popular bowling alley. The fire, which began in the furnace room, burned so hot that the occupant of the house next door could feel the heat through her walls. No one was hurt, but the 47-year-old building was a total loss. (Courtesy of Henderson House Museum, No. 1056.)

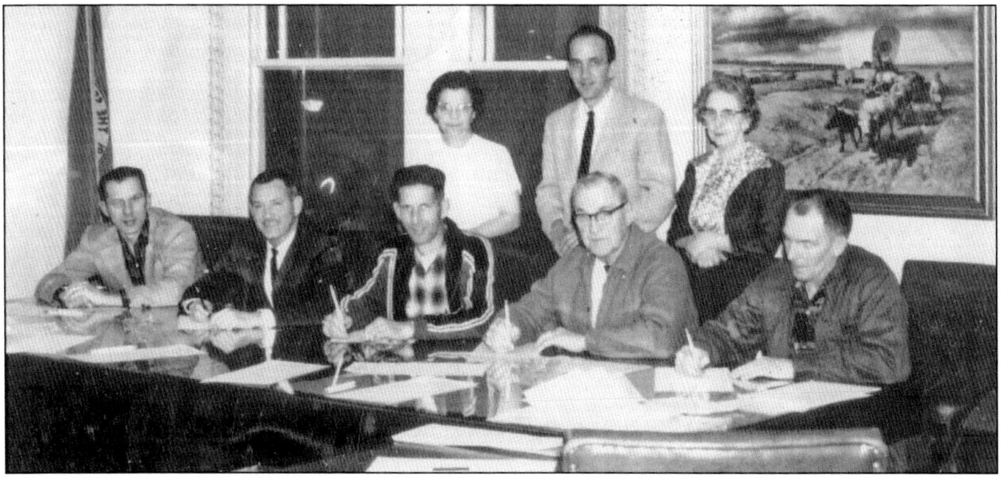

Tumwater's elected officials meet in 1962, around the time Tumwater voted to change its status with the State of Washington from a town to a city. Among other things, the new classification permitted the city to annex new land; it also boosted the number of city council members from five to seven. Council members are, from left to right, (first row) Jim Brown, Wes Barclift, Robert Stewart, Bill Brenner, and Harley McWillians; (second row) city treasurer Celestia Bech, Mayor Ray Ensley, and city clerk Mida Erickson. Note the wagon-train print on the wall. (Courtesy of Henderson House Museum, No. 319.)

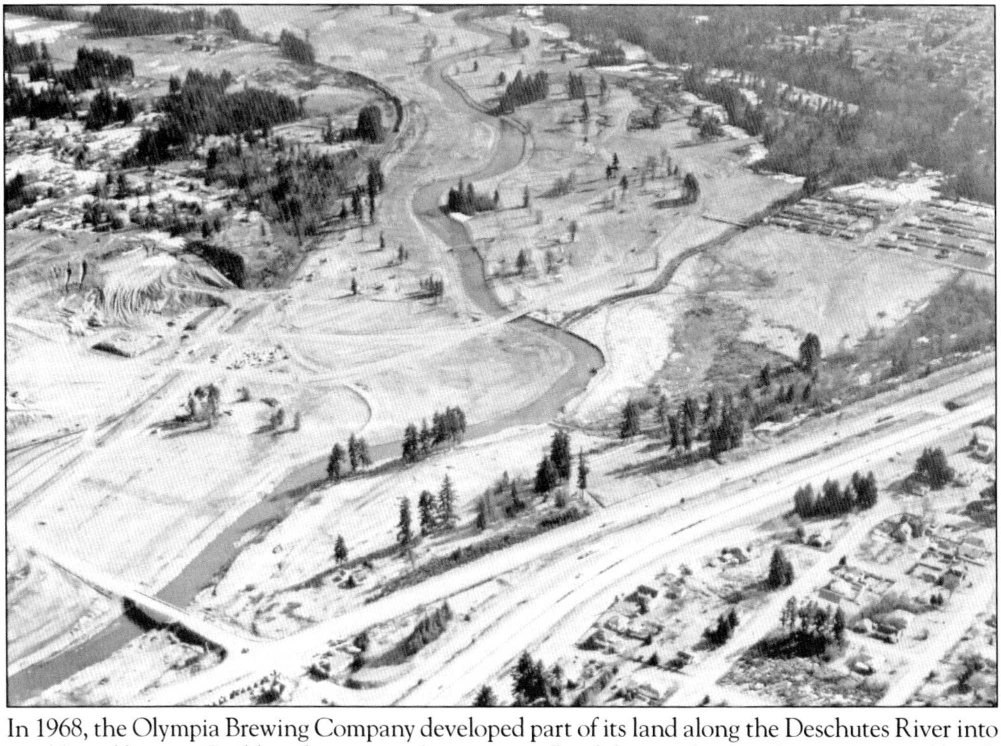

In 1968, the Olympia Brewing Company developed part of its land along the Deschutes River into a public golf course. Building fairways and greens in a floodplain took some doing. Trees and brush were cleared from the site, the river channel was embanked with volcanic rock, and enough sand was hauled in to raise the entire site 5 feet above its original level. The Tumwater Valley Golf Course was purchased by the City of Tumwater in 1996. (Courtesy of Olympia Tumwater Foundation.)

Six

Trails, Rails, and Automobiles

When Interstate 5 carved its way through Tumwater in the mid-1950s, it followed a route people had traveled—on foot, by canoe, and on horseback—long before cars were invented. Drivers who rush down the freeway today follow in the historic tracks of American Indians, Hudson's Bay Company traders, and optimistic Americans who made their way north to Puget Sound from the end of the Oregon Trail.

As early as 1830, British fur traders used American Indian trails to travel between Fort Vancouver on the Columbia River and Fort Nisqually (near present-day Dupont). By the mid-1800s, American settlers, arriving with livestock and wagons, had widened the Hudson's Bay Company trail into the primary wagon road between Portland and Puget Sound.

When the Northern Pacific Railroad laid track into Washington Territory, the new line followed the old wagon route only as far as Tenino before heading north to Tacoma, missing Tumwater and Olympia by more than 10 miles. Local citizens, determined to have a railroad, built a narrow-gauge spur to Tenino. Passenger trains ran through Tumwater from 1878 until 1916, one year after a new highway bridge was built across the river at what is now Boston Street. As the railroad era was ending, the auto age had begun.

The original Pacific Highway (Old 99) ran south from Olympia along Capitol Boulevard, zigzagged over the Boston Street Bridge, and funneled cars down the main street of Tumwater. In 1938, a new concrete bridge extended Capitol Boulevard in a straight line over the river, relieving traffic congestion but also carrying business away from the central town core. Ten years later, state highway engineers were discussing a four-lane freeway that would bypass troublesome stoplights in downtown Olympia. When a proposed tunnel under the capital city proved too expensive, planners fell back on their second choice: an interstate highway that sliced through the historic heart of Tumwater. The freeway opened to traffic on December 12, 1958, changing Tumwater—and South Puget Sound—forever.

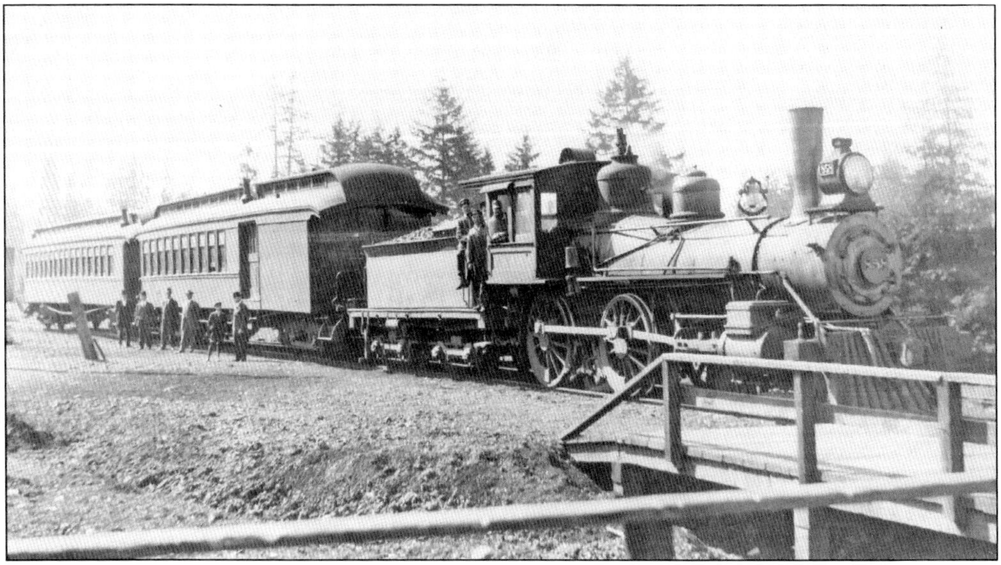

A steam locomotive from Olympia/Tumwater pulls into the station at Tenino in the early 1900s. A mix of paid and volunteer laborers, including 20 hired Chinese workers and at least one volunteer crew of Squaxin Island Indians, graded the bed for a spur line to Tenino in 1874. Rails were laid a few years later, and the first passenger train made its way from Olympia to Tenino on August 1, 1878. Several pioneer reminiscences mention a Chinese man living in Tumwater during the 1880s; it is likely he first came to town to work on the railroad. (Courtesy of Henderson House Museum, No. 697.)

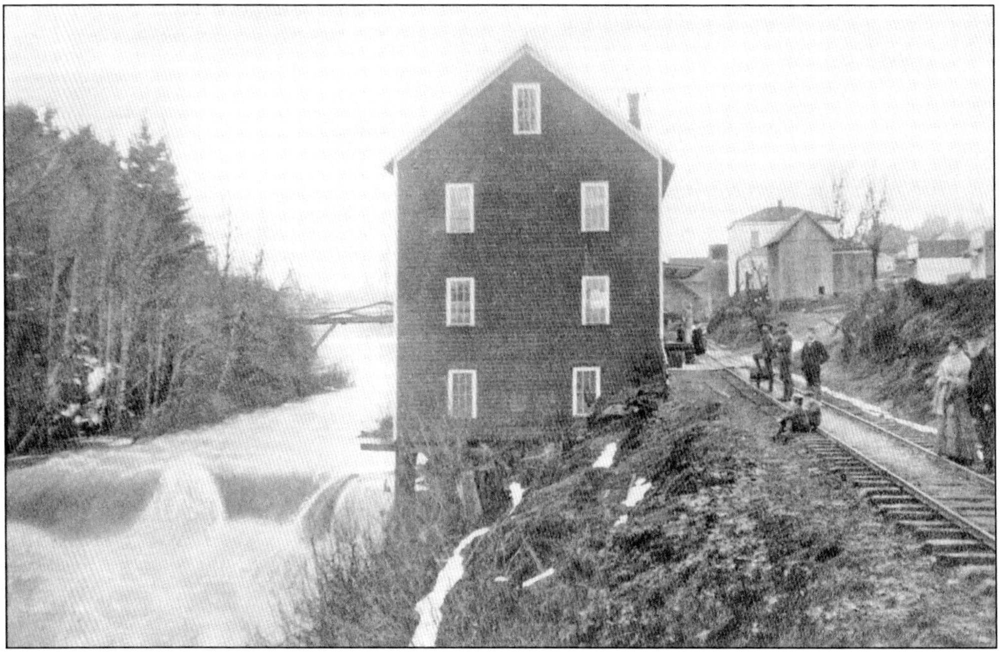

Passengers wait outside Gelbach's mill in the winter of 1879 for the southbound train to Tenino. Raw materials and finished goods—logs, lumber, shingles, and eventually beer—were shipped on the railroad as well. Standard-gauge track replaced the original narrow-gauge rail in 1890. (Courtesy of Henderson House Museum, No. 032.)

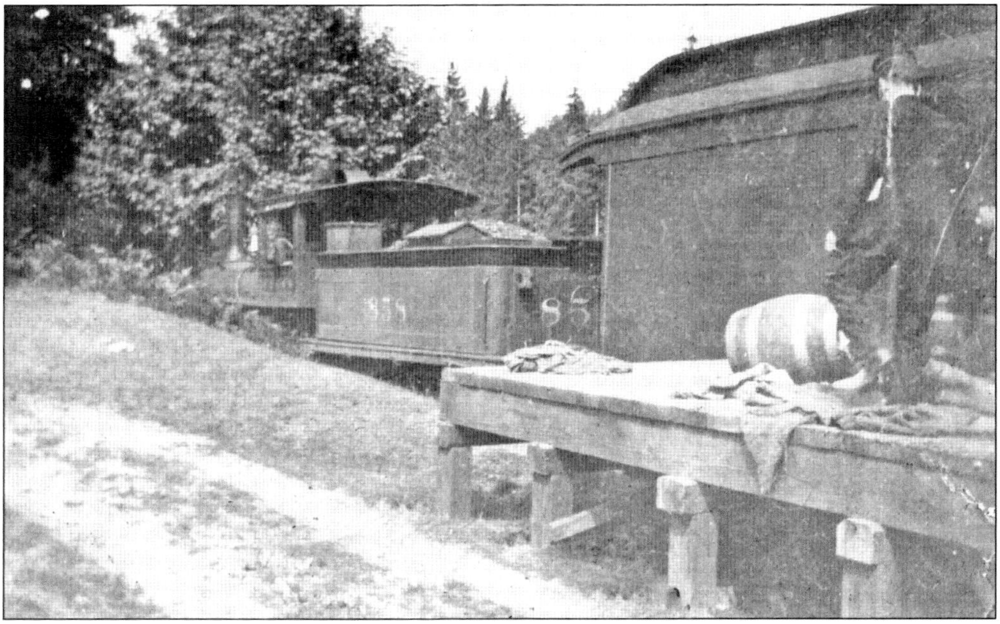

A simple wooden platform, located between Gelbach's mill and the wagon bridge, was the official rail stop in Tumwater. Here conductor Ed Kevin tends to business on the Tumwater platform while a train stops on its way north to Olympia. (Courtesy of Henderson House Museum, No. 844.)

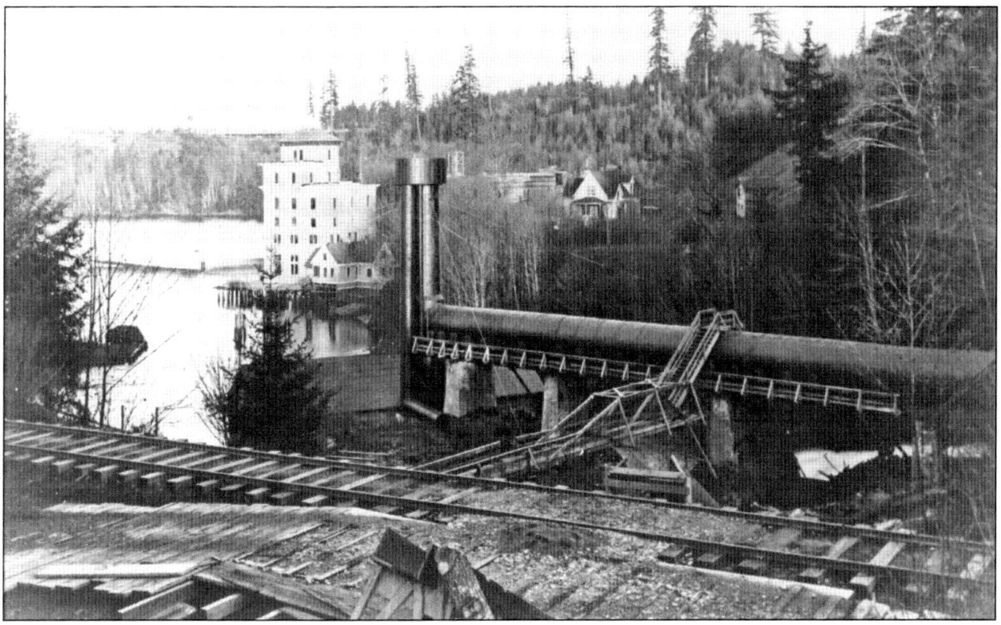

The rail line from Tenino to Olympia ran through Tumwater along the west bank of the river, parallel to the town's main street, and then on pilings along the west side of the tidal waterway (later Capitol Lake). The original line terminated at the west end of Olympia's Fourth Avenue bridge, although trains eventually did cross the waterway into downtown Olympia. This view, looking east, shows the Tumwater train tracks, the penstock of Powerhouse No. 2, and the 1906 brewhouse all crowding the mouth of the river. The Biles house, at the water's edge, has not yet been moved from its original site. (Courtesy of Henderson House Museum, No. 1299.)

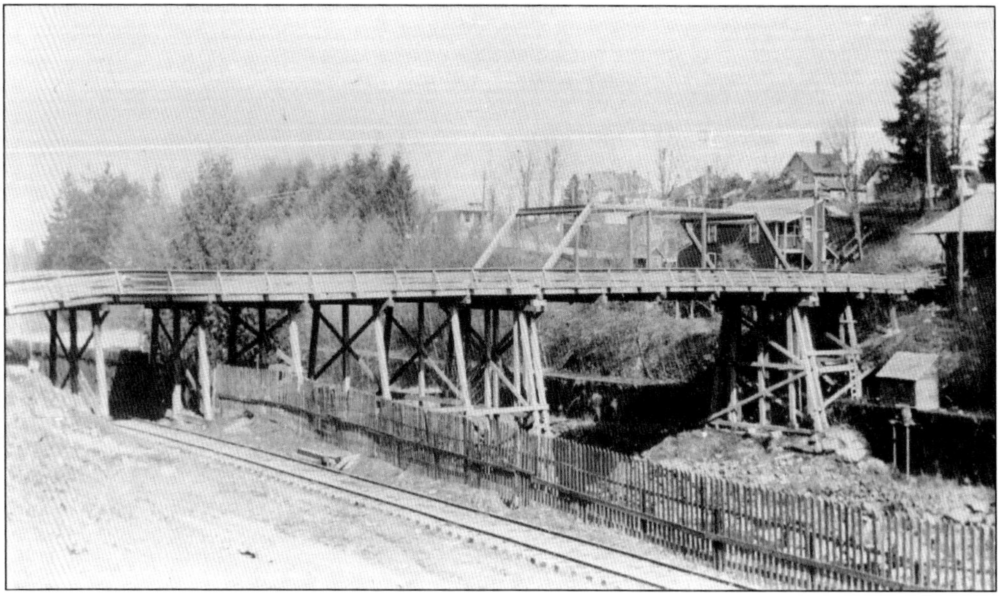

The tracks of the Olympia-Tenino Railroad run beneath the west end of the wagon bridge (at what is now Boston Street) about 1910. The Tumwater streetcar station—the end of the line from Olympia—stands at the east end of the bridge (far right). In another 30 years, the Olympia Brewing Company complex will replace the houses at the top of the hill. (Courtesy of Henderson House Museum, No. 650.)

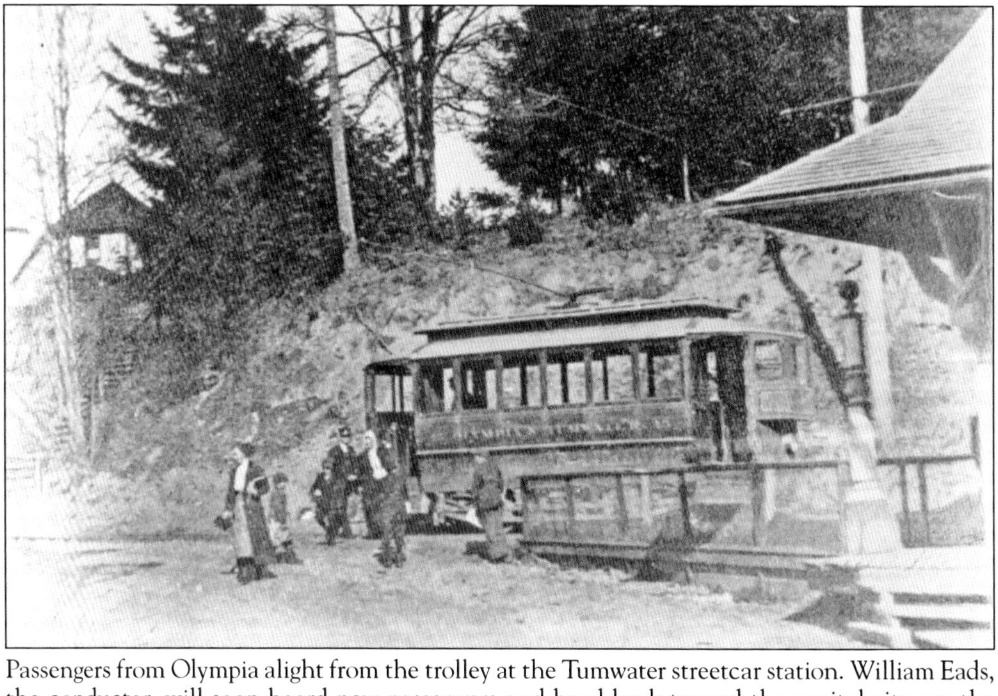

Passengers from Olympia alight from the trolley at the Tumwater streetcar station. William Eads, the conductor, will soon board new passengers and head back toward the capital city: up the hill on Boston Street, right on Custer Way, left on Cleveland Avenue, and then straight down Capitol Boulevard. The young woman in the white blouse carrying books is Edwina Lloyd Myers. (Courtesy of Henderson House Museum, No. 709.)

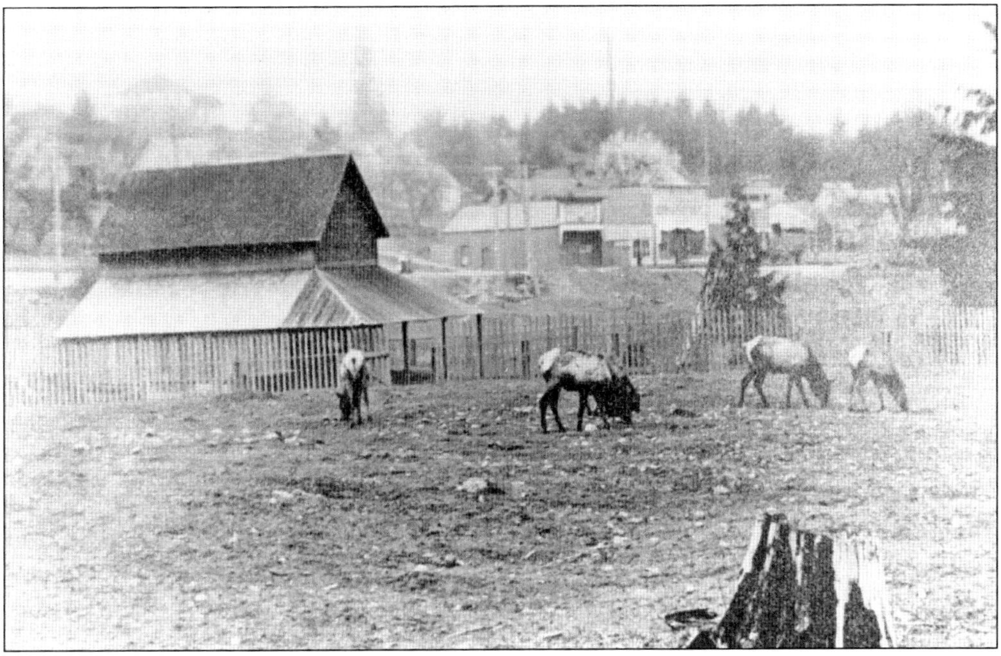

Businessman Hazzard Stevens, son of territorial governor Isaac Stevens and part-owner of the streetcar company, installed live elk at the Upper Falls as a way of enticing passengers to ride to the end of the line. The fence of the elk pen can be spotted in many local photographs from the late 1800s. Note the wooden storefronts along Reserve Street (Deschutes Way) in the background. (Courtesy of Henderson House Museum, No. 627.)

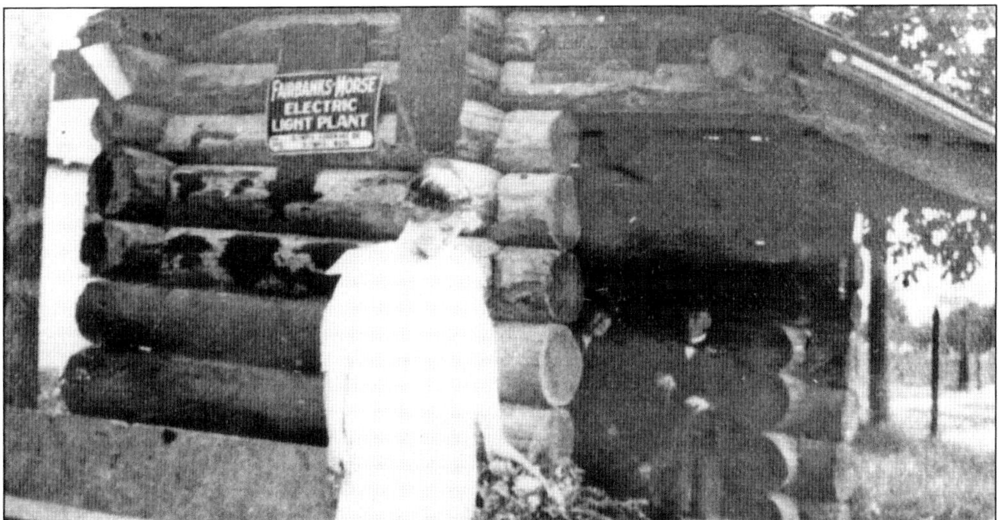

Riders wait for the trolley at the "log cabin" streetcar stop on the northeast corner of North Street and Cleveland Avenue across from the Masonic Cemetery. North Street was once known as Log Cabin Road, presumably after the streetcar stop; the old name persists where the road makes a jog, a mile or so to the east. (Courtesy of Henderson House Museum, No. 710.)

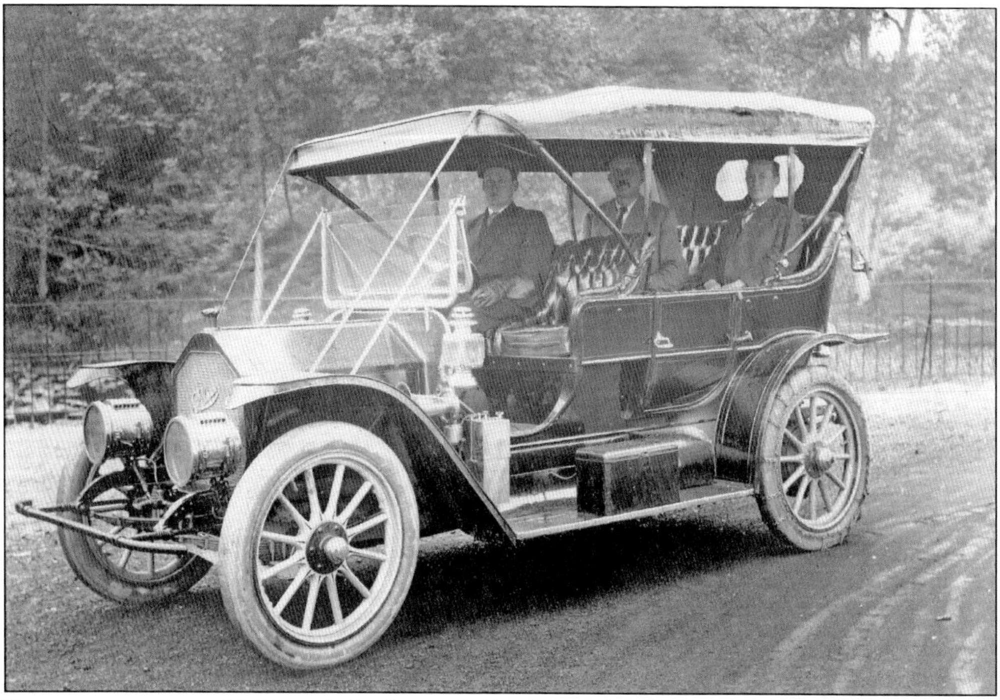

Brewery owner Leopold Schmidt (back seat, left) is being chauffeured in style to the 1909 Alaska Yukon Pacific Exposition in Seattle. Expensive automobiles like this were still out of reach for most Americans, but Henry Ford's assembly-line production would soon make cars available at an affordable price. (Courtesy of Olympia Tumwater Foundation.)

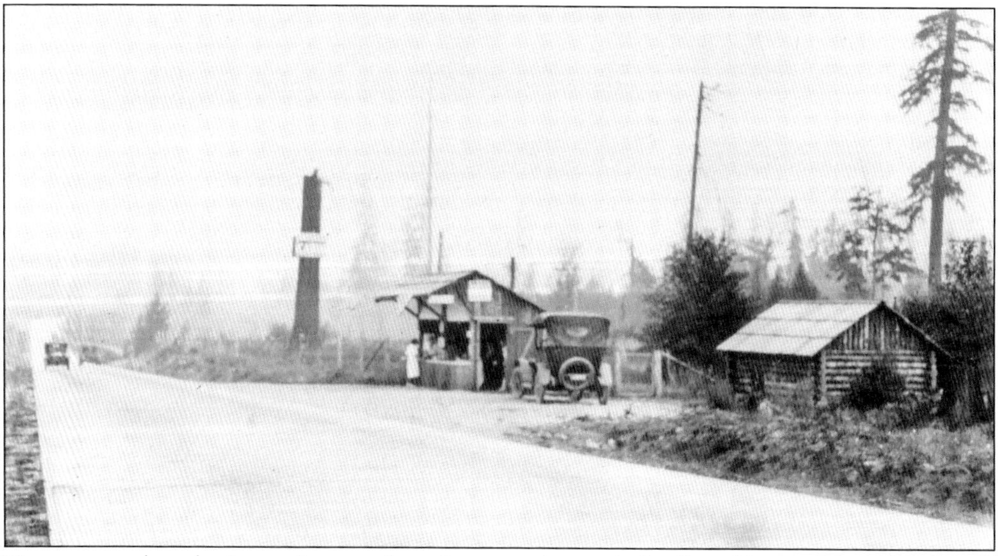

To accommodate the increasing number of cars on the road, the State Department of Highways completed a two-lane road through western Washington from Canada to Oregon in 1919. South of Tumwater, the new Pacific Highway (Old 99) followed the route of the old American Indian and pioneer trail. In this view from 1921, a Model T Ford stops at the roadside refreshment stand called Sheldon's Cabin halfway between Tumwater and Tenino. (Courtesy of Henderson House Museum, No. 756.)

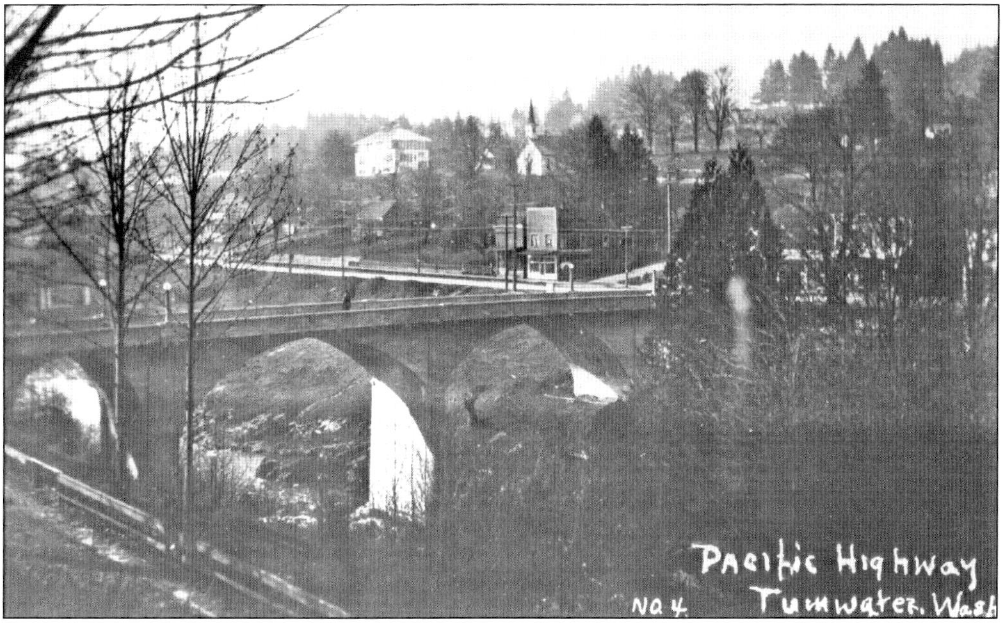

The Boston Street Bridge, rebuilt in concrete in 1915, carried the Pacific Highway across the Deschutes River. Cars driving south from Olympia made their way down the east bank, crossed the bridge, and turned left onto Deschutes Way in order to pass through town. Local boys delighted in watching frequent crashes, as drivers miscalculated the turn at the west end of the bridge. (Courtesy of Henderson House Museum, No. 638.)

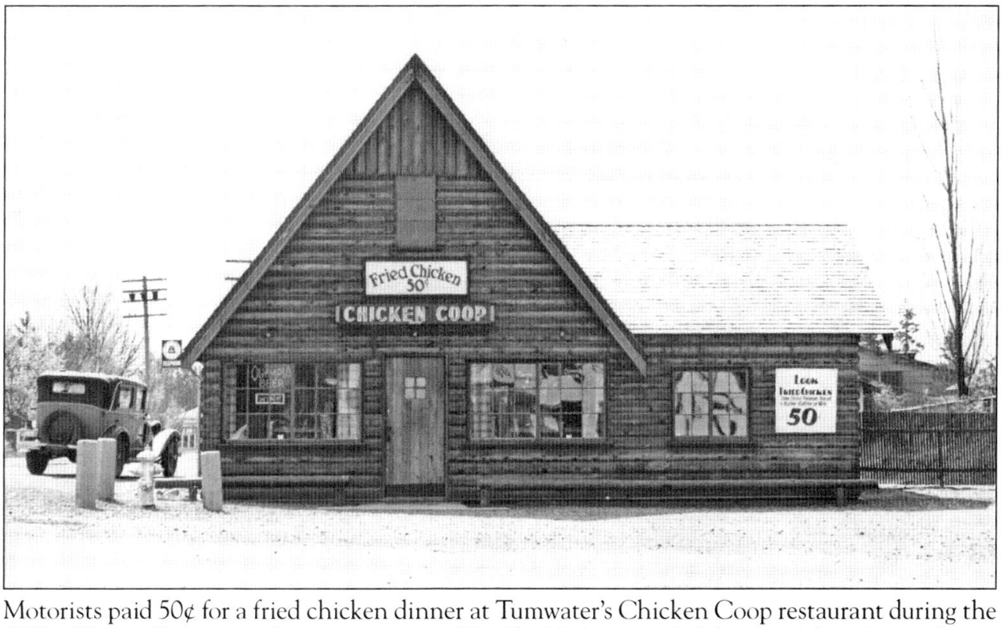

Motorists paid 50¢ for a fried chicken dinner at Tumwater's Chicken Coop restaurant during the 1930s. The café stood at the intersection of Pacific Highway and Yelm Road (on the southwest corner of present-day Cleveland Avenue and Custer Way). The log cabin style of the restaurant echoed that of the streetcar stop at the same intersection, though the rise of the gas-powered automobile brought an end to the trolley system. Streetcar service was discontinued in 1933. (Courtesy of Henderson House Museum, No. 1032.)

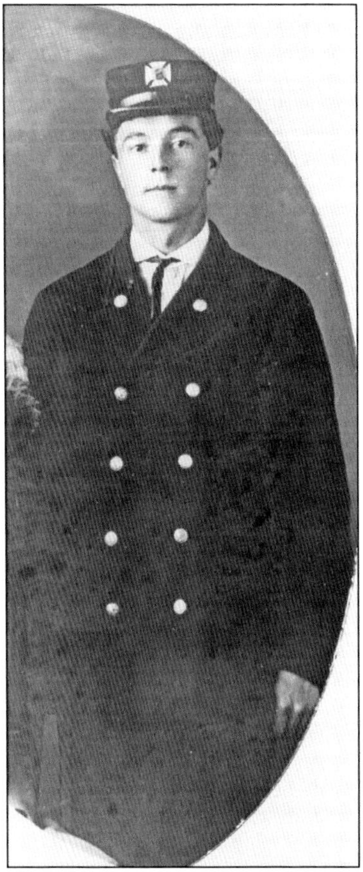

As more and more households acquired automobiles, American families clamored for new destinations. Nathan Trosper (at left) and his wife, Isabelle, opened the Olympic Auto Camp south of town on the new Pacific Highway (Old 99), near present-day Trosper Road. The camp offered cottages, tent camping, kitchens, stove rentals, car repair, groceries, and gas. (Both, courtesy of Henderson House Museum. At left, No. 961; below, No. 694.)

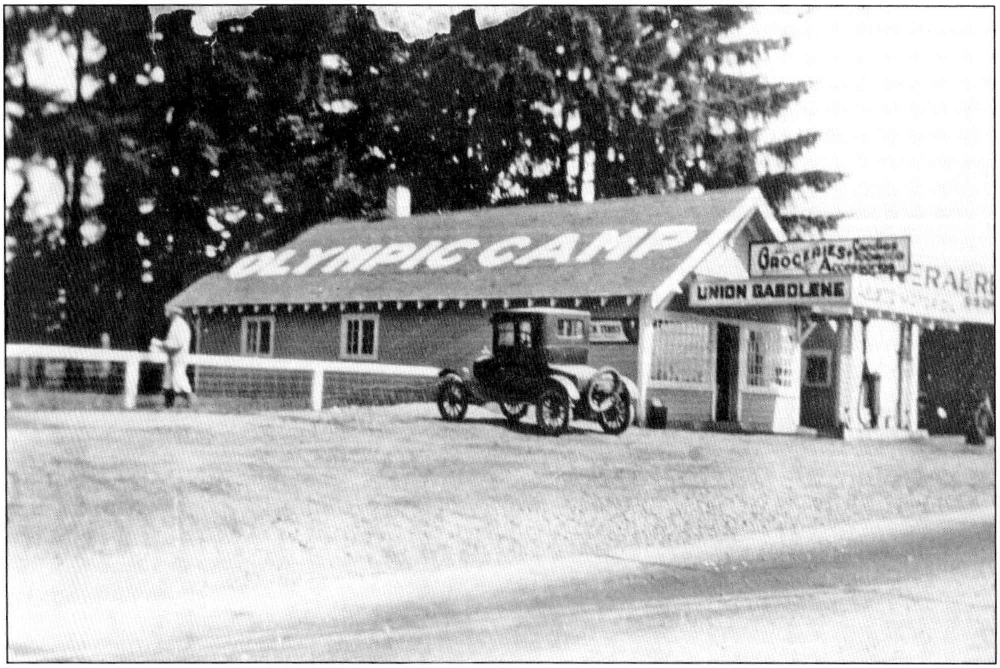

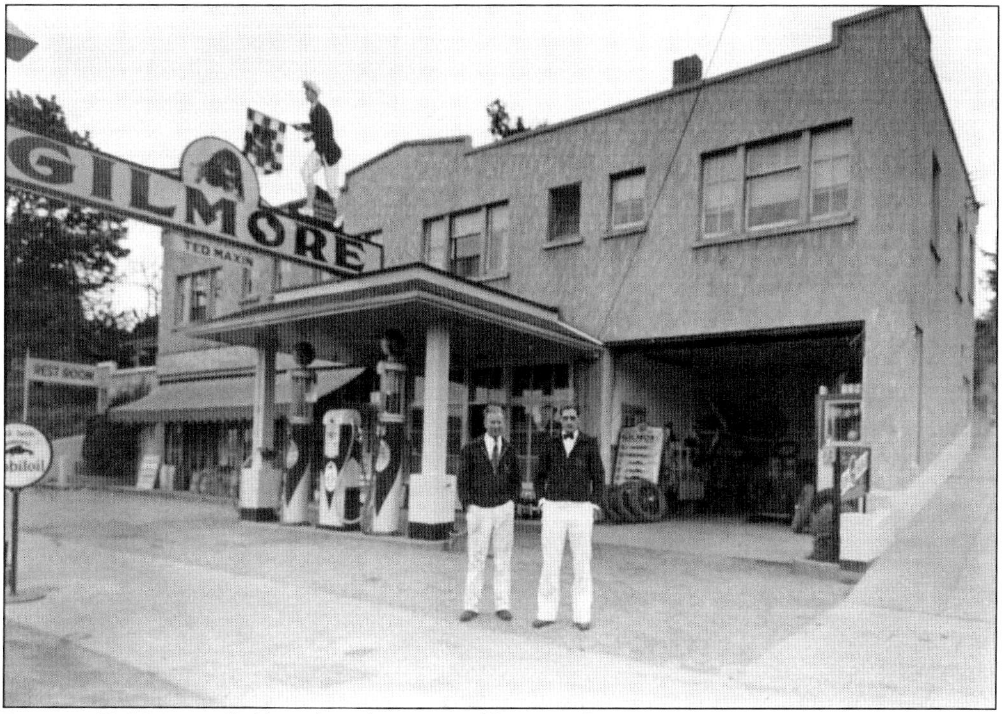

Partners Ted Maxin (left) and Walt Romanofski owned two gas stations on Deschutes Way at Division Street during the 1930s. The one shown here stood on the west side of the street in a two-story building that also housed the O'Hare Brothers grocery (see page 82). Their other service station stood directly across the street, allowing the partners to tap both northbound and southbound traffic. (Courtesy of Washington State Historical Society, C2010.0.4.)

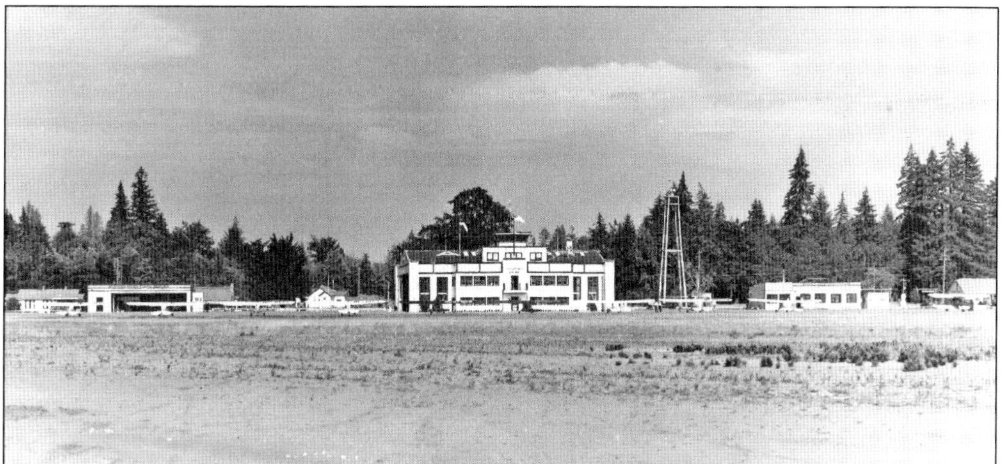

Spurred by a group of local businessmen (including brewery founder Leopold Schmidt's sons Peter G. Sr. and Adolph), the City of Olympia purchased a field south of Tumwater in 1928 for a municipal airport. The large hangar (center), which still stands, was built with federal government funds during the Great Depression of the 1930s. The Olympia Airport, now owned by the Port of Olympia, was annexed into Tumwater in 1987. (Courtesy of Port of Olympia.)

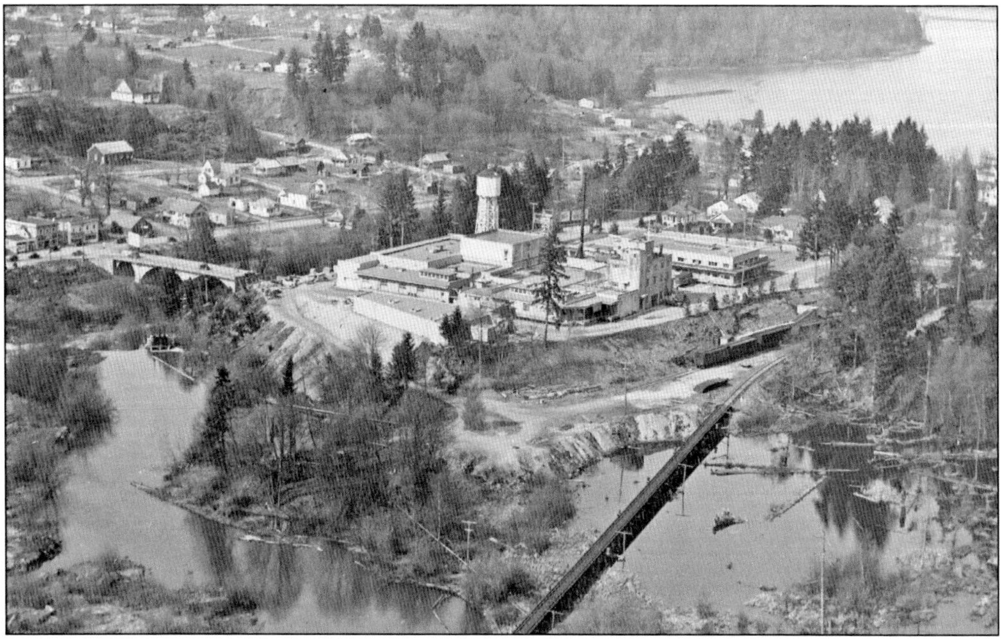

This aerial photograph of Tumwater, taken in the late 1930s, shows the "new" Olympia Brewery already growing on the top of the bluff. Train tracks cross the Deschutes River east of the brewery complex, but the Capitol Boulevard car bridge has not yet been built. Drivers must still wind their way behind the brewery, over the Boston Street Bridge (left), and along Deschutes Way in order to pass through town. (Courtesy of Henderson House Museum, No. 080.)

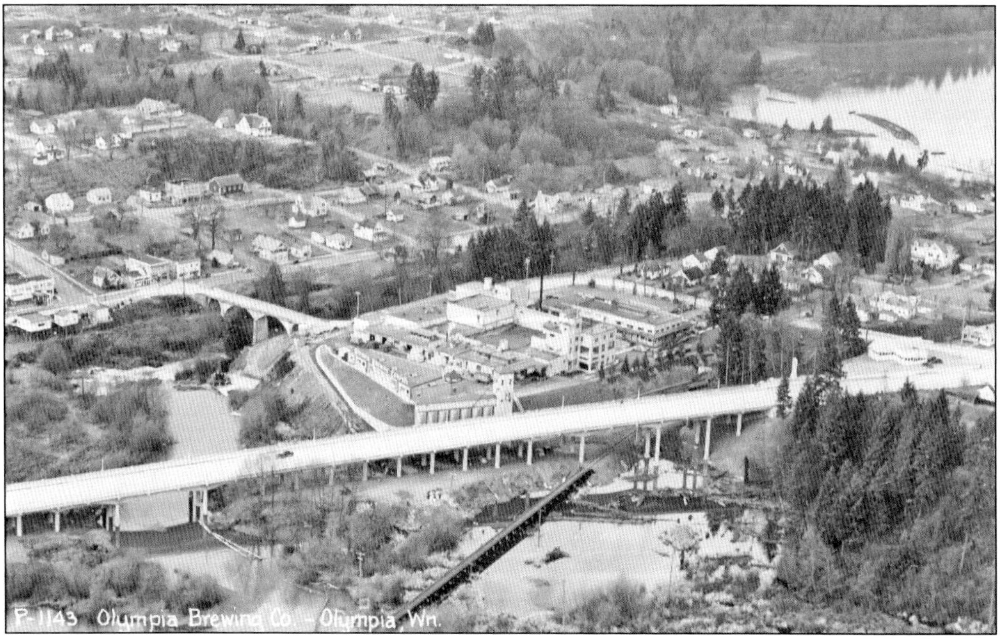

In 1938, the Washington State Department of Highways straightened out the local kinks in the Pacific Highway by building a four-lane bridge across the Deschutes River. Drivers were now able to speed straight ahead on Capitol Boulevard, bypassing the old part of Tumwater completely. (Courtesy of Henderson House Museum, No. 078.)

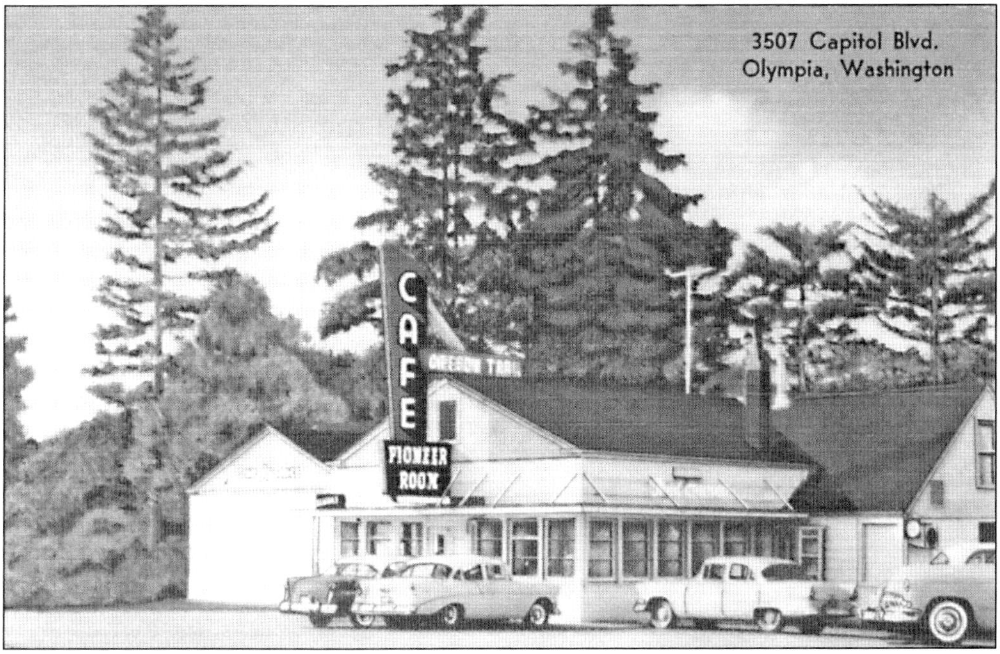

To take advantage of the increased highway traffic, the owners of the Chicken Coop Restaurant closed their older establishment and moved to the north end of the Capitol Boulevard Bridge. While modern cars were literally changing the shape of Tumwater, the new restaurant's name—the Oregon Trail Café—gave a nod to the town's oxcart past. Later the building would house the long-standing South Pacific Restaurant. (Postcard courtesy of private collection.)

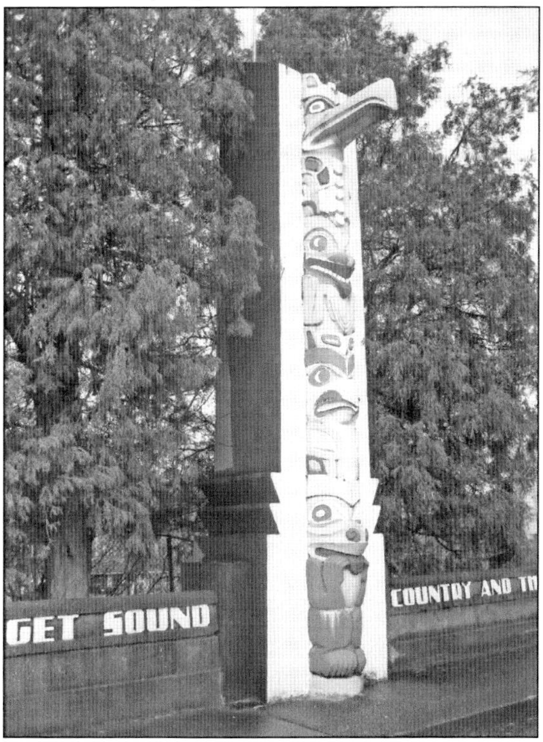

Cast-concrete details on the Capitol Boulevard Bridge borrowed both art deco and North Coast Indian design motifs. Decoration included four painted totem poles and deco-style geometric borders. Lettering on the guardrails touted Tumwater as the gateway to Puget Sound country, the Olympic Peninsula, and the Inside Passage to Alaska, as well as proclaiming it the "Site of the First American Pioneer Settlement in Washington." (Courtesy of Henderson House Museum, No. 1537.)

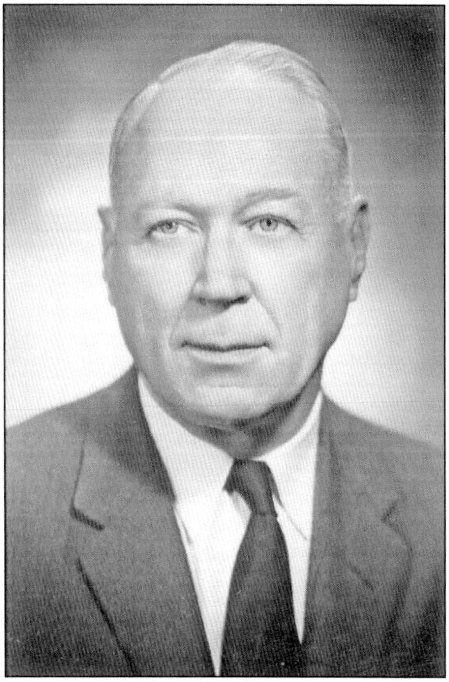

Ray Johnson was mayor of Tumwater from 1923 to 1927 and again from 1941 to 1957. It was during his final term that the state chose a route for Washington's first interstate freeway, a decision that ultimately split Tumwater in two. "If they come this way, they're going to have to help us," Johnson told residents at a town meeting in 1954. Under his leadership, the city received sewer and water improvements, an overpass and an underpass to accommodate east-west traffic, a bridge across the freeway at Custer Way, and a full-service interchange at Trosper Road. (Courtesy of Henderson House Museum, No. 333.)

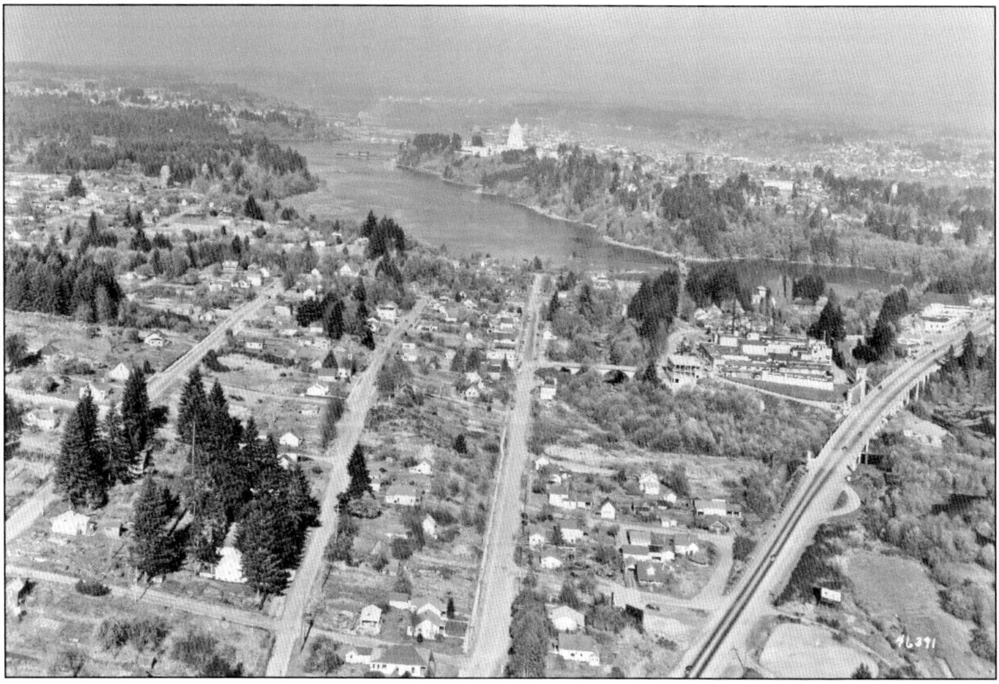

The original plan for Interstate 5 took the new freeway west of Tumwater (to the left of this photograph), then east across Capitol Lake (seen at center), and through a tunnel beneath the capital city of Olympia. When that concept proved too costly, an alternate plan was chosen that routed the freeway straight through historic Tumwater (foreground) and installed a multilevel highway interchange at the south end of Capitol Lake. (Courtesy of SWRA, Washington State Department of Transportation.)

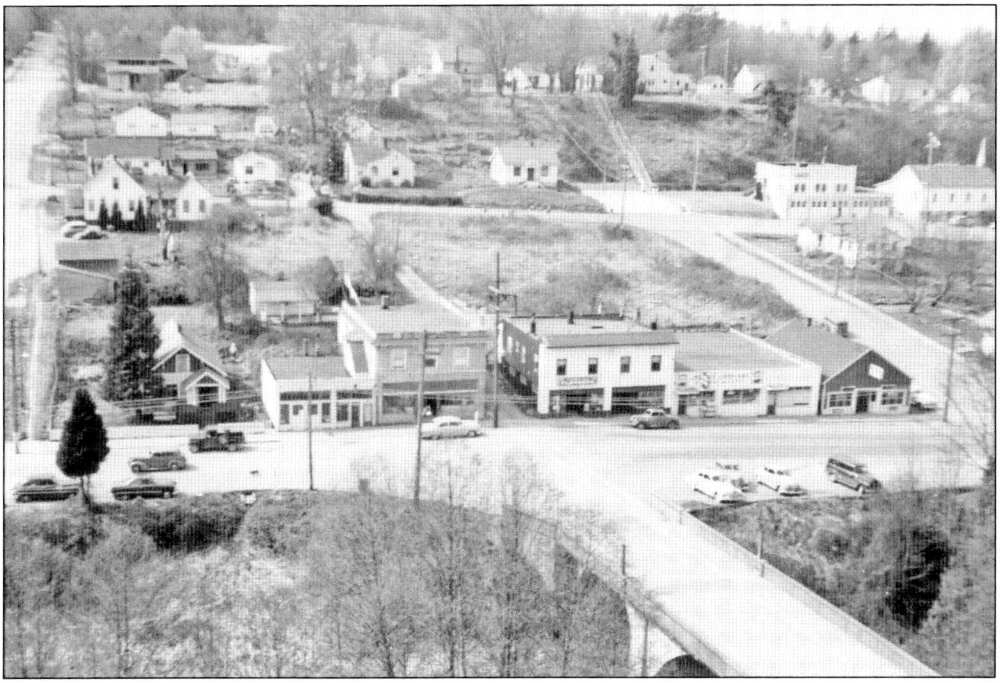

Downtown Tumwater is captured in February 1954, two months before a final decision was made on a route for Interstate 5. (Courtesy of Henderson House Museum, No. 1437.)

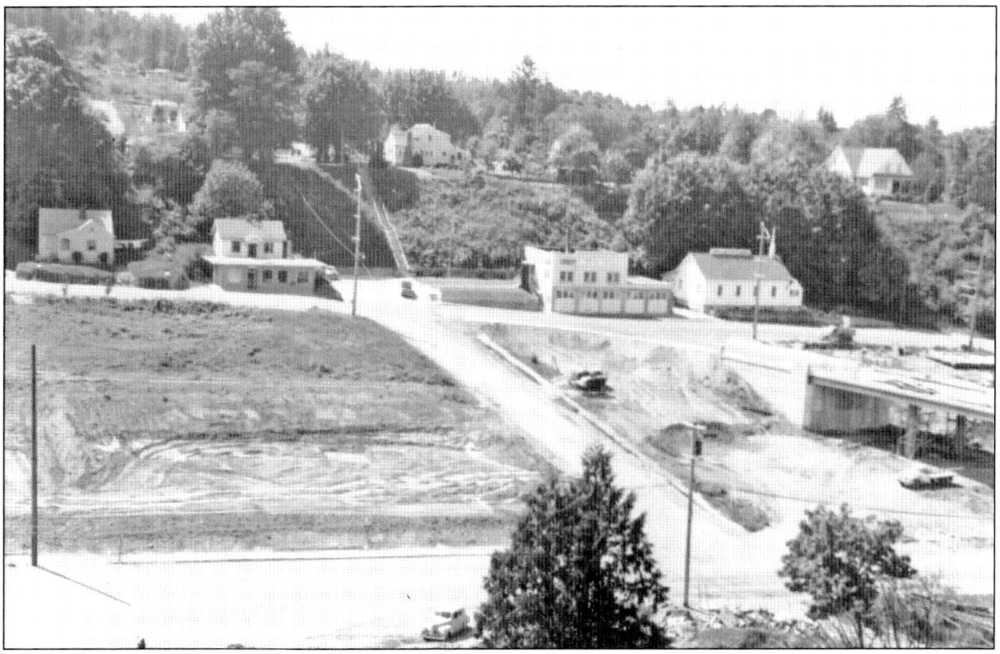

By January 1956, land clearance for freeway construction is well underway. All the commercial buildings on Deschutes Way have disappeared, and the post office has moved to a new one-story, flat-roofed building on Second Avenue near the steps to Tumwater Hill. On the far right, construction has begun on the Custer Way Bridge that will eventually carry local traffic across Interstate 5. (Courtesy of Henderson House Museum, No. 1444.)

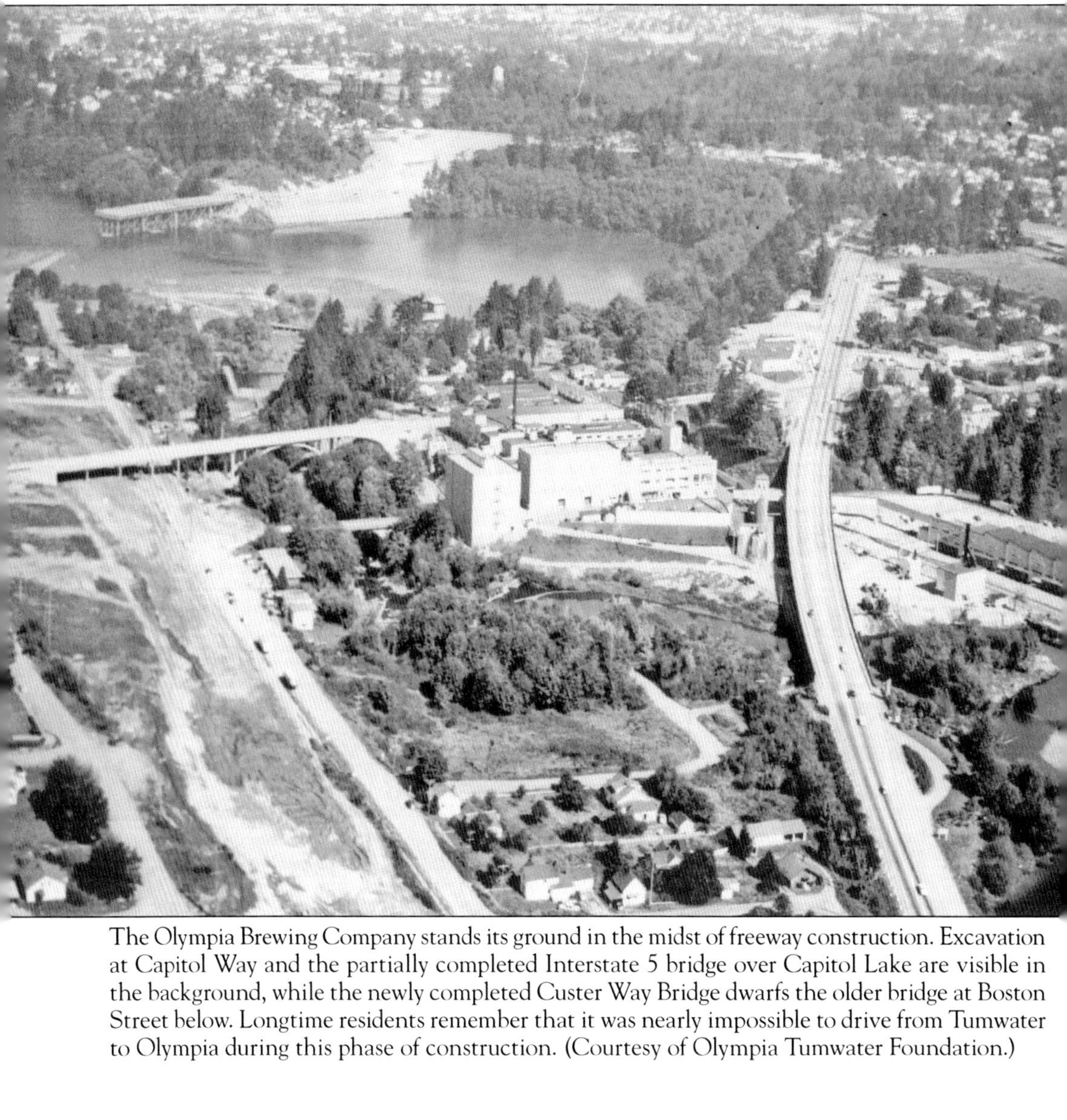

The Olympia Brewing Company stands its ground in the midst of freeway construction. Excavation at Capitol Way and the partially completed Interstate 5 bridge over Capitol Lake are visible in the background, while the newly completed Custer Way Bridge dwarfs the older bridge at Boston Street below. Longtime residents remember that it was nearly impossible to drive from Tumwater to Olympia during this phase of construction. (Courtesy of Olympia Tumwater Foundation.)

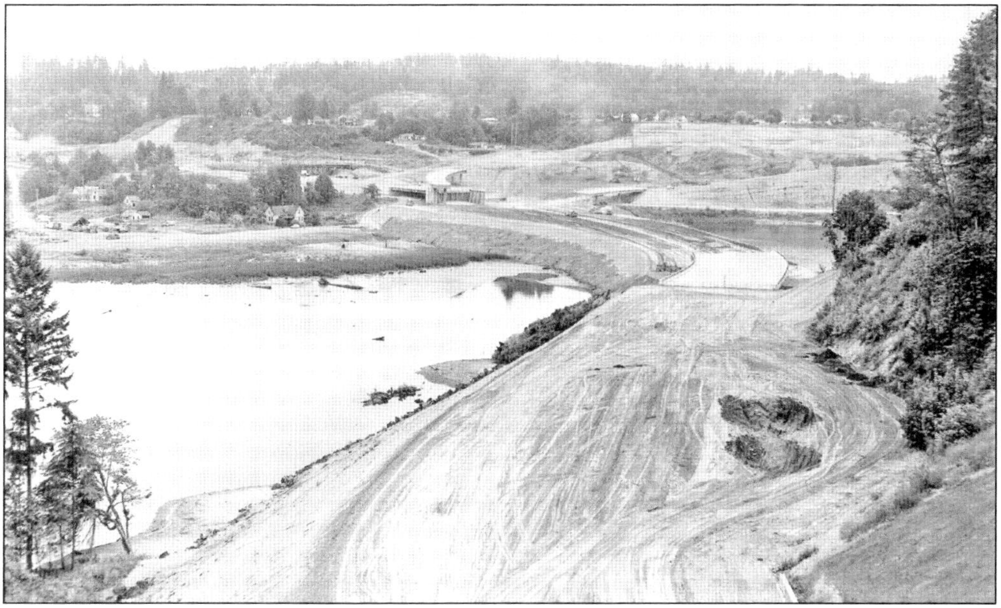

This view looking west toward Tumwater Hill, from the bridge over Interstate 5 at Capitol Way, shows the raw outline of the roadbed of the new Capitol Lake interchange. Massive embankments now squeeze the Deschutes waterway under the deck of a concrete bridge just to the right of center. (Courtesy of Washington State Department of Transportation.)

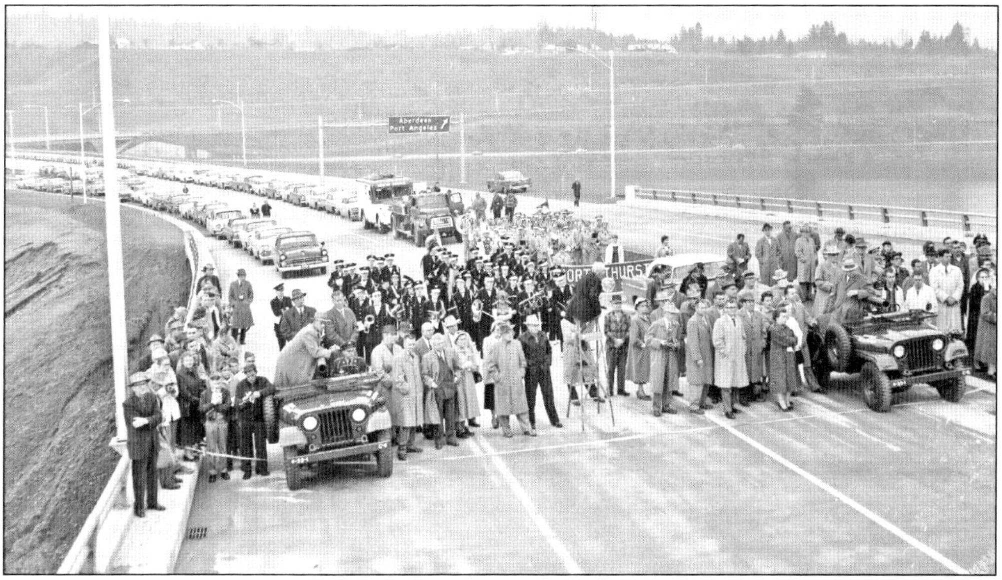

Elected officials, military brass, and local high school marching bands were on hand to celebrate Freeway Day—December 12, 1958—when the 6.5-mile stretch of freeway through Tumwater and Olympia was officially opened to traffic. Dedication ceremonies were held on the bridge of the Capitol Lake interchange, where Gov. Albert Rosellini declared the new highway "a work of art as well as a thing of utility." Ironically, the first accident on the new stretch occurred only a few hours later, when a confused motorist tried to enter the freeway via an exit and got his car stuck in the median while attempting a U-turn. (Courtesy of the Susan Parish Collection of Photography.)

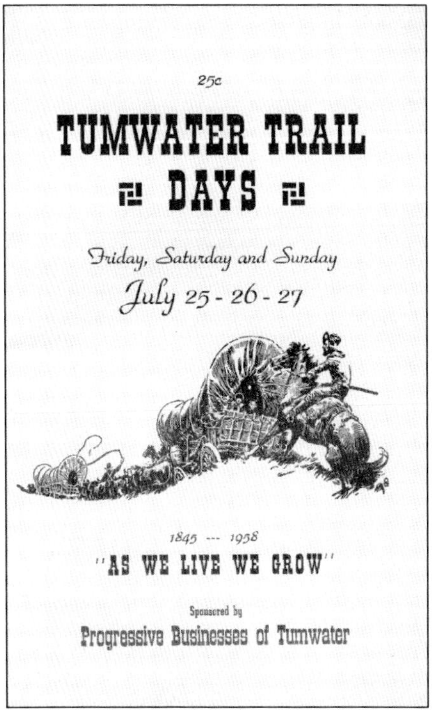

The first Tumwater Trail Days were celebrated in the summer of 1958 as the freeway neared completion. After more than two years of road construction, local business owners and residents were ready for some fun. Ironically, just when the historic heart of Tumwater disappeared forever, citizens seized the idea of dressing up as pioneers and celebrating the town's past. (Courtesy of Henderson House Museum, 2010.15.)

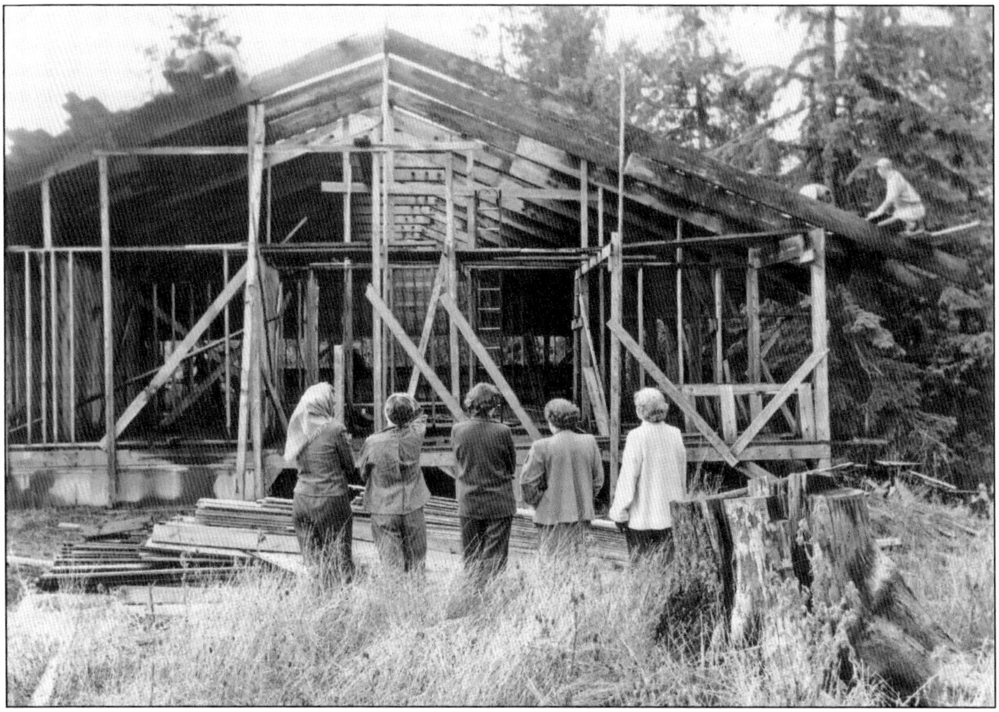

Interstate 5 wasn't the only thing under construction in Tumwater during the mid-1950s. Volunteers from a half-dozen service organizations, led by the Tumwater Rotary Club, banded together to build a "Community House" on what is now X Street as a meeting hall for the city's Boy and Girl Scouts. (Courtesy of Henderson House Museum, No. 1151.)

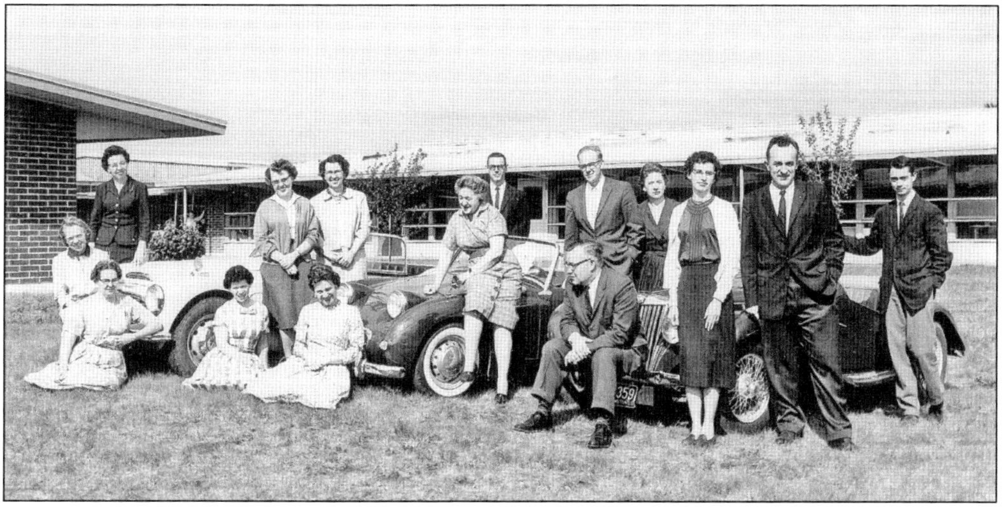

For the first time, Tumwater grew large enough to support more than a single school. Peter G. Schmidt Elementary School opened in September 1957 and was followed in 1961 by Tumwater High School. Both schools were built well to the south of Tumwater's original center, reflecting a trend in development away from the river and falls. The Schmidt School staff is pictured here in 1961. From left to right are (first row, seated) E. Clara Hagen, Helen Pinson, Mae Couch, Willadine Radke, and Lloyd McElvain; (second row, standing) Katherine Proctor, secretary Modie Madison, Maxine Hart, Mabel Sundberg, Lawrence Fisher, George Lasswell, Gretchen Cloud, Caroline Lattin, principal Jim Pill, and James Kemp. (Courtesy of Tumwater School District.)

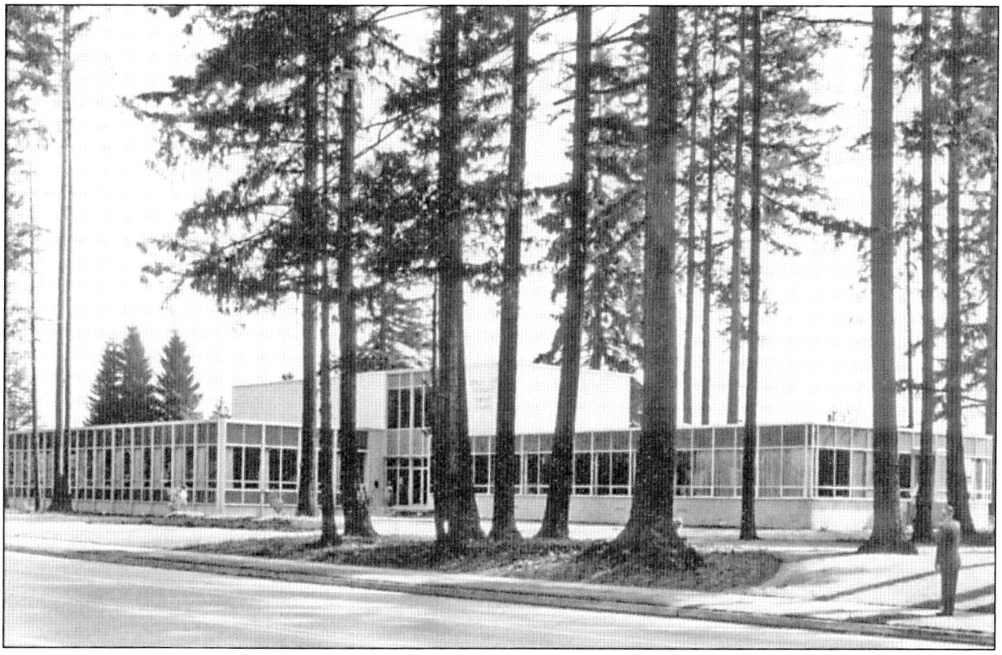

Sunset Life Insurance Company moved its home office from Olympia to Tumwater in 1959, building a modern glass corporate headquarters on Capitol Boulevard. The elegant home of real estate developer Fred Carlyon (see page 69) was razed to make way for the new building, although many large trees on the site were saved. Sunset Life remained a major local employer, until the company was sold in 1999. (Courtesy of Henderson House Museum, 87.7.17.)

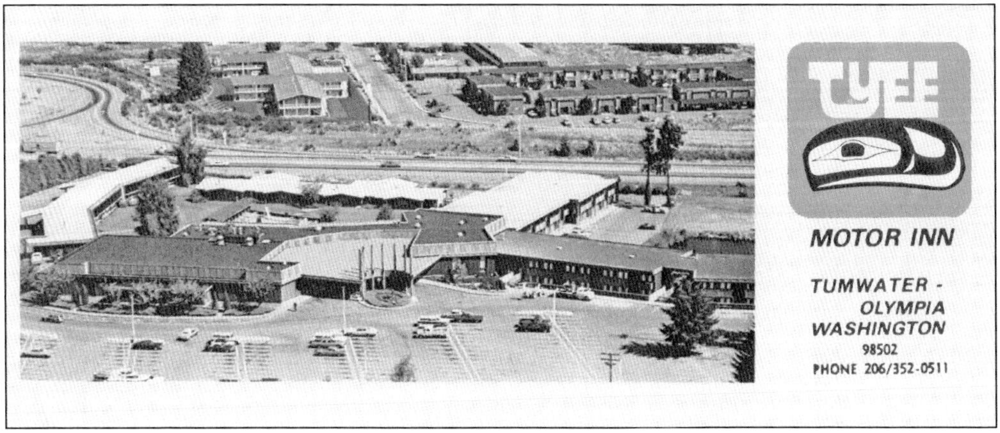

Brothers Ralph and Jim Swanson originally planned to build houses on acreage they owned at the south end of town; when the freeway came through their property, they built a hotel instead (above). The Tyee Motor Inn, opened in 1958, catered to lawmakers from Olympia as well as to out-of-town tourists. So much state business was conducted there that the Tyee Motor Inn was jokingly dubbed "the unofficial state capitol." The hotel survived two fires but was torn down in 2000 to make way for a Fred Meyer store. The road behind the shopping center is still called Tyee Drive. (Both, courtesy of LaVera Hart.)

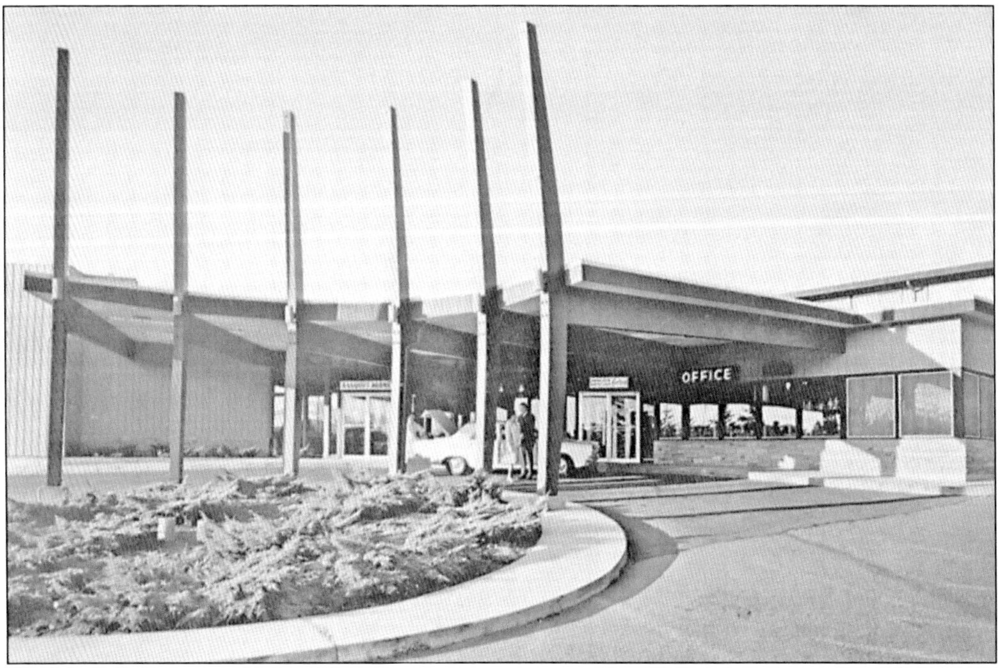

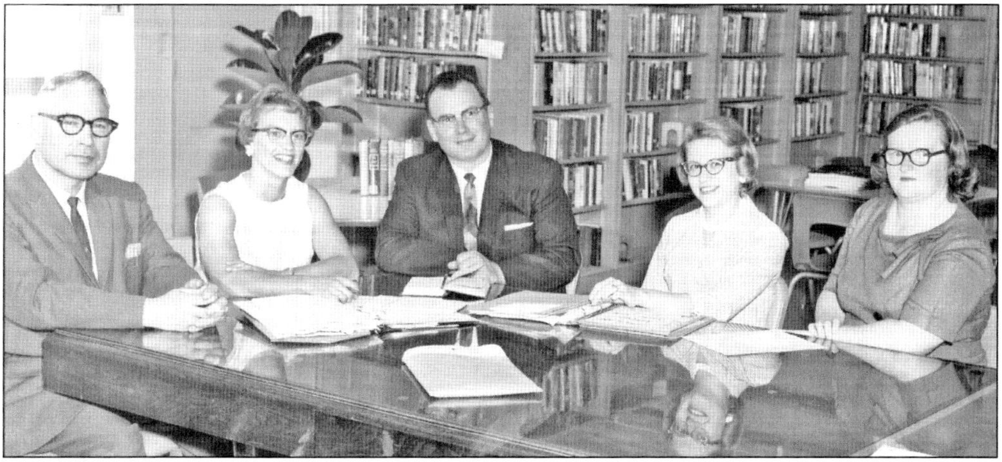

The first Tumwater Timberland Library opened in 1965 in a storefront next to the freeway in Southgate Shopping Center. Members of the first library board were, from left to right, Rollo Walters, Donna Unwin, Dale Johnson, Arlene Gardner, and Dee Dick. The tremendously popular library remained in rented space at the shopping center for 30 years before moving to a purpose-built structure on Israel Road. (Courtesy of Tumwater Timberland Library.)

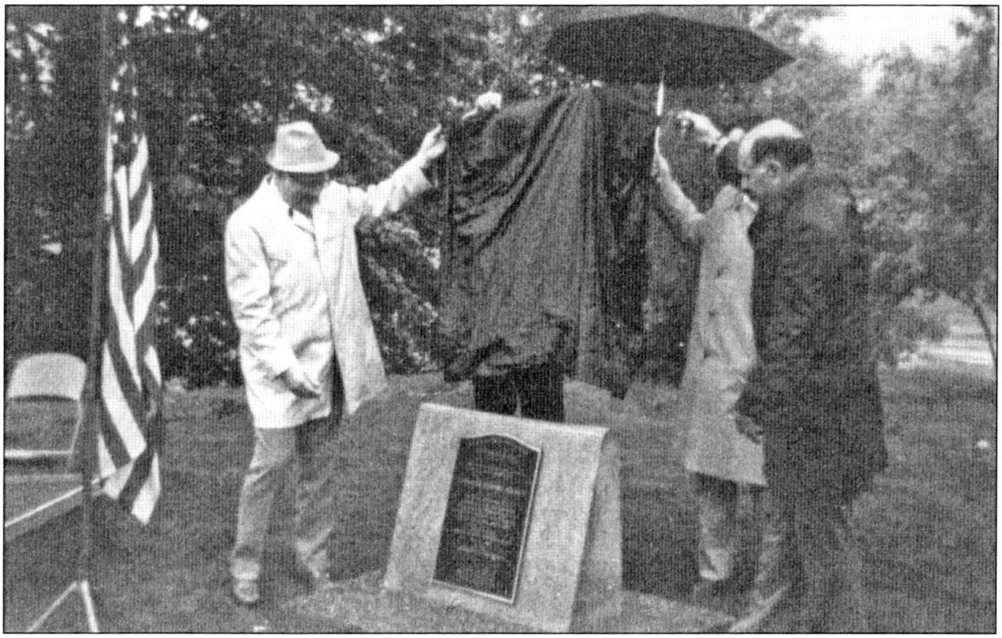

On August 18, 1979, the City of Tumwater dedicated the Tumwater Historic District, which stretches along both sides of the river from the Upper Falls to Capitol Lake. Included within the district are the Crosby House Museum, the Naumann/Henderson House Museum, the 1906 brewhouse of the Olympia Brewing Company, the Schmidt House, a section of roadbed from the Olympia-Tenino Railroad, the Boston Street Bridge, and the sites of nearly two dozen pioneer-era homes and businesses. In this photograph from the dedication, State Historic Preservation officer Louis Guzzo unveils the historic district marker (left) while the Honorable Hewitt Henry (far right) looks on. Judge Henry was the son of Laura (Hewitt) and Phil Henry, who are featured on page 81. The Tumwater Historic District is listed on both the National and Washington State Registers of Historic Places and on the Tumwater Historical Register. (Courtesy Henderson House Museum, No. 1347.)

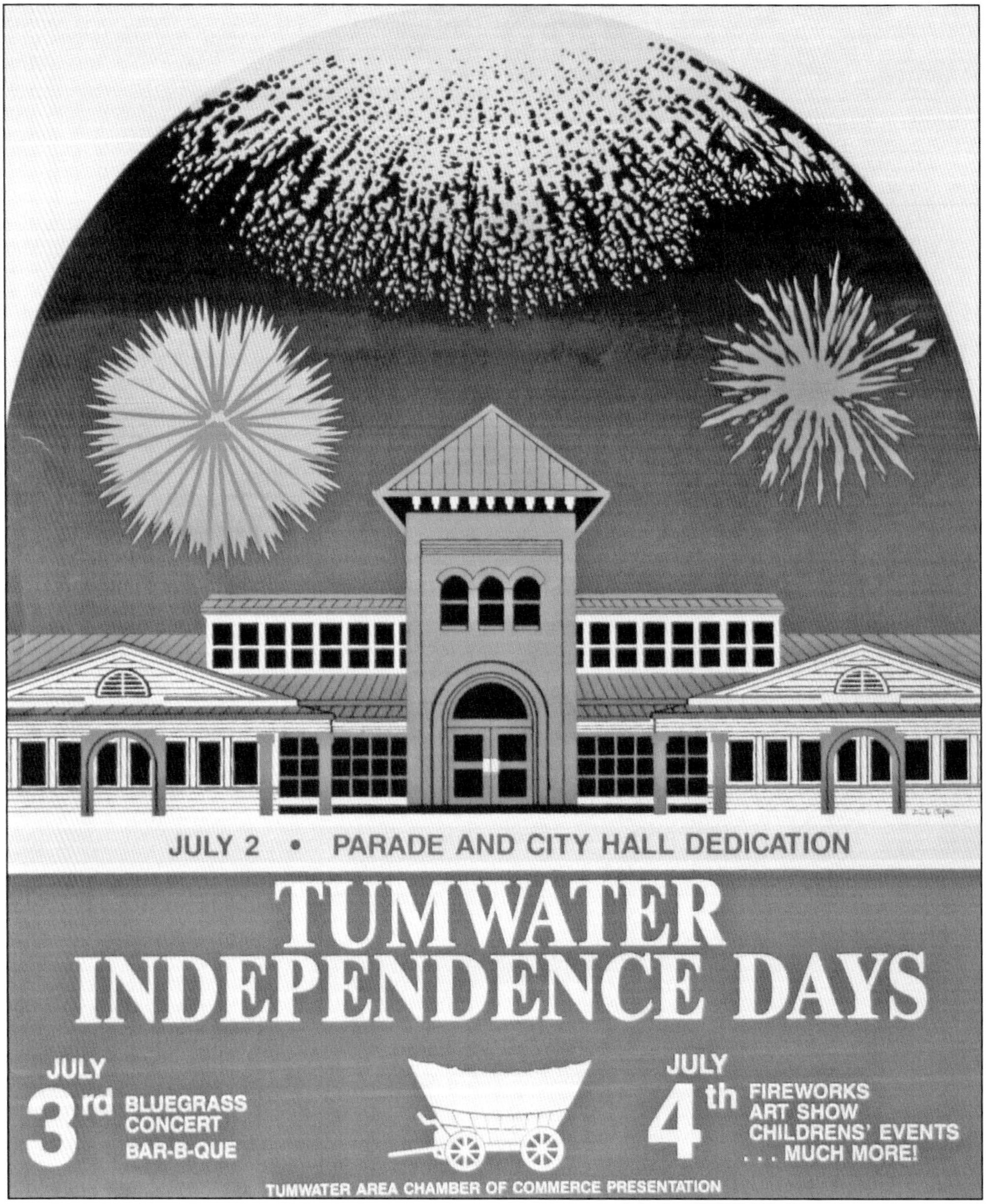

Tumwater city government moved out of the old city hall and fire station (now Tumwater Old Town Center) in 1988 and into a new city hall complex on Israel Road not far from Tumwater High School. The Tumwater Timberland Library followed in 1995, securing Israel Road's status as the new municipal center of town. The design of Tumwater City Hall was inspired, in part, by the tower of the 1906 brewhouse of the Olympia Brewing Company—a link between present-day Tumwater and the town's rich, textured past. (Poster by Richard Clifton; courtesy of Henderson House Museum, 2010.14.)

Bibliography

Hannum, James S. *Delusions of Grandeur: The Olympia and Tenino Railroad*. Olympia, WA: Hannum House Publications, 2009.

History of Thurston County Pioneers before 1870. Washington Rural Heritage Collection, Washington State Library Digital Archive.

Kangas, Jill, and Don Trosper. *Tumwater Oral Interviews 1994–1995* (transcripts of recorded interviews with Ray Ensley, Tom Lozier, Philip "Skip" Schmidt, and Jim Brown). Tumwater, WA: Henderson House Museum Collection.

Newell, Gordon. *Rogues, Buffoons & Statesmen*. Seattle, WA: Superior Publishing, 1975.

Palmer, Gayle L., ed. *The River Remembers: A History of Tumwater 1845–1995*. Virginia Beach, VA: The Donning Company, 1995.

Schmidt, Peter G. Jr. *Growing Up in Tumwater: Memories of Childhood During Prohibition and the Great Depression Years of the 1930s*. Tumwater, WA: Olympia Tumwater Foundation Collection. (unpublished lecture notes, 2002.)

Stevenson, Shanna. *Olympia, Tumwater and Lacey: A Pictorial History*. Norfolk, VA: The Donning Company, 1996.

Trosper, Don. *A Rich Heritage: Tumwater Area Schools since 1845*. Tumwater, WA: Tumwater School District, 2008.

Wulfsberg, Carla. *Oral Interviews* (transcripts of recorded interviews with Margaret Henderson Lee (2004) and Virginia Henderson Walton (2005). Tumwater, WA: Henderson House Museum Collection.

Archives and Repositories

Clipping and pamphlet files, Henderson House Museum Collection, Tumwater, WA.

Washington birth, death, and cemetery records, Washington State Digital Archives.

INDEX

About the Organization

The Henderson House Museum is home to the City of Tumwater's historic photography collection, research archive, and collection of local artifacts. The museum also sponsors a variety of programs for the public, including illustrated history talks, regular tours of the Naumann/Henderson House, a documentary film series airing on Tumwater's government-access cable-television channel, special tours for school groups, and other educational events.

The museum is always looking for additional historic images for its local photography collection, which is used by researchers, businesses, students, and interested members of the public. Individuals are encouraged to bring in photographs that document Tumwater's past—from local families and neighborhoods to businesses and community events. The museum is particularly interested in adding photographs of Tumwater from the period between 1950 and 1990. If you have a photograph that tells a story about Tumwater, or if you can offer more information on any photograph in this volume, please let us know. Donations of photographs and other materials are always welcome, but we would also be happy to scan the original for the museum's collection and return it to you.

The Henderson House Museum is located in the historic Naumann/Henderson House, 602 Deschutes Way, Tumwater, Washington. More information about the museum can be found on the City of Tumwater Web site at www.ci.tumwater.wa.us.

For more about the museum and its programs or to inquire about volunteer opportunities, call (360) 754-4217 or e-mail museum@ci.tumwater.wa.us. Mail should be sent to:

Henderson House Museum
c/o City of Tumwater
555 Israel Road SW
Tumwater, WA 98501

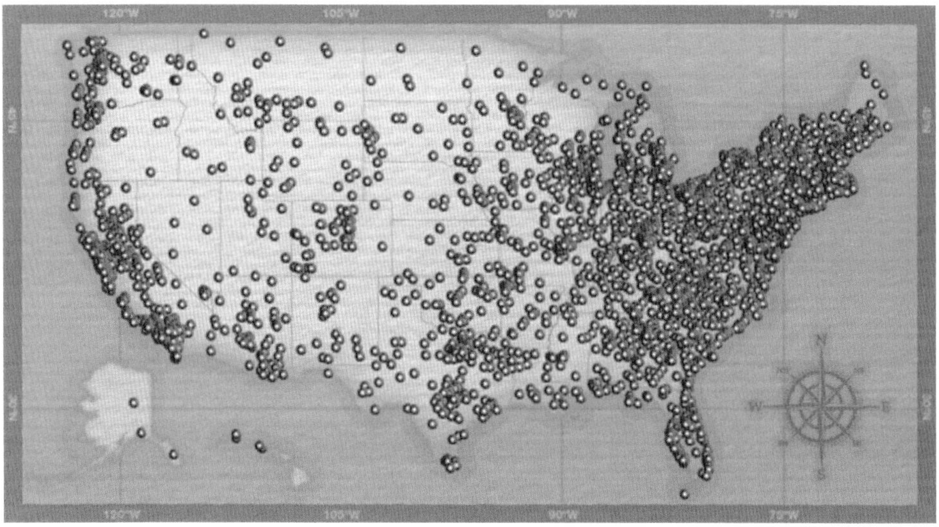